MODERN PALESTINIAN
LITERATURE AND CULTURE

To Umm Samir
in the Galilee

Modern Palestinian Literature and Culture

AMI ELAD-BOUSKILA

Chairman of the Department of Arabic Language and Literature, Beit-Berl College, Israel

FRANK CASS

LONDON • PORTLAND, OR

First published in 1999 in Great Britain by
FRANK CASS PUBLISHERS
Newbury House, 900 Eastern Avenue
London, IG2 7HH

and in the United States of America by
FRANK CASS PUBLISHERS
c/o ISBS, 5804 N.E. Hassalo Street
Portland, Oregon, 97213-3644

Website: www.frankcass.com

British Library Cataloguing in Publication Data

Elad-Bouskila, Ami
Modern Palestinian literature and culture
1. Palestinian literature – Israel – 20th century – History and criticism 2. Palestinian Arabs – Social life and customs – 20th century 3. Intifada, 1987– – Social aspects
4. Palestinian Arabs – Intellectual life
I. Title
892.7'09'006

ISBN 0-7146-4956-2 (cloth)
ISBN 0-7146-8015-X (paper)

Library of Congress Cataloging-in-Publication Data

Elad, Ami.
Modern Palestinian literature and culture / Ami Elad-Bouskila.
p. cm.
Includes bibliographical references and index.
ISBN 0-7146-4956-2 (cloth). – ISBN 0-7146-8015-X (paper)
1. Arabic literature–Palestine–History and criticism. 2. Arabic literature–20th century–History and criticism. 3. Authors, Palestinian Arab–Israel–Political and social views.
4. Palestinian Arabs–Israel–Intellectual life. I. Title.
PJ8190.E42 1999
892.7'0989274–dc21 99-20736
CIP

Typeset by Regent Typesetting, London

Contents

Acknowledgements

Various individuals and institutions have provided assistance during the writing of this book. I would like to express my gratitude, first and foremost, to the Research Committee of Beit Berl College, which made it possible for me to carry out a large part of this research. In addition to Dr Aharon Seidenberg, Rector of Beit Berl College, I would like to thank Professor Moshe Ma'oz, director of the Harry S. Truman Research Institute for the Advancement of Peace of the Hebrew University of Jerusalem, and Professor Avraham Friedman, head of the Jerusalem Institute for Israel Studies, who provided research fellowships at various stages of the writing of this book. My gratitude also to the Middle East Centre, St Antony's College at Oxford University, through the Israeli Junior Visiting Fellowship for 1997–8 that enabled me to complete my research, and especially to Dr Derek Hopwood, director of the Middle East Centre, Dr M. M. Badawi for our fruitful discussions and Dr Ahmed Al-Shahi for his assistance. I would also like to thank my colleagues who read the manuscript and provided valuable insights: Professors Irene Eber, Moshe Piamenta, Shmuel Moreh and Jacob M. Landau of the Hebrew University; Dr Ifrah Zilberman of Beit Berl College and the Jerusalem Institute for Israel Studies; and Dr Yizhak Schnell of Beit Berl and Tel-Aviv University. My thanks to my research assistants at various stages of the writing: Zeev Klein, Shany Payes, Ibrahim Khouri, and Elah Velstra. I would also like to thank those who made available various resources during the course of the writing: the library of Beit Berl College; the Information Center at Givat Haviva and its head, Ronit Barzilai; Yossi Amitay; As'ad al-As'ad, Secretary-General of the Association of Palestinian Writers in Gaza and the West Bank; Dr Kamal Abd al-Malek from Brown University in the United States; and, last but not least, the skilful editing by Gila Svirsky is deeply appreciated.

Ami Elad-Bouskila
St Antony's College, Oxford

INTRODUCTION

Palestinian Culture in the Middle East

Between Arabism, Westernism and Israelism

Many studies have focused on various aspects of Palestinian society and culture: history, politics, political science, the refugees, relationships between Palestinians and other Arabs, Palestinian education and literature, and so forth. The field of literature has been only partially explored, and most of that in Arabic, with only a few studies in other languages, primarily Hebrew and English.[1] The present work seeks to add another dimension to the study of Palestinian society, especially in the last decade. It is not intended to be a definitive survey of modern Palestinian literature, but rather originated in a series of articles and essays about modern Palestinian literature that have been reworked as a book, with all the necessary updates.

This Introduction provides an overview of the development of all types of Palestinian literature, with a special focus on writing during the intifāḍa period. In order to provide a broad, comparative perspective, the Introduction will include not just genres of Palestinian literature, but it will touch upon modern Arabic literature in general as well as Israeli-Arab culture. Any discussion of Palestinian literature must reach beyond purely literary issues into areas that cast light not just on its literature, but on Palestinian society itself. Therefore, this Introduction – and some chapters as well – incorporate a discussion of Israeli-Jewish and Israeli-Arab society, attempting to outline the problems of identity of both Palestinian and Israeli-Jewish societies, and the fabric of relations between the two which are not always strained, and indeed often struggle with the same problems.

This book has six chapters, most of them originally published as articles and essays in several languages (see Bibliography). Chapter 1 grapples with the dilemma of Arabs who live in Israel in sorting out their Arab, Israeli and Palestinian identities, as observed from the perspective of literature and culture.[2] This chapter addresses three main questions: (1) For whom do Israeli Arabs write? (2) Where do they publish their writing? (3) What do they write about? Chapter 2 examines the multifaceted issue of Israeli Arabs who write for publication not only in Arabic, but in Hebrew as well. Writing in the language of the other is a complex, delicate and problematic issue, as 'the other' represents a nation in conflict with several Arab states. Thus, an Arab writing in Hebrew can evoke powerful negative reactions, at least among part of the Arab world, as well as among some Arab citizens of Israel. Chapter 3 looks at one prominent author among the younger generation of Arab writers in Israel.[3] A survey of the literary career of Riyāḍ Baydas (1960–) in the decade 1980–90 can illuminate trends in the writing of Israeli Arabs, though it clearly does not reflect all the writers of his generation, let alone the older generation of Israeli-Arab writers, pre-eminently Emile Ḥabībī (1921-96) and Samīḥ al-Qāsim (1939–). In Chapter 4 Palestinian writing is surveyed from the outbreak of the intifāḍa in 1987 until the Gulf War, as reflected in *al-Kātib*, the journal of the Association of Palestinian Writers in Gaza and the West Bank.[4] This does not reflect all the writing of the intifāḍa, as a journal by nature is limited in scope and cannot encompass genres such as the novel. Furthermore, works by both Palestinians and non-Palestinians were published during the intifāḍa (and before) in other Palestinian and non-Palestinian periodicals, literary and otherwise. Chapter 5 explores the image of the Jew and/or Israeli in Palestinian literature during the intifāḍa. It notes that Palestinian writers – like Israeli-Hebrew writers – draw to a large extent upon clichés and stereotypes created during the conflict and maintained for over a hundred years between the Palestinian and Israeli communities. The Palestinian perception of Israeli society, especially the security forces, settlers and leftists, is reflected in their writing, particularly during the intifāḍa. In a sense, the intifāḍa restored to Palestinian literature its pre-occupation with the image of the Jew. While in the beginning this image was negative, after the second year of the intifāḍa, even positive Jewish figures are depicted. In Chapter 6 I examine the myth of Jerusalem in Palestinian society during the intifāḍa period.[5] This myth is more religious than political, and thus Jerusalem differs in the collective memory of Palestinian society from other important Palestinian cities that do not have religious standing, such as Jaffa and Haifa. Palestinian writers write with religious and political passion about Jerusalem and yet with less extremism and vehemence than Arab writers who are not Palestinian.

Finally, there is an Epilogue in which I attempt to sum up the chapters and reflect upon trends in modern Palestinian literature, especially during the last decade of the twentieth century. Drawing upon additional material about Palestinian and Arab affairs enriches and varies the analysis, as this is not intended to be an orderly presentation of the development of Palestinian literature but rather an attempt to cast light on some aspects of Palestinian society and culture as mirrored in the literature during various periods of writing.

MODERN ARABIC LITERATURES – PLURAL

The study of modern Palestinian literature would be lacking were it explored without reference to two additional cultures and their literatures: modern Arabic literatures, which include modern Palestinian literature, and Israeli-Jewish society and its literature. The thesis of this book is that there is no one Arabic literature, just as there is no one English literature, but there are rather modern Arabic literatures. By 'modern Arabic literatures', we refer to the Arabic writing that began to appear in the 1870s, hence this writing is young, just over a century old. Chronologically, then, the development of modern Arabic literatures parallels to a great extent the history of modern Hebrew literature, more than it does the history of modern European literature.

Modern Arabic literatures did not develop *ex nihilo*. These literatures are intrinsically related to classical Arabic literature, both prose and poetry. Arabic literature dates back to the pre-Islamic period (before the seventh century). This was primarily an oral tradition of poetry that developed in the Arabian peninsula. Classical Arabic literature reached its peak in the tenth and eleventh centuries with all genres of prose and poetry.[6] The period from the fourteenth until the nineteenth century is generally viewed as a period of decline, when Arabic literature was stagnating. During this period, content was sacrificed on the altar of style and linguistic virtuosity. From the beginning of the nineteenth century, Arabic literature began to revive, first in imitation of the classical literary heritage and later drawing upon Western literature.[7]

Modern Arabic literatures are embedded in the political, social and economic processes that began in the late eighteenth century and continue to this day. These concern the complex of relations between Western countries and the Arab world. Central to these relations were the European military conquests of Asian and African countries, in particular, of Egypt, the Levant and the Maghrib. This encounter with Western culture, especially science and technology, had a profound impact on many aspects of Arab society. Of foremost significance was the economic involvement of Western countries, and the changes this wrought in the social fabric. The encounter led many Arabs, especially the intelligentsia, to a deep ambivalence about the culture of Western society. Attitudes toward Western culture split the Arab intellectual elite into three groups:

(1) Those who advocated an enthusiastic borrowing from the West, belittling or ignoring Arab culture. In other words, imitation out of self-effacement, but also the attempt to establish a semi-secular nation-state.
(2) Those who totally rejected Western culture. This group was made up primarily of the religious elite, based in al-Azhar, the prestigious religious seminary in Egypt.
(3) Those who advocated an integration of the two cultures, attempting to synthesize the best of both worlds. This third group was, and still is, the dominant one, although within it there are various shades and differences in emphases.

The 1960s can be regarded as an important milestone in the development of modern Arabic literature: a time of change in both style and content. Whereas the mainstream of writing in the early twentieth century was romantic, this yielded to realism in the 1940s and 1950s. The realistic style of writing waned in the 1960s, making way for montage, stream of consciousness, and other styles. The change was reflected in themes, not just in style of writing. Since the 1960s many writers have focused on the individual rather than the community at large, and the literature has reflected questions about the meaning of life and a search for personal and cultural identity.[8] The individual at the centre is engrossed in problems of alienation, loneliness and estrangement, especially in urban existence – together with questions of tradition, style of life, customs and religion, especially in the rural areas.[9]

The exposure of Arab writers to European and American literatures, as well as their openness to this influence, gained momentum in the 1960s. The most influential European and American writers on Arab writing were Camus, Dostoevsky, Kafka, Faulkner, Joyce, Proust and Robbe-Grillet. There was also a growing audience of more educated and sophisticated Arab readers, ripe for a higher standard of writing in Arabic. This increasing awareness and openness also affected publishing houses and journals which published and promoted modern Arabic literatures.

The Arab world is currently undergoing major transformations in the spheres of politics – the decline of pan-Arabism and Nasserism; economics – increased industrialization at the expense of agriculture, open-door policies; and society – increased urbanization, social and religious polarization, urban Westernization which parallels growing Islamicism, a faster pace of living, and the alienation of the individual – especially city-dwellers. As a result of these processes, literature is less in the service of ideology and has a more personal orientation. These changes have also made possible the development of a 'woman's literature'. Although Arab women writers were active in the first third of this century, and as a group have significant, though not major, standing, they began to flourish only in the 1960s.[10]

Clearly there is more in common than is different among these literatures: after all, the 22 different literatures are almost entirely written in Arabic for an Arab audience. However, we cannot ignore the many differences among them. A close look at modern Arabic literatures reveals two major categories: that of the Mashriq – the eastern part of the Arab world – and that of the Maghrib – the western part of the Arab world. Common to both are the language of writing (usually Arabic) and Islam, which is the religion of most of the writers there as revealed in their work. Nonetheless, the differences are significant. First, many of the Maghrib dialects differ from the Mashriq dialects, as evident in the dialogue of much Maghrib writing. Second, the language of writing of some Maghrib writers is Arabic and French, or sometimes only French or Berber. Third, the heritage of Mashriq writers, besides Islam, includes Phoenician, Pharaonic and Babylonian cultures, as well as African culture in the case of Egypt and Sudan. Whereas the cultural heritage of the Maghrib world is drawn primarily from African and Berber sources, besides the cultures of Islam and French (or Italian) in their various manifestations.[11]

The Mashriq category is not homogeneous; Syrian literature, for example, is not identical or even very similar to Sudanese literature. Nevertheless, Syrian literature does resemble Lebanese, Iraqi, Jordanian and Palestinian literatures, just as Egyptian literature and modern Sudanese literature have a lot in common. In general, the story of modern Mashriq literature or, more accurately, the modern Mashriq literatures, is to some extent the story of modern Egyptian literature. From the beginning of modern Arabic literature, Egypt was the cultural, political and social centre of the Arab world. The changes that took place in Egypt in the course of the century generally reflect – with some difference – the changes that swept across the Arab world. Milestones in the development of Egypt in the twentieth century are the revolution of 1919, the *coup d'état* of July 1952, the war with Israel in 1967, the 'open door' policy of the early 1970s, another war with Israel in 1973, the peace agreement with Israel in 1979, and the assassination of President Sadat in 1981. These landmarks, mostly political, mark some major convulsions in Egyptian society as well as other Arab societies, and these are reflected in the literature.

With the development of modern Arabic literature, two cultural centres emerged – Cairo and, of secondary importance, Beirut. However, from the mid 1970s, and particularly since the civil war in Lebanon (1976), the centre in Beirut has declined, while other centres have risen in importance to rival that of Cairo. One cultural centre evolved in Morocco, with a flourishing industry of newspapers, periodicals and books. Important Arab cultural centres have also sprung up in non-Arab countries such as Cyprus (although this has waned since the Oslo Agreement), France and England. These centres emerged in the wake of the Palestinian diaspora that developed there, especially following the Lebanon War in 1982. The political, social and cultural circumstances were fertile for their growth – large numbers of Arab *émigrés* who sought channels of expression. These cultural centres often saw the publication of literary works, periodicals and newspapers that could not be printed in Arab countries.

With the rise of the centres, one can observe the impressive cultural revival of Arab states that until then had been in the literary hinterland, notably the Gulf states, Kuwait and Saudi Arabia. The vast income of these oil-producing countries enabled a surge in development that Arab states had never before known. Inevitably, this economic development also spilled over into the field of literature. It should also be noted that besides the cultural centres of Cairo and Beirut, major cultural centres evolved in the second half of the nineteenth century, especially in the American diaspora (*mahjar*: diaspora; *al-adab al-Mahjarī*: the literature of the diaspora).[12] Young Arab writers and poets emigrated to the West, either because of persecution by the Turks or to seek a better life. The most celebrated among them were young Christians from Syria and Lebanon. Some of these immigrants reached New York and created a northern Mahjar literature (Mikhā'il Nu'ayma, Jubrān Khalīl Jubrān). Others settled primarily in Brazil and Argentina, creating the southern Mahjar literature (Michel al-Ma'lūf, Jūrj Ṣaydaḥ).

North African – or in its other name, Maghrib – literature is unique.[13] First and foremost it is written in three languages: Arabic, French and Berber, a fact which has had a great impact on its development in the past, the present, and presumably will continue to do so in the future. Maghrib literature draws from two primary sources: modern Arab literature of the Mashriq, which is primarily Egyptian, and French literature dating back to the nineteenth century. While Mashriq literature was influenced at the beginning of its development by various European literatures – primarily in matters of form – and even by American literature, modern Maghrib literature written in Arabic and French has been totally immersed in French literature. There has also been evidence in the recent decade of other influences on Maghrib literature, particularly Latin American and British. And lately we are witness to a revival of Berber culture and its literary treasures.

Much of the population of Morocco, Algeria and Tunisia feels ambivalent toward French culture – attracted and repelled by it. Nevertheless, Algeria and Tunisia are significantly different from Morocco. (I do not explore the modern literatures of Libya and Mauritania, which are again different from the three main Maghrib literatures, and on which there was minimal European influence.) This difference is reflected in the fact that most Algerian and Tunisian literature is written in French, while Moroccan literature is generally written in Arabic, though important writers such as Ṭāhir Ben Jallūn (1944–) reside in France and garner recognition from French culture for their French Maghrib writing, even winning the Prix Goncourt.

From the 1970s, two different cultural centres evolved in the Arab world, although they were intertwined: the major literary centre in the Maghrib in general, Morocco in particular; and the second centre, written primarily in French, in Paris. Maghrib literature in Arabic and French was written in both locations and, to a lesser extent, in Berber as well. The extensive literary activity in Morocco from the late 1970s transformed Casablanca into a significant Arab cultural and literary centre, together with the literary centre in Cairo. There were two reasons for this. First, the quantity of writing by Moroccan writers – in Arabic especially – has increased since the late 1970s, and the quality of this writing in comparison with Arabic literature from the Mashriq is noteworthy. The second reason relates to the decline of the cultural centre in Beirut, which began before the civil war in Lebanon, but accelerated markedly during the war. As noted, the decline of Beirut as a centre paralleled not just the rise of the cultural–literary centre in Casablanca, but also the increased importance of the literary centres in the Gulf states and in non-Arab countries, especially Nicosia and London. Ironically, prominent Arab capitals such as Damascus and Baghdad did not – for reasons that are not purely literary –

become cultural centres.

Research into modern Maghrib literature written in Arabic is in its infancy. Comprehensive studies have been carried out only since the 1970s. Until then, interest in Maghrib literature was marginal, for reasons rooted not just in the quality of the literature, but in non-literary factors as well. In the Maghrib itself, however, studies about Maghrib literature are more numerous and comprehensive. Moreover, these studies relate to Maghrib writing as literature written in two and sometimes even three languages, with a tendency to emphasize the literature written in Arabic. Conversely, the French studies of Maghrib literature highlight the works written in French.

One of the important phenomena in modern Maghrib literature concerns the fact that the themes and techniques are very similar in the French and the Arabic writing. The main themes in modern Maghrib literature also do not significantly differ from the main themes of Mashriq literature. Both focus on the struggle of the Arab with Western culture and all that this implies – migration from the village to the city, the decline of agriculture in favour of industry and services, the status of women, education, progress versus tradition, and attitudes toward religion. The singularity of modern Maghrib literature is related to the dilemma of the Maghrib individual, especially the well-educated one, and the mixed feelings of attraction – repulsion concerning French culture centred in Paris. This derives from the fact that many Maghrib writers are intrinsically linked to Paris from all points of view. (Bear in mind the small physical distance between France and the Maghrib and the fact that some Maghrib writers reside permanently in Paris, while others alternate their residence between France and the Maghrib. This proximity greatly affects their writing.) Indeed, French influence on the poetics of Maghrib writing is enormous, not to mention the influence of French literary-philosophical thought, especially existentialism, and the techniques of estrangement, intertextualism and the absurd. French scholarly criticism has also had a profound influence on Maghrib critical writing, which is distinctively different from the scholarly-critical writing of the Mashriq. This kind of scholarship is at a very high level, no less than its Mashriq colleagues.

MODERN PALESTINIAN LITERATURE ... OR LITERATURES?

There is no question that Palestinian literature is an inseparable part of modern Arabic literatures, just as it has been partially influenced by Israeli culture and literature. What is Palestinian literature? It is a literature written by Palestinians. This definition is no different from that of other modern Arabic literatures, as Egyptian literature is written by Egyptians and Iraqi literature by Iraqis. The problem, however, is that Palestinian literature demands a more precise definition of who is a Palestinian. Until 1948 every Palestinian engaged in literary activity, whether inside or outside Mandatory Palestine, was writing Palestinian literature. These included writers such as Isḥāq Mūsā al-Ḥusaynī (1904–90), Khalīl al-Sakākīnī (1878–1953), Khalīl Baydas (1874–1959), and others. The change took place in 1948, when the Palestinian population was split into two. One group included Palestinians who lived and created with a local perspective from outside Israel, whether in Arab states (especially Lebanon, Jordan, Egypt, Iraq and Syria) or in Arab population centres outside Arab countries (Europe or the United States). The second group included the Palestinian-Arab population who lived within the borders of Israel. This latter, it should be noted at this stage, were marginal to the Arab states and indeed to other Palestinians; they gained stature only after 1967 and especially, 1969, as we shall see later. This division also holds for Palestinian writers. Many Palestinian writers and poets worked outside Israel: in Lebanon this included Samīra ʻAzzām (1927–67) and Ghassān Kanafānī (1936–72); in Iraq there was Jabrā Ibrāhīm Jabrā (1920–94); and in the area of the West Bank that had been annexed to Jordan, it included Fadwā Ṭūqān, the poetess from Nablus (1923–). For ʻAzzām, Kanafānī and Ṭūqān, the question of territorial, geographical or national definition never arose, as they were, and are, clearly perceived to be Palestinian writers. The case of Jabrā Ibrāhīm Jabrā, however, reflects some of the complexity of the issue, since Jabrā was educated, worked, and has created primarily outside of Palestine (like other writers mentioned above), but he writes and publishes poetry and narrative in Arabic and English (see Chapter 2), which leads Arab writers, especially Palestinians, to view him as an Arab or Iraqi writer rather than a Palestinian. This claim may also be affected by irrelevant considerations that influence scholars and writers who address this phenomenon. In my view, the only valid consideration is the language of the writing, and hence there is a parallel here with Maghrib-Arab writers who write in French, such as Ṭāhir Ben Jallūn, who is presented (with justification) as a Moroccan and not a French writer. (See Chapter 2 for further discussion of the issue of bilingualism.)

The second group includes Palestinian-Arab writers who remained in the newly founded Israel and were artistically active there. The work of these writers was not conspicuous in the 1950s, the first decade of the state, and was fairly modest, with writers such as Emile Ḥabībī, Samīḥ al-Qāsim (1939–), Michel Ḥaddād (1919–97), and others. Jews who immigrated to Israel from various Arab countries, especially Iraq, made a significant addition to the Arabic literary and cultural activity there.[14]

Palestinian writing both inside and outside Israel made significant progress in the 1960s like other modern Arabic literatures and modern Hebrew literature as well.[15] Palestinian literature has traversed the same stages as other modern Arabic literatures: first, the influence of the romantics; in the second stage, realism or social realism; and then the use of writing techniques influenced by stream of consciousness, existentialism, the absurd and montage. Palestinian literature during this period – like other Arabic literatures – was influenced by two primary sources: Arab, especially Egyptian, literatures, and European and American literatures.

If 1948 is the first watershed in the development of modern Palestinian and Arabic literatures, then 1967 is the second, though each took its own course, as we shall see. The war that erupted in 1967 between Israel and the Arab states was a landmark not only for political–historical affairs, but in cultural–literary terms as well. The Arab world, particularly its intellectuals, used up reams of paper analysing the reasons for the defeat [*naksa*] of the Arab armies. The soul-searching among Arab policy-makers was mirrored among Arab writers and thinkers.[16] The 1967 defeat had a marked impact on the Palestinian community. The geographic changes entailed by the war were reflected in the literary activity of the two branches of Palestinian literature – one outside the borders of Israel and the other within it. Now a third branch was added, the occupied territories of the West Bank and the Gaza Strip, with its own literature. Palestinian cultural activity flourished in these territories, as did other kinds of activity catalysed by the new political situation. Thus, in mapping Palestinian literature after 1967, one can delineate three main branches: literature written by Palestinians in Arab countries and in centres of Palestinian culture in Europe and the United States, exemplified by the work of Jabrā Ibrāhīm Jabrā and Afnān al-Qāsim; literary activity in the West Bank and Gaza, exemplified by the writing of Rashād Abū-Shāwir (1942–) and Yaḥyā Yakhluf (1944–); and Palestinian literature written in Israel, exemplified (apart from prominent veterans like Emile Ḥabībī) by

Maḥmūd Darwīsh (1941–) – until he left Israel in 1972 – and Zakī Darwīsh (1944–). This tripartite division is analogous to a tree with three branches, each representing one division of modern Palestinian literature, all three originating in the trunk deeply rooted in the earth. One could also describe post-1967 Palestinian literature as it had been before the war, with only two divisions: work written outside Israel and work written within its borders. Whatever the division, there is justice to the claim that there is no single modern Palestinian literature, but rather there are several. This assertion is not politically motivated; on the contrary, political motivations (but not exclusively such) underlie the claim that there are no divisions and that it is incorrect to speak of a plurality of modern Arabic literatures.

The changes in Palestinian society outside Israel after the 1967 war were also felt by Palestinians inside Israel. Indeed, Israel's lifting of the military regime over Israeli Arabs in late 1966 and the war of June 1967 wrought enormous changes in Arab society (as well as Jewish society) in Israel. These changes were reflected in the work of local Arab (as well as local Jewish) writers. This marked the opening up of the greater Arab world to the local Palestinian-Arab community, and the beginning of the process of legitimation not just for Arabs who live in Israel, but also for their creative efforts. Following incisive debates in the Arab world in the late 1960s, especially among Palestinians and the PLO itself, their writing was accorded the title 'the literature of resistance', first used by the Palestinian writer and critic Ghassān Kanafānī. One may question the accuracy of the term 'the literature of resistance' [*adab al-muqāwama*] for the case at hand, but this is not the place to explore this. Nonetheless, after the 1967 war, 'the literature of resistance' was applied to Palestinian writing in the West Bank and Gaza.

The 1967 war brought Israeli Arabs into much greater contact with other Arabs than they had been before. And the new-found relations between Palestinian citizens of Israel and other Arabs – including Palestinians in Arab countries and especially those in the West Bank and Gaza – were also experienced by Arab writers in Israel, who forged links with Arab writers in other countries. This change in target audience also affected the choice of themes for Israeli-Arab writing. From then on, Israeli Arabs often wrote for the audience of readers in Cairo and Beirut, and less for their traditional target audience at home – other Israeli Arabs. An interesting dynamic was set into motion in which Israeli Arabs sought acceptance among the writers, scholars and publishers of the Arab countries, while the Arab literary community worldwide heaped love and praise on Israeli Arabs, repenting the former ostracism of them. It should be noted that even prior to June 1967, works by Israeli-Arab writers had appeared in publications throughout the Arab world, primarily in Egypt and Lebanon, the most prominent being Emile Ḥabībī and the poets Samīḥ al-Qāsim, Maḥmūd Darwīsh and Tawfīq Zayyād (1932–94).

The June 1967 war catalysed far-reaching changes in all segments of the Palestinian community and its culture, especially in strengthening the bonds among the three branches of the Palestinian people. The rise in stature of the PLO in the international arena, predominantly in the early 1970s, expedited this process. The sense of solidarity of the Palestinian community, some of whom lived in the Palestinian homeland within the state of Israel or under Israeli rule in the occupied territories and some of whom lived without a homeland or a state, left a profound impression on modern Palestinian literature. The solidarity and cooperation increased during the 1970s and early 1980s. One expression of this is the fact that Palestinian writers and critics from the occupied territories – Asʿad al-Asʿad (1947–), al-Mutawakkil Ṭāha (1958–), Ḥanān ʿAwwād (1951–), Jamāl Bannūra (1953–), and others – agreed to appear in Arabic periodicals and newspapers in Israel such as *al-Jadīd*, *al-Mawākib* and *al-Ittiḥād*. This was also true for Palestinian writers from the various diasporas, such as Afnān al-Qāsim whose essays and criticism about Palestinian affairs appeared in Arabic periodicals and newspapers in Israel. Conversely, Israeli-Arab writers such as Samīḥ al-Qāsim, Emile Ḥabībī, Zakī Darwīsh, Riyāḍ Baydas, and others were published in journals in the occupied territories such as *al-Kātib*, and in periodicals in the various diasporas such as *al-Karmil*, *Shu'ūn Filasṭīniyya*, *Filasṭīn al-Thawra* and *Balsam*.

The intifāḍa that erupted in October 1987 is the third watershed in Palestinian society, accelerating processes and changes that had existed under the surface in the three branches of the Palestinian community. The uprising was launched by Palestinians in Gaza and the West Bank, and although the violence did not spill over into Israel proper, it definitely affected the Arabs of Israel and their ties with the other two branches of the Palestinian people. The impact of the intifāḍa on Palestinians in the various diasporas was manifested on the level of personal and collective Palestinian identity as well as concrete assistance, primarily economic, to those participating in it. The bonds forged among the three parts of the Palestinian nation were clearly felt among the members of the literary community. Since then, there has been virtually no distinction between the writing in the three branches of Palestinian literature. Intifāḍa writing encompasses writers from all three, without noting or emphasizing to which branch the writers belong. Similarly, anthologies of intifāḍa writing published in Israel do not distinguish among the three branches of contributors.[17] In short, the contacts and links among the branches of the Palestinian people have consolidated and this was reflected in Palestinian literature during the period of the intifāḍa. Besides writers from the Arab world, this literature has ties with 'revolutionary' writers from outside it, as well as with Israeli-Jewish writers who identify with the goals of the intifāḍa and the Palestinian struggle for independence.

The Declaration of Principles signed by Israel and the PLO in September 1993, and the peace treaty with Jordan from October 1994, changed the political map in the Middle East once again, and constitute the fourth watershed in the development of the Palestinian community. The special circumstances of the Palestinian community together with their sense of identity have consolidated into a demand for political and cultural independence, which they seek to achieve through a comprehensive peace process. This process has had a two-pronged effect: it led the Palestinians to acknowledge the demands of the Israelis and, likewise, led Israel to acknowledge the claims of the Palestinians. The relationship between the Palestinians and the Israelis points up the singularity of the Palestinians as a political and cultural entity, as well as their link to the Arab nation, though they are fated to live with Israeli Jews. And within this complex situation, Israeli Arabs are unique within the already unique circumstances of the Palestinian nation.

The present study is largely devoted to the literature of Israeli Arabs for two primary reasons: first, because of the important and special role their works play in modern Arab literatures in general and in Palestinian literature in particular; and, second, because studies about Palestinian literature that have appeared so far in Arabic, Hebrew and English have not, in my opinion, sufficiently focused on the literature of Israeli Arabs.

THE CULTURE OF THE OTHER – ISRAELI JEWS

In the context of research about modern Palestinian literature, I think it proper to devote part of the Introduction to Israeli-Jewish culture, as my perspective of Israeli-Jewish society is influenced by my preoccupation with Arab culture. I believe that examination of the problems of identity of Israeli-Jewish society can shed light from the opposite direction on the culture and identity of the Palestinians, especially Israeli Arabs.[18]

The first question that should be asked is if an Israeli culture in fact exists. And if so, what is it? Israeli society is not homogeneous, but is without exaggeration the most heterogeneous society in the Middle East.[19] And in the face of this diversity, efforts are underway through the Israeli establishment to impose a particular world view and culture, as had been done in the past, i.e., to bestow a Western orientation to the nation in Zion. This had been the approach of the founding fathers, and remnants of it are still evident both in the government and among a significant number of intellectuals. Two illustrious examples: Abba Eban, the former Foreign Minister of Israel, a writer and intellectual well versed in Arabic, treats with contempt anything that is Arab and advocates a Western orientation.[20] Similarly, Amos Oz, one of Israel's most celebrated authors since the 1960s, and one who identifies with the Israeli left (like Eban), bemoans the loss of Western cultural hegemony.[21]

The shattered dreams of the Jewish founders, who believed in establishing a state that would not be Levantine, stemmed from their basic lack of understanding of Middle Eastern reality. This shortcoming was rooted in both ideological motives and practical sources – because they were educated and brought up in a Western cultural milieu. Their descendants, who have dominated the most powerful cultural, economic and political positions, have inordinate influence in Israel over what to do and how to do it. And the predominant approach of the founding fathers and most of their followers was to close themselves off to Middle Eastern and Mediterranean cultures in favour of a culture based on that of central or at least Eastern Europe. This ideological and pragmatic approach had a profound influence in the fields of policy, society and economics, shaping many levels of Israeli culture. The approach still dominates the various programmes of culture and music, whose editors ignored and eliminated the Middle Eastern component from the Israeli cultural canon.

The desire of many Israelis, especially intellectuals, to distance themselves from things Eastern and to espouse everything Western calls for a re-examination of the terminology, such as the word 'Levant' and its derivatives. Levant is, of course, a term with a specific geographical definition, to which some have attached pejorative meanings, such as a superficial or shallow cultural style. This is how the term is translated in Israel, and when the term 'Levant' or 'Levantine' appears, it has an immediate negative connotation. For example, the former Chief Justice of the Supreme Court, Moshe Landau, when giving the acceptance speech on behalf of the recipients of the Israel Prize for 1991, warned against 'the Levantinization poised outside the door of Israeli society and the pursuit of material pleasures'.[22] Clearly, we are again facing a recurring phenomenon

– the sense of superiority and ethnocentrism of most educated Israeli Jews who feel that everything of the East is inferior, superficial, common and crude, while everything at the opposite pole, i.e. Western culture, is positive.

As we near the end of the second millennium, the controversy over Arabs, Arabic, the teaching of Arabic and translations from Arabic literature into Hebrew are among the most important issues in Israeli society. Arabic is an official language of Israel, like Hebrew, but only in a formal sense. In some middle schools, Arabic is studied in the Jewish sector, but to this day has not been made mandatory in schools, not withstanding all declarations to the contrary. The only explanation for this can be the attitude of the policy-makers toward teaching Arabic to the Jewish population of Israel. What is revealed is alienation, if not ignorance. One might have expected that the rise to power of the Labour Government in 1992, many of whose members define themselves as liberal and progressive, would give substance to the claim that Arabic is an official language of Israel. But as of this writing, the teaching of Arabic in Israel is going nowhere, and attitudes about it are no more positive than they have been in the past. This corroborates my belief that policy-setters – not just politicians – seek to divorce themselves from the Middle East, preferring the Western values and norms, and apply Israeli ethnocentrism as they understand it.

One of the most intriguing questions is why most Jewish intellectuals in Israel do not know Arabic. This is an anomaly. One would expect that those who define themselves as progressive, liberal and leftist would study the language and culture of their (around 200 million) Arab neighbours and of the Arabic minority in Israel. Instead, there is an interesting dialectical process in which those who express solidarity with the 'other side' – the Arabs – consistently refuse to acknowledge the need to know its language and culture. Logically, one would expect the opposite. The explanation seems to be that these people were raised in, educated about, and networked with the various Western cultures and hence relate with arrogance and alienation toward the Arab or Muslim cultural heritage. Since these individuals occupy powerful positions in the fields of culture, society, politics and the media, this attitude trickles down and influences many others in Israeli society. This is true, for example, of publishers and cultural programmes on radio, television and in the newspapers. The editors know about, and concentrate primarily on, local Hebrew literature, usually ignoring Arabic literature entirely, unless there happens to be a political context. One can discern a difference between the literary programmes on the radio and, to a lesser extent, in the newspapers which show some interest in Arabic literature and culture, while programmes on television completely disregard the subject. Even when important political events are relevant, they do not lead to literary or cultural programmes about Arab society. The most glaring example of this was the Declaration of Principles with the Palestinians and the peace accord with Jordan. One would think that during the years of these treaties (1993 and 1994), Israelis would be deluged with programmes about Palestinian and Jordanian literature, but amazingly (or not), almost nothing was done in the field. Perhaps with regard to Jordanian literature, it could be argued that few Israelis are specialists in their literature, but regarding Palestinian literature, a great many Israelis (both Jewish and Arab) have expertise on the subject. One would have expected some curiosity from the literary editors, but nothing was forthcoming.

The central problem that has faced Israel throughout its modern history is the continuation of the main obstacle that faced the Jewish community in Palestine before the founding of the state – its acceptance or more accurately lack of acceptance, into the Middle East. The peace treaty between Israel and Egypt in 1979 began the process of lifting the taboo on the Jewish community that had existed prior to the founding of Israel and ever since. As of this treaty Israel was accepted not by all the Arab states, but, at least formally, by Egypt. Significant segments of Egyptian society – the intellectuals and trade unions, for example – continue to boycott Israel. Thus the agreement is one between governments with common interests, rather than between the peoples. Nevertheless, the agreement did manage to percolate down to some of the other Arab states. The Oslo Agreement of September 1993 was a turning point in the acceptance of Israel, not just in the Arab region, but in the Muslim world at large, and indirectly helped Israel in its relations with countries in Africa, Asia and even Europe and Japan. The peace treaty signed between Israel and Jordan in October 1994, like the negotiations between Israel and Syria, is another building block in the growing acceptance of Israel in the Arab region and in some parts of the Muslim world. Clearly the dialogue begun with Egypt in 1977 has expanded to include not only the Arab countries bordering Israel, but some north African countries and Gulf states as well, including Kuwait and Saudi Arabia. The significance of this is that the dialogue is no longer only between Israel and the Arab world, but between Israel and the Muslim world.

Acceptance of Israel in the Middle East is clearly a two-directional problem. On the one hand, as noted above, it is related to the willingness of the Arab and the Muslim countries to acknowledge the Israeli entity as a state having the right to exist with its unique views and principles. On the other hand, the acceptance of Israel is not up to the Arab and Muslim world alone, but to a large extent depends on the willingness of Israel's inhabitants to integrate into the Middle East. The fact is that many Israeli-Jewish intellectuals, as well as wide sectors of the population who came originally from Arab countries and were socialized to mockery, haughtiness and hostility toward their culture, place obstacles in the way of this integration, and of accepting Arab culture among Israeli Jews.[23]

Another problematic issue is the acceptance in Israel of Arabic literature in the Arabic language. In the social, cultural and political circumstances of Israel today, what conditions must obtain for there to be a major corpus of translations from Arabic into Hebrew?[24] Our point of origin is that literature is an important window to the culture of a nation and that translated literature can break down the ethnocentric stereotypes that permeate society. Arabic literature is no different in this respect than any other literature.[25]

NOTES

1. Kāmil al-Sawāfīrī, *al-Adab al-'Arabī al-Mu'āṣir fī Filasṭīn min Sanat 1860–1960*, Cairo, Dār al-Ma'ārif, 1979. Fārūq Wādī, *Thalāth 'Allāmāt fī al-Riwāya al-Filasṭīniyya*, 2nd edn, Acre, Dār al-Aswār, 1985. 'Abd al-Raḥmān Yāghī, *Fī al-Adab al-Filasṭīnī al-Ḥadīth qabla al-Nakba waba'dahā*, Kuwait, Sharikat Kāẓima li'l-Nashr wa'l-Tarjama wa'l-Tawzī', 1983. Maḥmūd Ghanāyim, *Fi Mabnā al-Naṣṣ, Dirāsa fī Riwāyat Emile Ḥabībī al-Waqā'i' al-Gharība fī Ikhtifā' Sa'īd Abī al-Nahs al-Mutashā'il*, Jatt, Manshūrāt al-Yasār, 1987. Muṣṭafā 'Abd al-Ghanii, *Naqd al-Dhāt fī al-Riwāya al-Filasṭīniyya*, Cairo, Sīnā li'l-Nashr, 1994. Ami Elad [-Bouskila] (ed.), 'Sifrutam Shel Ha'Aravim BeYisrael', *HaMizraḥ HeḤadash*, 35 (1993). Shimon Ballas, *HaSifrut Ha'Aravit BeTsel HaMilḥama*, Tel-Aviv, 'Am 'Oved, Ofakim, 1978. Mattityahu Peled, 'Annals of Doom: Palestinian Literature 1917–1948', *Arabica*, XXIX, 2 (1982), pp. 141–83. Hanan Ashrawi, *Contemporary Palestinian Literature Under Occupation*, Bir Zeit, Bir-Zeit University, 1976. Stefan Wild, *Ghassan Kanafani: The Life of a Palestinian*, Wiesbaden, Otto Harrassowitz, 1975. Salma Khadra Jayyusi (ed.), *Anthology of Modern Palestinian Literature*, New York, Columbia University Press, 1992.
2. This chapter is based on my article, 'HaḤipus Aḥar HaZehut: Mipui Sifrutam Shel Ha'Aravim BeYisrael', *Alpayim*, 11 (1995), pp. 173–84; and on my article 'La littèrature Palestienne d'Israël: Une Littèrature en quête de légitimation', *Levant*, 7 (1994–95), pp. 146–49.
3. This chapter is based on my article, 'Bein 'Olamot Mesoragim: Riyāḍ Baydas VehaSipur Ha'Aravi HaKatzar BeYisrael', *HaMizraḥ HeḤadash*, 35 (1993), pp. 65–87.
4. Parts of this chapter are based on my article 'Avanim 'Al Mitzḥa Shel HaMoledet: 'Al HaSifrut HaPalestinit BeTekufat HaIntifāḍa', *Alpayim*, 7 (1993) pp. 96–117. See also

my article, 'Al-Kâtib – eine Palästinensiche Kulturzeitschrift als Forum der intifāḍa-Literature', *Orient*, 36 (1995), pp. 109–25.

5. This chapter is based on my article 'Kedushata Shel 'Ir: Yerushalayim BeSifrut HaIntifāḍa', *HaMizraḥ HeḤadash*, 34 (1992), pp. 151–61.
6. Reynold A. Nicholson, *A Literary History of the Arabs*, Cambridge, Cambridge University Press, 1930.
7. M. M. Badawi (ed.), *Modern Arabic Literature*, Cambridge, Cambridge University Press, 1992, pp. 1–23. Pierre Cachia, *An Overview of Modern Arabic Literature*, Edinburgh, Edinburgh University Press, 1990, pp. 29–42.
8. Ami Elad [-Bouskila], 'Maḥfūẓ's Za'balāwi: Six Stations of a Quest', *International Journal of Middle East Studies*, 26 (1994), pp. 631–44. Menachem Milson, 'Najīb Maḥfūẓ and the Quest for Meaning', *Arabica*, 17 (1970), pp. 155–86. Sasson Somekh, 'Za'balāwī: Author, Theme and Technique', *Journal of Arabic Literature*, I (1970), pp. 24–35. Muḥammad Siddiq, 'The Process of Individuation in al-Ṭayyib Ṣāliḥ's novel *Season of Migration to the North*', *Journal of Arabic Literature*, XVII (1986), pp. 126–45.
9. Ami Elad [-Bouskila], *The Village Novel in Modern Egyptian Literature*, Berlin, Klaus Schwarz, 1994.
10. For more about women's literature in modern Arabic, see Miriam Cooke, 'Arab Women Writers', in Badawi (ed.), *Modern Arabic Literature*, pp. 443–61; Mineke Schipper (ed.), *Unheard Words: Women and Literature in Africa, the Arab World, Asia, the Caribbean and Latin America*, London, Allison & Busby, 1985, pp. 69–120; Fedwa Malti-Douglas, *Woman's Body, Woman's World: Gender and Discourse in Arab-Islamic Writing*, Princeton, Princeton University Press, 1991; Kamal Boullata (ed.), *Women of the Fertile Crescent: Modern Poetry by Arab Women*, Colorado, Three Continents Press, Colorado Spring, repr. 1994 (1st edn 1982); Nadje Sadig al-Ali, *Gender Writing/Writing Gender: The Representation of Women in Selections of Modern Egyptian Literature*, Cairo, American University in Cairo Press, 1994; Roger Allen, Hillary Kilpatrick and Ed de Moore (eds), *Love and Sexuality in Modern Arabic Literature*, London, Saqi Books, 1995; Joseph T. Zeidan, *Arab Women Novelists: The Formative Years and Beyond*, New York, State University of New York Press, 1995.
11. On modern Mashriq and Maghrib literatures, see Ami Elad-Bouskila, *Sifrut 'Aravit BeLevush 'Ivri*, Jerusalem, Ministry of Education, Culture and Sport, 1995, pp. 14–37. Ami Elad-Bouskila, 'En Deux Langues, La Littérature Moderne d'Afrique du Nord', in Ami Elad-Bouskila and Erez Biton (eds), *Le Maghreb, Littérature et Culture (Special Issue)*, *Apirion*, 28 (1993), pp. 86–7.
12. 'Īsā al-Nā'ūrī, *Adab al-Mahjar*, 3rd edn, Cairo, Dār al-Ma'ārif, 1977. Anṭwān al-Qawwāl, *Jubrān Khalīl Jubrān*, Beirut, Dār Amwāj li'l-Ṭibā'a wa'l-Nashr, 1993.
13. 'Abd Allāh Khālifa Rakībī, *al-Qiṣṣa al-Qaṣīra fī al-Adab al-Jazā'irī al-Mu'āṣir*, Cairo, Dār al-Kitāb al-'Arabī li'l-Ṭibā'a wa'l-Nashr, 1969. Muḥammad 'Azzām, *Ittijāhāt al-Qiṣṣa al-Mu'āṣira fī al-Maghrib*, *Dirāsa*, Damascus, Manshūrāt Ittiḥād al-Kuttāb al-'Arab, 1978. Najīb al-'Awfī, *Muqārabat al-Wāqi' fī al-Qiṣṣa al-Qaṣīra al-Maghribiyya, min al-Ta'sīs ilā al-Tajnīs*, Beirut and Casablanca, al-Markaz al-Thaqāfī al-'Arabī, 1987. Muḥammad Adīb al-Salāwī, *al-Shi'r al-Maghribī, Muqāraba Ta'rīkhīyya 1830-1960*, Casablanca, Ifrīqiyā al-Sharq, 1986.
14. Shmuel Moreh, *al-Qiṣṣa al-Qaṣīra 'Inda Yahūd al-'Irāq 1924-1978*, Jerusalem, Magnes Press 1981. Reuven Snir, 'We Were Like Those Who Dream: Iraqi-Jewish Writers in

Israel in the 1950s', *Prooftext*, 11 (1991) pp. 153–73.

15. Gershon Shaked, *HaSiporet Ha'Ivrit 1880–1980, BeḤevlei HaZeman*, vol. 4, Tel-Aviv and Jerusalem, HaKibbutz Ha-Artzi, Keter, 1993.
16. Ballas, *HaSifrut Ha'Aravit BeTsel HaMilḥama*, pp. 145–278. Ṣādiq Jalāl al-'Aẓm, *al-Naqd al-Dhātī ba'd al-Hazīma*, Acre, Dār al-Jalīl li'l-Ṭibā'a wa'l-Nashr, 1969. Nizār Qabbānī, *Hawāmish 'alā Daftar al-Naksa, Qaṣīda Ṭawīla*, 3rd edn, Beirut, Nizār Qabbānī, 1968.
17. *Ibdā'āt al-Ḥajar*, vol. 1, Jerusalem, Ittiḥād al-Udabā' wa'l-Kuttāb al-Filasṭīniyyin, 1988, vol. 2, 1989. Muḥammad 'Alī al-Yūsufī, *Abjadiyyat al-Ḥijāra*, Nicosia; Mu'assasat Bīsān li'l-Ṣiḥāfa wa'l-Nashr wa'l Tawzī', 1988. *Wahaj al-Fajr: Min Adabiyyāt al-Intifāḍa*, Nazareth, Rābiṭat al-Kuttāb wa'l-Udabā' al-Filasṭīniyyin fī Isrā'īl, 1989. 'Ādil Abū-'Amsha (ed.), *Shi'r al-Intifāḍa*, Jerusalem, Ittiḥād al-Kuttāb al-Filasṭīniyyin fī al-Ḍaffa wa'l Qiṭā', 1991.
18. For an interesting perspective, see Ammiel Alcalay, *After Jews and Arabs, Remaking Levantine Culture*, Minneapolis, University of Minnesota Press, 1993.
19. For further discussion of this theory, see Ami Elad-Bouskila, 'Petiḥut USegirut Shel HaḤevra HaYisraelit BaMizraḥ Ha Tikhon Be'Et Shalom', *Moznayim*, 70, 3 (December 1995), pp. 3–7.
20. Abba Eban, *Voice of Israel*, 1969, p. 76, as cited in Sammy Smooha, 'Nikur Tarbuti BeYisrael', *Apirion*, 2 (Winter 1983/84), p. 28.
21. 'Mumḥeh LeRomantika', *Ha-aretz*, (13 July 1990).
22. *Yediot Aḥaronot*, (19 April 1991).
23. One expression of this point of view can be found in the writing of the poet and critic Menaḥem Ben, 'HaShalom HaMe-ayem 'Aleinu', *Yerushalayim* (28 October 1994).
24. For an important article on this subject, see Sasson Somekh, 'Sifrut 'Aravit BeTirgum 'Ivri' in Jacob Mansour (ed.), *Meḥkarim Be'Aravit UveIslam*, vol. 1, Ramat-Gan, Bar-Ilan University, 1973, pp. 141–52.
25. For a fuller discussion, see Ami Elad [-Bouskila], 'HaMar-a HeSeduka: LeVa'ayat Hitkabluta Shel HaSifrut Ha'Aravit BeYisrael', *Moznayim*, 64:8 (April 1990), pp. 27–30. Ami Elad-Bouskila, 'Infitāḥ wa-Inghilāq al-Mujtama' al-Isrā'ilī fī al-Sharq al-Awsaṭ fī zaman al-Salām', *Mashārif*, 10 (August 1997), pp. 35–43.

I

The Quest for Identity
Three Issues in Israeli-Arab Literature

No nation or people seems entirely free of the struggle over problems of identity, both on the collective and the individual levels. The contemporary Arab world continues to grapple with issues of identity, the roots of this struggle harking back to Napoleon's invasion of Egypt in 1798, bringing a renewed encounter between Arab and Western culture. Then the struggle was evoked by the intrusion of a European-Christian power into a predominantly Muslim-Arab world that had been immersed for quite some time in a technological, scientific and cultural malaise. The ensuing upheaval only deepened with the conquest of large parts of the Muslim-Arab world in the Mashriq and the Maghrib in the nineteenth and twentieth centuries. Thus the Arab world has undergone almost two centuries of soul-searching with regard to national, cultural, religious, social and economic identity. And Palestinian-Arab society has undergone a special kind of upheaval, as its century-long struggle with the Jewish community ended in defeat, leading to the establishment of the state of Israel and leaving all Palestinians without a state and some without a homeland. In the context of this search for national and individual identity, and the special situation of Palestinian society, the turbulent search for identity by the Israeli branch of the Palestinian community is unique.[1]

This chapter looks at three issues in the literature of Israeli Arabs that relate to their quest for identity in both Palestinian-Arab and Israeli-Jewish societies: (1) for whom do Israeli Arabs write? (2) where do they publish their work? and (3) what do they write about? The complexity of these issues is compounded by the fact that, with the establishment of the state of Israel in 1948, this society was transformed from majority to minority status.[2]

The identity of Palestinian literature, particularly that written in Israel, is problematic and complex. As noted in the Introduction, Palestinian literature has three branches. However, while Palestinian literature written in the various diasporas can be considered a 'literature without a homeland', that written in the occupied territories has a partial homeland but lacks a state, and that written in Israel is produced in historical Palestine that is now a country with a Jewish majority and a Palestinian minority. Thus, the identity of Palestinian literature written in Israel is controversial, and various writers and scholars, not surprisingly, refer to it differently: 'Palestinian literature written by Israeli Arabs', 'the literature of Israeli Arabs', 'the literature of the 1948 Arabs', 'the literature of occupied Palestine', and so on. These appellations reflect more than semantic issues; indeed, since 1967, not only have different scholars used different terms, but sometimes the same scholar uses different terms on different occasions, especially in light of the changes brought about by the intifāḍa in Israel and the Arab world.[3] The Arabs themselves, especially Palestinians who live outside Israel and publish about this subject, are not tied down to any one formulation regarding what can loosely be referred to as 'the literature of resistance' [*adab al-muqāwama*].[4]

The bond among the three branches of contemporary Palestinian literature, including the contribution of Israeli Arabs to the 'literature of resistance', was strengthened in the early 1970s and came to the fore during the intifāḍa. The Palestinian uprising in the occupied territories vividly highlighted the links between Israeli Arabs and the other two branches, and also underscored the status of Israeli Arabs as a national and cultural minority that is subject to (or subjects itself to) rules of the game that the other two branches do not accept.

FOR WHOM DO ISRAELI ARABS WRITE?

The fundamental assumption of this chapter is that an examination of the above three questions can shed light on the basic orientation of Israeli Arabs. The question for whom Israeli Arabs write has, broadly speaking, two answers: some write in Arabic for Arabic-readers, and some write in both Arabic and Hebrew, the latter for a Hebrew-reading public (more about this in Chapter 2). Until 1967 writers in the first group wrote for the Arabic-reading audience inside Israel, which included Israeli Arabs as well as Jewish intellectuals who had recently immigrated to Israel from Arab countries, especially Iraq. However, the target audience of these

Israeli-Arab writers has changed since 1967, particularly since the early 1970s, when the Arab states 'discovered' Israeli Arabs, dropped the unflattering labels that had been applied to them, and began to heap undeserved praise on their creations. Maḥmūd Darwīsh became a bitter opponent of this trend, expressed by the title of his article 'Save us from this Cruel Love'.[5] Two complementary processes began at this time: Arab cultural centres outside Israel began to publish Arab works written in Israel, sometimes even competing for the honour (as happened to Samīḥ al-Qāsim and Emile Ḥabībī, for example), while, on the other hand, Palestinian literature in Israel became directed not only toward the local audience but primarily toward those outside Israel. Thus, many Israeli-Arab writers began to publish in foreign newspapers and periodicals, and used publishers within the Arab world.[6]

The question for whom Israeli Arabs write assumed a new significance during the intifāḍa. This period has been of great importance for Israeli Arabs – as for other Palestinians and Israelis. The literature published during the intifāḍa reflects the social, political and cultural processes which the Palestinian people have been experiencing.[7] In a series of Palestinian anthologies called *Ibdā'āt al-Ḥajar* [the stone creations] published by the Association of Palestinian Writers in the Territories, which so far includes two volumes (in 1988 and 1989), works by Israeli Arabs appear. The first volume, for example, includes 'al-Bū'ra' [the focus] – a short story by Riyāḍ Baydas – and the poems 'Risāla ilā Ghuzāt lā Yaqrā'un' [a letter to occupiers who do not read] by Samīḥ al-Qāsim' and 'al-'Unwān al-Jadīd' [the new address] by Jamāl Q'awār.[8] An example of Palestinian literary activity outside the occupied territories, especially Cypriot writing, is the series *Filasṭīn al-Thawra*, which appeared in Nicosia under the auspices of the PLO. This series, which included eight volumes of poetry and prose as well as political tracts and articles about the intifāḍa itself, does not distinguish between the different branches of the Palestinian people, and quite a few pieces have been written by Israeli Arabs.[9]

The extensive literary activity of Israeli Arabs during the intifāḍa also found an outlet in Arab magazines and periodicals in Israel, especially the journal *al-Jadīd* and the literary supplement of the daily *al-Ittiḥād*, both of which belong to the Israeli Communist Party. At the same time, Arab writers from the West Bank and the Gaza Strip such as the poet and author As'ad al-As'ad (editor of the journal *al-Kātib* and former Secretary-General of the Association of Palestinian Writers in the Territories) publish in Israeli-Arab newspapers and periodicals, particularly *al-Ittiḥād*. In general, evidence of the close ties among the three branches and the blurring of boundaries between them can be found in the various anthologies published during the intifāḍa, particularly during the first two years, in Gaza and the West Bank, in Israel and in Cyprus. In the first volume of *Ibdā'āt al-Ḥajar*, for example, appear poets from the territories such as al-Mutawakkil Ṭāha and 'Abd al-Nāṣir Ṣāliḥ together with the Israeli-Arab poets Samīḥ al-Qāsim and Jamāl Q'awār. And in the anthology *Wahaj al-Fajr* [the brilliance of dawn], published by the Association of Palestinian Writers in Israel, Israeli Arabs Zakī Darwīsh and Michel Ḥaddād appear together with Palestinians from the territories al-Mutawakkil Ṭāha and Ḥanān 'Awwād.[10] Another indication of this activity during the intifāḍa is the large number of books published by the Association of Palestinian Writers in Israel and by private publishers, primarily in the Galilee and the Triangle (a region in central Israel heavily populated by Arabs).

WHERE DO ISRAELI-ARAB WRITERS PUBLISH?

The second question, where do Israeli-Arab writers publish their work, is directly connected to the question of who constitutes the target audience for these writers. The picture is quite clear: until the late 1960s and early 1970s, Palestinian writers in Israel wrote for Arabic-readers in Israel, both Arabs and Jews, and hence appeared in the journals and newspapers of the Israeli establishment, including the dailies *al-Yawm* and *al-Anbā'*, periodicals such as *Ḥaqīqat al-Amr*, *Ṣadā al-Tarbiya*, *al-Hadaf*, *Liqā'-Mifgash* and *al-Sharq*, as well as the publications of the Israeli Communist Party – *al-Ittiḥād* and *al-Jadīd*.[11] Most of their books were printed by publishers sponsored or supported by the establishment, such as Dār al-Nashr al-'Arabī [Arab publishing house] that published from the 1960s not only books by local writers and poets, but also major works of modern Arabic literature.[12] There are, however, several exceptions to this: Israeli-Arab writers and poets who were published outside Israel in the Arab world, mainly Egypt (*al-Hilāl*, *al-Majalla*) and Lebanon (*al-Adīb*, *al-Adāb*). Among the most prominent of these are Tawfīq Zayyād, Samīḥ al-Qāsim, Maḥmūd Darwīsh (who left Israel in 1971), and Emile Ḥabībī (who won the Israel Prize for literature in 1992).

A significant change occurred in the late 1960s and early 1970s with regard to where Israeli-Arab writers published their work. Three factors contributed to this. The first was the 1967 war, which eliminated the barrier between Israeli Arabs and other Arabs, particularly Palestinians in the West Bank and Gaza. Emile Ḥabībī illustrates this in one chapter of his diary (published in *al-Jadīd*), describing how he found in West Bank bookstores not only books that he had never heard of, but an Arabic translation of Voltaire's *Candide*, which influenced him when he wrote his acclaimed novel *al-Mutashā'il*.[13] The second factor was the changed attitudes of Arabs outside Israel, who 'discovered' the Israeli Arab in the late 1960s, a trend strengthened as the PLO legitimized the Palestinian identity of Israeli Arabs. This legitimacy had an impact on intellectuals and writers in the Arab world, including journal editors, particularly in Egypt and Lebanon. Third, as a result of the two preceding factors, most Israeli-Arab writers who had previously written for periodicals of the Israeli establishment now abandoned them; hence, most of these periodicals ceased to appear by the late 1960s. Thus, both famous and less famous Israeli-Arab writers began to publish their work entirely in non-establishment periodicals in Israel or, increasingly, in the Arab countries.

The October War of 1973, the Lebanon War of 1982, and the intifāḍa that erupted in 1987 intensified the dynamic of change in Israeli-Palestinian literature, deepening the bond with Arab literature in general and with the two other branches of Palestinian literature in particular. This is reflected in the target audience, the venue of publication and the subject matter of Israeli-Arab literature. Much writing by Israeli Arabs now appears in periodicals of the major Arab cultural centres, both in Arab cities (Beirut, Cairo, Casablanca) and beyond (London, Paris, Nicosia). Thus a reciprocal process took place: Arab cultural centres took an increased interest in the writing of Israeli Arabs, and this impelled Israeli Arabs into prolific creativity. This process accelerated in the 1980s, especially with the start of the intifāḍa. In parallel, Israeli-Arab establishment periodicals – *al-Sharq* (1982) and *al-Anbā'* (1985) – were dying out. Although *Liqā'-Mifgash* reappeared in a new incarnation in 1984, by the late 1980s and early 1990s it was in a moribund state. Although *al-Ittiḥād* and *al-Jadīd* continued to publish, new periodicals began to flourish, such as *al-Aswār* (1988), *48* (the periodical of the Association of Palestinian Writers in Israel – 1988), *al-Thaqāfa* (1992-93), *Iḍā'āt* (1993–), and *Mashārif* (1995-97).

This trend was particularly evident during the intifāḍa, with Palestinian writers from the diaspora and the occupied territories publishing their works in Israeli-Arab periodicals, while Israeli-Arab authors appeared in Palestinian periodicals in and out of the territories, publishing poetry, prose and various anthologies in the Arab world and beyond.[14] Thus an interesting dialectic developed in which, on the one hand, the fences were falling between Palestinian writers in Israel and their kin in the diaspora and the territories; and, on the other hand, a nagging question could no longer be avoided: whether these citizens of Israel were Israelis against their will or by choice.

Although the intifāḍa blurred the boundaries between the three branches of the Palestinian people, it also heightened the sense of self of the Palestinians in Israel. The bond among the three branches is especially strong in the area of literary activity and publishing. Palestinians from the diaspora, such as the writer and scholar Afnān al-Qāsim in France, publish in *al-Ittiḥād* and *al-Jadīd*, which, as noted, belong to the Israeli Communist Party; and Palestinian poets and writers from Israel such as Emile Ḥabībī, Samīḥ al-Qāsim and Riyāḍ Baydas publish in Palestinian periodicals in the territories such as *al-Kātib* and in diaspora Palestinian periodicals such as *al-Karmil* and *Filasṭīn al-Thawra*. These relationships deepened during the period of the intifāḍa, involving not only periodicals but also anthologies published in the occupied territories, Israel and Cyprus. Thus, anthologies published in Israel contain prose and poetry written by Palestinians from the diaspora and the territories, while anthologies published in the territories and the diasporas contain writing by Israeli Arabs.[15]

WHAT DO ISRAELI ARABS WRITE ABOUT?

The third question under discussion is what do Israeli Arabs write about? One can broadly distinguish two main periods of Israeli-Arab literature: the first from 1948 until the late 1960s, and the second, from the late 1960s to the present. Before the establishment of the state of Israel, Palestinian literature dealt with two main subjects: the clash with the British colonial power and the generation gap in Palestinian society. Until the late 1960s, Israeli-Arab literature reflected the ideological identification of Israeli Arabs with the Arab world, especially support for Communist ideology (Emile Ḥabībī, Tawfīq Zayyād, Samīḥ al-Qāsim, Maḥmūd Darwīsh); since the late 1960s, however, the Palestinian factor has been more pronounced in this literature. In the first period, the writing was concerned with the problems of the refugees, the land, the Israeli military administration, Jewish–Arab relations, the status of women, and the struggle between old and new.[16] After the military regime over Israeli Arabs was lifted in 1966 and following the political, social and cultural upheavals in the wake of the 1967 war, both the techniques and themes of Israeli-Arab writing have altered. The renewed encounter of Israeli Arabs with the Arabs in the territories sharpened the awareness among Israeli Arabs of the uniqueness of their situation. Their writing now focused on other themes: identity, alienation and familiarity, the renewed interaction with Arabs in the territories, the wars of 1967, 1973 and 1982, the intifāḍa, and discrimination and racism.[17]

Some themes remained constant over the two periods: primarily the relationship of Israeli Palestinians to the land. Despite the processes of urbanization undergone by the Arab population in Israel (actually a process of transforming a village into a satellite of a metropolis), most remained in rural areas. Although the land has remained a central theme since the late 1960s, the emphasis shifted from the role of land as a source of livelihood to land as a focus of emotional attachment in a time of rapid change in Israel and the world. Thus, Israeli Arabs have continued to write about land from their original viewpoint, though less intensively – as in the work of major writers like Samīḥ al-Qāsim, Muḥammad Naffā‘, Riyāḍ Baydas, and others. One example is the writing about 'Land Day', commemorated first by Israeli Arabs on 30 March 1976: in contrast with the earlier period, land has here been transformed into an ethos and a symbol – political, social and even religious.

Other major themes of the first period have also undergone transformation: the refugee problem, the status of women, relations between Arabs and the establishment, Jewish–Arab relations and the confrontation between old and new. The theme of refugees and infiltrators (refugees who tried to return illegally), which had been central for many Israeli-Arab writers in the 1950s and early 1960s, lost its popularity in the late 1960s,[18] although after the 1967 war it still served as the subject of a few short stories.[19] But by the 1970s and 1980s, few writers addressed this issue, with the exception of Ḥabībī and Baydas. Not only did interest in the theme diminish, but it was also treated differently. In recent years the presentation was less ideological and took on a more sentimental character of nostalgic memories.

Subjects that during the 1970s and 1980s were more or less relegated to the margins of literature include the processes of modernization of Israeli-Arab society. Concern with the status of women and the struggle between old and new has, in general, waned. This dynamic is visible not only in Israeli-Arab literature, but in Arab literature in general. These issues had once been central in Arab writing, particularly prose in the 1950s and 1960s; since the 1970s, however, Arab literature has dealt with them much less, or even dismissed them as belonging to the general transformation undergone by the Third World. Recent writing has focused more on the individual and the relationship between the individual and the community-at-large or the surrounding Jewish society. Outstanding events such as the intifāḍa and the Gulf War have also had an impact on the writing of Israeli Arabs, giving it a more collective and national orientation.

The subject of Jewish–Arab relations, on both the personal and collective levels, has also been treated differently since the late 1960s (more about this in Chapter 5). The image of the Jew appears less frequently in Israeli-Arab literature,[20] and there is less of a tendency to demonize and dehumanize Jews. From the mid 1970s, however, this subject was somewhat revived, mainly in prose; and with the outbreak of the intifāḍa, the unflattering characterization of the Jew, typical of 1950s literature, began to reappear in prose and poetry. This applies to the writing of non-Palestinians such as Sa'd Di'bis, Farīd 'Aqīl, and Su'ād al-Ṣabāḥ, as well as to Palestinian writers such as 'Alī al-Jarīrī, and Tawfīq Fayyāḍ.[21]

Examination of the three main issues in this chapter attests to the fact that Israeli Arabs live and write in three dimensions: (1) the Arab world; (2) the three branches of the Palestinian people; and (3) Israel. The year 1967 was a watershed: until then, Israeli-Arab literature put more emphasis on the Arab dimension; in the 1970s, following the 1982 Lebanon War, and since the intifāḍa, the Palestinian element has come to the fore.

For Israeli-Arab writers from the 1950s onward, the three constituent elements of literary activity – target audience, place of publication and subject matter – have reflected these changes. Until 1967, the isolation of Israeli Arabs from the Arab world forced these writers to publish mainly in Israel for Arabic-readers – Jews as well as Arabs – which was limited in scope and fostered attention to more local themes that were singular to Israeli Arabs. In the late 1960s and early 1970s, with the renewal of contact between Israeli Arabs and the Arab states, and after Arab intellectuals partly recognized that this was not treasonous literature but rather a 'literature of resistance', Israeli Arabs won the legitimation they had longed to obtain. Ironically, this very recognition only intensified their problem of identity. Vacillation between national distinctiveness and their Israeli identity together with, intermittently, their desire for legitimization from both Arabs and Israelis continues, despite their ongoing process of Palestinization. Awareness of their status as a national minority with ties to the Arab world and to the other branches of the Palestinian people has not resolved their situation, but rather enhanced their sense of its uniqueness and complexity.

With a few exceptions such as Emile Ḥabībī, Tawfīq Zayyād, Samīḥ al-Qāsim and Maḥmūd Darwīsh, Israeli-Arab writing is not directed primarily toward the Arab minority in Israel, but rather toward the Arab cultural centres in the Arab states and beyond. This change in audience and publication venue since 1967 has led to changes in both the techniques and themes of the literature. Its focus is now more universal, while preserving the sense of the singular situation of a community that constitutes a national minority within an Israeli-Jewish majority that is, in itself, a minority in the sea of Arabs in the Middle East. And yet, Israeli-Arab writing is part of Palestinian literature that has a homeland but no state, in contrast with the writing of Palestinians in the occupied territories who have no state and only a partial homeland, and the writing of diaspora Palestinians who have neither. This special situation of Israeli Arabs, reflected in their literature, is regarded by some as enabling them to enjoy the best of two worlds – the Israeli and the Arab – by others as lacking both worlds, and by others as living poised between the two. In any case, both the pre- and post-1967 Palestinian literature in Israel has been influenced very little by the new Hebrew literature; the main influence on it today, as on Arab literatures in general, is that of world literatures.

As noted, repeal of the military regime and the processes of modernization undergone by Israeli-Arab society brought it into contact with modern Israeli-Jewish society, at the same time that it renewed its contact with Palestinians living in the territories. Thus, the problematic situation of the Palestinians in Israel was complicated still further. Yet most of the Arab community in Israel remains rural, so that its contact with Israeli Jews is limited and superficial. The images of both Palestinians and Jews in Israeli-Arab literature remain, for the most part, stereotypical, reflecting a lack of will or perhaps desire to change this in any substantial way. This, however, reflects another aspect of the uniqueness of the Palestinian literature written in Israel – vacillation between the two poles, Israeli and Arab. The quest for legitimization from both the Arab world and Israeli society, and the struggle with the problem of identity on both the collective and personal levels, are ongoing. The intifāḍa, which at first pushed Israeli Arabs and their writers toward the Palestinian pole, as well as the Oslo Agreements and the peace with Jordan, now impel them toward the conclusion that at least part of the answer to their fundamental problem will be found at the Israeli pole. Some evidence of this will be presented in Chapter 2, which deals with an important phenomenon in the literature of Israeli Arabs: the bilingual – Hebrew and Arabic – work of some of its writers.

NOTES

1. For more on the identity problems of Israeli Arabs, see: Yizhak Schnell, *Perceptions of Israeli Arabs: Territoriality and Identity*, Aldershot, Arbury, 1994; Sammy Smooha, *Arabs and Jews in Israel*, vols 1 and 2, Boulder, Westview Press, 1989, 1992; and Alouph Hareven (ed.), *Eḥad MeKol Shisha Yisraelim: Yaḥasei Gomlin Bein Hami'ut Ha'Aravi VehaRov HaYehudi BeYisrael*, Jerusalem, Van Leer Institute, 1981.
2. Ami Elad [-Bouskila] (ed.), *Sifrutam Shel Ha'Aravim BeYisrael, HaMizraḥ HeḤadash*, 35, 1993. Shmuel Moreh, 'Arabic Literature in Israel', in Shmuel Moreh (ed.), *Studies in Modern Arabic Prose and Poetry*, Leiden, E.J. Brill, 1988, pp.161–72. Emile Nakhleh, 'Walls of Bitterness: A survey of Israeli-Arab Political Poetry', in Issa J. Boullata (ed.), *Critical Perspectives on Modern Arabic Literature*, Washington DC, Three Continents Press, 1980, pp. 244–62.
3. For example, the terms 'the literature of Israeli Arabs' or 'Arab literature in Israel' are used by scholars such as Sasson Somekh in 'Batim Gvohim, Karim: Dmut HaShakhen HaYehudi BeYetziratam Shel Sofrim 'Aravim MeḤaifa VehaGalil', *Mifgash* 4–5 (8–9) (Winter 1986), pp. 21–3; Avraham Yinon, 'Tawfīq Zayyād: Anaḥnu Kan haRov', in Aharon Layish (ed.), *Ha'Aravim BeYisrael: Retzifut u-Temurah*, Jerusalem, Magnes Press, 1981, pp. 213–40; and Hannan Hever, 'Lehakot Ba'Akevo Shel Akhiles', *Alpayim* 1 (June, 1989), pp. 186–93. The term 'Palestinian-Arab literature in Israel' was used by Reuven Snir, 'Petza' MePtza'av: HaSifrut Ha'Aravit HaPalastinit BeYisrael', *Alpayim* 2 (1990), pp. 244–68. George Kanazi used the term 'the literature of Israeli Arabs' in his article 'Be'ayat HaZehut BaSifrut Shel 'Arviyei Yisrael', in Alouph Hareven (ed.), *Eḥad MiKol Shisha Yisraelim: Yaḥasei Gomlin Bein HaMi'ut Ha'Aravi VehaRov BeYisrael*, Jerusalem, Van Leer Institute, 1981, pp. 149–69, but eight years later he wrote an article 'Yesodot Idyologyim BaSifrut Ha'Aravit BeYisrael', *HaMizraḥ HeḤadash*, 32 (1989), pp. 128–38, in which, despite the title ('Ideological elements in Arabic literature in Israel'), he uses the term 'Palestinian literature in Israel'.
4. The term 'literature of resistance' was coined by the Palestinian writer and journalist Ghassān Kanafānī in reference to the literature of Israeli Arabs. See his *Adab al-Muqāwama fī Filasṭīn al-Muḥtalla, 1948–1966*, 2nd edn, Beirut, Mu'assasat al-Abḥāth al-'Arabīyya, 1982. An acrimonious debate developed in the Arab world around this term in the late 1960s and early 1970s, focused on the question of how to refer to Israeli Arabs: 'the Arabs in Israel', 'the Arabs of the land conquered before June', 'the Palestinians in Palestine that was occupied in 1948', 'the Arabs of Palestine', and so on. Since the 1973 war, official PLO publications have taken the emphatic position that Israeli Arabs are first and foremost Palestinians. See Gideon Shilo, *'Arviyei Yisrael Be'Eynei Medinot 'Arav Ve-Ashaf*, Jerusalem, Magnes and the Truman Institute, 1982, pp. 63–9.
5. *al-Jadīd* (June 1969), pp. 2–4.
6. This process is evident among young and veteran Arab writers alike who live in Israel. One striking example is Riyāḍ Baydas of Shfaram, whose writing appears in newspapers, periodicals and publishers mainly in the Arab world, but also in Israel. See Chapter 3 for a discussion of this writer.
7. On the literature of the intifāḍa, see Ami Elad [-Bouskila], 'Avanim 'Al Mitzḥa Shel HaMoledet: 'Al HaSifrut HaPalestinit BeTekufat HaIntifāḍa', *Alpayim*, 7 (1993), pp. 96–117; and Ami Elad [-Bouskila], 'Al-Kâtib eine palästinensische Kulturzeitschrift als Forum der Intifāḍa-Literatur', *Orient*, 36, 1995, pp. 109–25.

8. *Ibdā'āt al-Ḥajar*, vol. 1, Jerusalem, Ittiḥād al-Udabā' wa'l-Kuttāb al-Filasṭīniyyīn, 1988, pp. 57–68, 69–74, 89–90.
9. Edmūn Shiḥāda, *al-Ṭarīq ilā Bīr Zeit*, 2nd edn, Nicosia, Mu'assasat Bisān li'l-Ṣiḥāfa wa'l-Nashr, 1989; Zakī Darwīsh, *Aḥmad, Maḥmūd wa'l-Āakharūn*, 2nd edn, Nicosia, Mu'assasat Bīsān Press li'l-Ṣiḥāfa wa'l-Nashr, 1989; Muḥammad Watad, *Zaghārīd al-Intifāḍa*, 2nd edn, Nicosia, Mu'assasat Bīsān li'l-Ṣiḥāfa wa'l-Nashr, 1989.
10. *Wahaj al-Fajr: Min Adabiyyāt al-Intifāḍa*, Nazareth, Rābiṭat al-Kuttāb wa'l-Udabā' al-Filasṭīniyyin fī Isrā'īl, 1989.
11. Additional information on the Arabic-language dailies and periodicals that appear in Israel can be found in Shmuel Moreh, *al-Kutub al-'Arabīyya allatī Ṣadarat fī Isrā'īl (1948–1977)*, Haifa, Bet HaGefen, 1977, pp. 71–87, and in *Katalog 'Itonim 'Arviyim-Palestinyim 1930–1989*, Givat Ḥaviva: Merkaz Meida, n.d.
12. Examples of local works include the poetry collection by Michel Ḥaddād, *al-Daraj al-Mu'addī ilā Aghwārinā* (1969), or the short-story collection by various Israeli-Arab writers, *al-Bi'r al-Mashūra wa Qiṣaṣ Ukhrā* (1969), or the anthology of Arab poetry edited by Shmuel Moreh, *Alwān min al-Shi'r al-'Arabī al-Isrā'īlī*, Tel-Aviv, Dār al-Nashr al-'Arabī, 1967. Examples of works in Arabic include the novel *al-Arḍ* by the Egyptian writer 'Abd al-Raḥmān al-Sharqāwī, the novel *Anā Aḥyā* by the Lebanese writer Laylā Ba'labakkī, and the novel *al-Ḥayy al-Lātīnī* by the Lebanese writer Suhayl Idrīs.
13. Emile Ḥabībī, 'Ṣafaḥāt min Mufakkira', *al-Jadīd* (September–October 1969), pp. 20–6.
14. This trend was reflected in works by both veterans and the younger generation. Among veteran writers, we can cite Emile Ḥabībī, whose novel *al-Waqā'i' al-Gharība fī Ikhtifā' Sa'īd Abī al-Naḥs al-Mutashā'il*, first published in Israel (Maktabat al-Ittiḥād) in 1974, has appeared in many editions in the Arab world, including: Jerusalem, Manshūrāt Ṣalāḥ al-Dīn, 1977; Cairo, Dār Shuhdī, n.d.; Tunis, Dār al-Janūb, 1982; also *Ikhṭayya*, Nicosia, Kitāb al-Karmil, 1, 1985; and *Khurrāfiyyat Sarāyā bint al-Ghūl*, Haifa, Dār Arābesk, 1991; London, Riyāḍ al-Rayyis, 1992. An example among the younger writers is Riyāḍ Baydas, who has written five books with a range of publishers: *al-Jū' wa'l-Jabal*, Jerusalem, Manshūrāt Ṣalāḥ al-Dīn, 1980; *al-Maslak, Majmū'at Qiṣaṣ Qaṣīra*, Jerusalem, Intermīdiyā, 1985; *al-Rīḥ*, Nicosia, Dār al-Ṣumūd al-'Arabī, 1987, *Takhṭīṭāt Awwaliyya, Qiṣaṣ*, Casablanca, Dār Tūbqāl li'l-Nashr, 1988, and *Ṣawt Khāfit, Qiṣaṣ Qaṣīra*, Nicosia, Maṭbū'āt Faraḥ, 1990.
15. *Ibdā'āt al-Ḥajar*, 2 vols, 1988, 1989; *Wahaj al-Fajr*, 1989; Muḥammad 'Alī al-Yūsufī, *Abjadiyyat al-Ḥijāra*, Nicosia, Mu'assasat Bīsān li'l-Ṣiḥāfa wa'l-Nashr wa'l Tawzī', 1988.
16. Kanazi, 'Be'ayat HaZehut', in Hareven (ed.), *Ehad Mikol Shisha Yisraelim*, p. 157; Avraham Yinnon, 'Kama Nos'ei Moked BaSifrut Shel 'Arviyei Yisrael', *HaMizraḥ HeḤadash*, 15, 1–2 (57–8) (1965), pp. 62–3, 69–70, 75–82; Avraham Yinnon, 'Nosim Ḥevratyim BeSifrut 'Arviyei Yisrael', *HaMizraḥ HeḤadash*, 16, 3–4 (63–4), (1966), pp. 366–73; Shmuel Moreh, 'HaSifrut BaSafa Ha'Aravit BeMedinat Yisrael', *HaMizraḥ HeḤadash*, 11, 1–2 (33–4) (1958), pp. 33–8; Maḥmūd 'Abbāsī, *Hitpatḥut HaRoman VehaSipur HaKatzar BaSifrut Ha'Aravit BaShanim 1948–1976*, Jerusalem, Hebrew University, 1983, pp. 113–36, 160–80, 192–201; Nabīh al-Qāsim, *Dirāsāt fī al-Qiṣṣa al-Maḥalliyya*, Acre, Dār al-Aswār, 1979, pp. 87–8, 109–10. With the exception of the last work, in Arabic, all the foregoing are in Hebrew.
17. 'Abbāsī, *Hitpatḥut HaRoman VehaSipur HaKatzar*, pp. 103–4, 137–59, 181–6; Ḥabīb

Būlus (ed.), *al-Qiṣṣa al-'Arabīyya al-Filasṭīniyya al-Maḥaliyya al-Qaṣīra, Anṭolojiyā*, Nazareth and Shfaram; al-Maṭba'a a-Sha'biyya, Shfaram, Dār al-Mashriq, 1987, p. 149; Fakhrī Ṣāliḥ, *al-Qiṣṣa al-Filasṭīniyya al-Qaṣīra fī al-Arāḍī al-Muḥtalla*, Beirut, Dār al-'Awda, 1982, pp. 53–4.

18. One poignant and fascinating example of the problem of infiltrators appears in the story 'Mutasallilūn' [infiltrators] by Ḥannā Ibrāhīm (1927–) *Azhār Barriyya*, Haifa; Dār al-Ittiḥād, 1972, pp. 82–9.
19. Emile Ḥabībī, 'Bawwābat Mandelbāwm', *Sudāsiyyat al-Ayyām al-Sitta wa–Qiṣaṣ Ukhrā*, Haifa, n.d. (1st edn 1969), pp. 11–19; Qaysar Karkabī, 'Sittī', *al-Bi'r al-Mashūra wa Qiṣaṣ Ukhrā*, Tel-Aviv, Dār al-Nashr al-'Arabī, 1969, pp. 101–5; Muḥammad 'Alī Ṭāha, 'al-Khaṭṭ al-Wahmī', *Salāman Wa-Taḥiyya*, Acre, Dār al-Jalīl li'l-Ṭibā'a wa'l-Nashr, 1969, pp. 23–7.
20. Somekh, 'Batim Gvohim, Karim', *Mifgash*, pp. 21–5.
21. Sa'd Di'bis, *Qaṣā'id li'l-Islām wa'l-Quds*, Cairo, al-Markaz al-Islāmī li'l-Ṭibā'a, 1989; Farīd 'Aqīl, *Filasṭīn al-Ḥijāra*, Damascus, Maṭba'at al-Kātib al-'Arabī, n.d.; Su'ād al-Ṣabāḥ, 'Simfoniyyat al-Arḍ', *al-Kātib*, 95 (March 1988), pp. 91–2; 'Alī al-Jarīrī, 'Ajā al-Shaqiyy 'alā Sha'bī Yughālibuhu', *al-Kātib*, 108 (April 1989), p. 92; Tawfīq Fayyāḍ, 'al-Ṣabiyy Salāma', *al-Kātib*, 110 (June 1989), pp. 77–8.

2

The Other Face
The Language Choice of Arab Writers in Israel

In this chapter I shall examine one of the most intriguing issues in the study of literature, namely, the language of writing. Most literature is written by residents of a particular country or homeland and its language is usually the native tongue of the writers. Contemporary societies are not homogeneous, however, but made up of those who speak and write in the language of the majority and those who speak and write in other languages. Thus when a group of writers that is not part of the majority chooses to write in the language of the majority, the question of motivation arises. Why do they do it? One must also distinguish between those who write only in the majority language, which is not their native tongue, and those who write in both languages, i.e., their native tongue and the language of the majority. These categories encompass a host of very different cases and these differences are reflected in the attitudes to the writer of both the surrounding majority culture and the minority language group. There are several prominent examples of writers who were not native to the countries where they wrote and published, but who came as immigrants and ended up writing and publishing their work in the language of their adopted countries. One striking example of this in world literature is Joseph Conrad (1857–1924), born in the Ukraine to a Polish family, who lived part of his life in Russia, returned to Poland, and then moved to England where he wrote. Conrad is acclaimed not only in England, but also internationally. Another outstanding example is Vladimir Nabokov (1899–1977), who was born in Russia and moved to England, Germany, and finally the United States, writing in English and winning recognition not only in the English-speaking world, North America in particular, but internationally as well. Nabokov first wrote in Russian and then switched to English and has also translated works from Russian into English.

These are but two examples of a phenomenon characteristic of world literature in the nineteenth and twentieth centuries. This phenomenon, however, is not unique to the modern era, but has been around for centuries. In Arabic literature, for example, note the role of non-Arab writers and thinkers who wrote in Arabic, especially during the Middle Ages. These writers, though neither Muslim nor Arab, felt themselves to be an integral part of the rich Arab culture and hence some composed not just in the language of their own community (Hebrew or Greek), but also in the language of their cultural community – Arabic. Prominent among these were Rabbi Saadiah Gaon (882–942) and Rabbi Judah Halevi (1075–1141). Here was an integration of two languages that existed side by side. Although Arabic represented the language of the ruler and sovereign power, it also represented the language of the Arab nation and its culture in which Jews were involved, not by coercion, but out of a sense of belonging to the mainstream collective culture of the period. Jews living in the Aramaic and Greek cultures behaved similarly. Writing in the language of the majority was not perceived as politically incorrect or unworthy, and such authors were certainly not considered unfaithful to the language of their religious faith, i.e., Hebrew. In the words of Joshua Blau, 'Jewish Arabic as a whole served as the literary language of the organized Jewish community in the Arab countries, and therefore had a literary tradition of its own'.[1] Here was a cultural and literary expression of the social, cultural and political situation of a minority that contributed not just to its own culture, but to the broad mosaic of the magnificent Arabic culture of the Middle Ages.[2]

MODERN ARABIC LITERATURES – TO WRITE IN THE LANGUAGE OF THE OTHER

In the modern era, writing in the language of the other became an issue in Arabic literature in two major contexts: the literature of the Mahjar since the end of the nineteenth century and the literatures of North Africa at the end of the twentieth.

Mahjar literature was written in the Arab diasporas, mainly in North and South America, following the major migrations in the 1860s, primarily from Syria and Lebanon.[3] This migration to the West and to the United States in particular stemmed from both political–social and economic considerations. As part of large Arab communities in their new countries, these *émigrés* created important works of prose and poetry that served as models for emulation in Arab countries. In the first stage, the Mahjar writers, most of whom were Christian Arabs, composed in two languages – Arabic and the local language, i.e., English, Spanish or Portuguese. There is little dispute that the most important of the Mahjar authors was the Lebanese writer, composer and artist Jubrān Khalīl Jubrān (1883–1931).[4] The Mahjar writers preserved their religious, national and cultural heritage and, at the same time, they absorbed much political, social and cultural influence from their surroundings, which they expressed in their works. Jubrān, like many of his colleagues, wrote in both Arabic and English, but he had a greater impact on Arabic readers inside and outside Arab countries than on English readers. Not only did the literary flowering in the first quarter of the twentieth century not undermine the Arabic cultural heritage, it even revitalized modern Arabic literatures, especially the poetry of that period, and its impact is evident to this day. The Mahjar writers of this first generation freely chose their language of writing and were aware of their own cultural and linguistic heritage as well as the new cultural and literary milieu. The second generation of Mahjar writers was more distant from its cultural and linguistic roots, having grown up in a society dominated by the majority language and culture. These writers did not abandon their cultural and linguistic heritage, although they were more absorbed by the local culture, but assimilation was not absolute.

The other case of bilingual and even trilingual writing in modern Arab history was that of the Maghrib literatures from the end of the nineteenth century,[5] written in Arabic, French and Berber. Clearly, writing in the language of the former conqueror remained an open issue and preoccupied Maghrib writers as it does the students of Maghrib literature. The writers are aware of the problematic nature of this bilingualism and trilingualism in literature. One of the significant Moroccan writers of the younger generation, al-Muʿṭī Qabbāl, who writes in Arabic and French and translates from and into both languages, addresses this question:

> The issue of bilingualism in the Maghrib opens up an entire debate. On the one hand, the nationalists argue that with decolonization, there is no reason for French to continue its cultural dominance, that decolonization should also take effect in the writing, the literature. On the other hand, Maghrib authors who write in French treat the language not as an end but as a means, and believe that writing in French gives them distance from themselves, a chance to come out of themselves. The novels of Ṭāhir Ben Jallūn, Muḥammad Dīb, Kātib Yāsīn and others – who write in French – are all drawn from the cultural and ritualistic milieu of the Maghrib and portray it that way, i.e., through their

> writing . . . The question of bilingualism is not just cultural, but also political . . . Bilingualism as a philosophical question touches upon identity, the question of the other, and the role of the other in the cultural space of these countries, reflecting the hardship. Although the question is an open one . . . those who write in Arabic are the majority. They give voice to a political and cultural attitude replete with resentment for the language of the conqueror. But their desire to banish this language is an illusion . . . bilingualism is a window to modernity.[6]

As noted, Morocco, Algeria and Tunisia are ambivalent about French culture – they feel both attracted to and repelled by it. But how do the French view Maghrib literature written in the French language? In my view, the French are keenly aware of it and take an active role in determining the future of Maghrib literature – works written in Arabic, as well as those in French. In Paris, more than anywhere else except for the Maghrib itself, one can find special publications and anthologies of Maghrib writers and poets in both Arabic and French. The deep interest of the French in Maghrib literature, particularly works written in French, derives not only from its literary value, but from their belief that Maghrib culture, particularly that created in France, is part and parcel of French culture. What is more, they seem to have a parallel view of French-language Maghrib writers and Maghrib writers who use both languages. Although the French view this literature not as canonical but as a marginal literature of the French empire, on the other hand, they would like to espouse this literature for reasons that are not purely literary.

One of the most fascinating subjects in the study of modern Palestinian literature concerns the language used by Palestinian-Arab writers who live in Israel. Palestinian writers who reside in the other two Palestinian locales – the West Bank and the Gaza Strip – as well as those who live in the diasporas of Arab or other countries have clearly chosen to write in Arabic, with the exception of a few writers such as Jabrā Ibrāhīm Jabrā (1920–94) who composed – like the Maghrib writers – in two languages, in his case Arabic and English, in addition to his many translations from English to Arabic.[7] But Jabrā is a veteran Palestinian writer, and most Palestinian writers who were born in the various diasporas, especially in North America (like Arab writers in general), no longer write in Arabic but in English.[8] One prominent example is Naomi Shihab Nye (1952–), who published books of poetry and prose and has also translated from Arabic to English, most of it poetry.[9] Besides the literary activity of Palestinians writing in Arabic or one of the languages of North or South America, Palestinian writers are active in Europe in other languages, especially

French and German. One prominent Palestinian writer in France is the prolific writer, playwright and critic Afnān al-Qāsim, who generally writes in Arabic, with some of his criticism also in French.[10]

The twentieth-century phenomenon in which individuals move to another country, continue to write in their mother tongue, and then some begin to write bilingually while the younger generation born in the new community writes only in the new language, is universal and not unique to Arab or Palestinian writers. This phenomenon, related to economic, cultural and social elements that were factors in the immigration, are the primary reasons for bilingual writing. There is an additional universal phenomenon in which authors write not only in their native tongue or the local language, but in an additional language or the language of the conqueror. This takes place, of course, in countries that were under an extended period of foreign rule, such as African and Asian countries under European or American colonial powers. One dramatic example is India, where the British had great impact, predominantly in establishing English as the official language. The primary reason for the dominance of English there was the competition among the various Dravidian languages, such as Tamil. To avoid granting 'cultural imperialism' to Hindi, the use of English is maintained. As for the Arab states and the colonial powers, there was the English and French influence in the Middle East and the North African countries. In the first stage, the local writers composed in the language of the conqueror, considered the language of 'culture'. In the second stage when the colonial power left, a reaction set in and the local writers began composing in their own language. In the third stage, this writing that had been a reaction disappeared and some writers again began composing in the language of the other, this time as a deliberate choice in the new circumstances. And in the fourth stage, writers returned to composing in the local language following the increased religious climate and the rise of fundamentalist Islam. Algeria is a clear example of this.

The above examples from both the Arab and the non-Arab world sharpen the uniqueness of the phenomenon to be explored here, and also provide context and insight into it. We have already noted that Palestinian literature is different, not just in the sense that all Arab literature has its uniqueness and special qualities, but because it is not one literature, such as that of Syria, Egypt, etc. From 1948 Palestinian literature was composed of two separate Palestinian branches, and, as of 1967, three Palestinian branches. At any rate, one cannot speak of a 'normal' Palestinian literature with its own country. Within the singularity of Palestinian literature in the corpus of modern Arabic literatures, Palestinian literature written in Israel stands out.[11] This literature is unique by definition, since most Arabic literature is written in Arab lands or somewhere where a local Arab community demands it, as was the case with Mahjar literature. Modern Palestinian literature from its inception, however, was written not only in historical Palestine, but also outside it, in Arab capitals such as Cairo and Damascus. Egyptian literature, by contrast, is written only in Egypt, while modern Palestinian literature lacks a state and is written in various locations. Palestinian literature written in Arabic in Israel is different from its sisters in that it is written in a Middle Eastern country where Arabic is not the main language, but rather Hebrew is, with Arabic the second official language. This point can help us understand the choices made by Israeli Arabs about the language of their writing, as it has clarified the language choices made by Palestinians in other locations. Which language will be used for their writing by Arab Palestinians in Israel is an open question; while this is one of the fundamental issues related to the literary endeavour, it also belongs to the realm outside literature. The issue of the language of writing is related not only to language, but also to territory, the target audience, the goals of the writer, and the period of writing. Thus, it is important to examine if Arab writers in Israel write only in Arabic or in both Arabic and Hebrew, as there are no Arab writers who choose to write only in Hebrew. In either case, when do they choose to write in Arabic and when in Hebrew? These questions will be addressed later in this chapter.

ISRAELI ARABS WRITING IN HEBREW AND ARABIC

Most of the Arab writers who live in Israel write in Arabic, although a small number write both in Arabic and Hebrew. Why should this be unusual, as we have noted the existence of similar phenomena not just in the world at large, but even in the Arab world? Is it any different from the Mahjar authors writing in the language of their new community? Does it differ from a Maghrib author writing in French not just in France or Canada, but in one of the three Maghrib countries influenced by French culture? The answers to these questions are not simple in light of the political, social and cultural circumstances in which the Arab writer in Israel lives and works. Another parallel is that the Maghrib community is ambivalent about French culture – at the same time that some of its intellectuals admire it – as these two communities were in political and military conflict, and some claim that this confrontation passed into the cultural sphere, which is no less harsh.

There is a fundamental difference between the general phenomenon of writing in the language of the other and the phenomenon in Israel of Arab authors writing bilingually. The political situation in the Middle East – an extended conflict between the Arab and Israeli communities, the ongoing state of war between Israel and some of the Arab world – gives special significance to the fact that these authors write in Hebrew. What is more, these authors publish in and are acclaimed by the Hebrew reading community, although some (such as Na'īm 'Arāidī) are regarded by the Arab world, and by some Israeli Arabs, as traitors to Arab culture, and as such are condemned on every occasion. The issue of writing in Hebrew did not exist before the birth of the state of Israel, but first cropped up in the 1960s. It is hard not to tie in this phenomenon with the social and political changes in Israel and in Arab society, in particular. The process of Israelization of Israeli Arabs – or at least some of them – accelerated significantly in the 1960s, together with demographic, economic and cultural changes and the lifting of the military regime over the Arab sector. There is clearly a connection between the significant changes in the 1960s that made it possible for an Arab author living in Israel to write in Hebrew. This option did not exist in the 1950s, in my opinion, because of the recent birth of the state of Israel – and attendant animosities between the two cultures – and thus it took until the 1960s and the concomitant changes that affected the Arab community in Israel as well. Note that this phenomenon encompassed only a limited number of Arabs writing in Hebrew, and took place prior to and together with their writing in Arabic which ensued. This is characteristic of some prominent writers such as the veteran 'Aṭāllāh Manṣūr (1934–) and the younger writers Na'īm 'Arāidī (1948–) and Anton Shammās (1950–). Note that together with the Arab writers who write in Hebrew there is also a group of Israeli-Arab writers who use Arabic for their literary work, but Hebrew for their non-fiction articles. This includes, for example, Emile Ḥabībī (1921–96) and Samīḥ al-Qāsim (1939–) – who have achieved prominence not just in the Arab Palestinian world, but also in the Hebrew-speaking world and media.

This raises the important and significant difference between writing fiction or poetry and writing articles for the newspaper. Once an author writes even one article in Hebrew, this testifies to cultural and intellectual involvement in the majority culture. The conscious decision of Emile Ḥabībī and Samīḥ al-Qāsim to use Arabic for fiction, in the case of Ḥabībī, and for poetry, in the case of al-Qāsim, was presumably based on cultural and political considerations, and not just because they are more fluent in Arabic than in Hebrew. Moreover, Emile Ḥabībī – who is considered not just one of the major twentieth-century writers of Palestinian literature, but of the entire Arab world – wrote an autobiographical text in Hebrew. But this did not prevent one of the respected publishing houses in the Arab world from publishing it in Arabic, and mentioning its linguistic roots.[12] Both these authors write for the Hebrew press, give frequent interviews in Hebrew on Israeli radio and television, and appear in literary evenings and interviews on subjects broader than Arabic literature, all of which indicates beyond doubt their involvement in the spiritual, social and political life of Israel. Moreover, Samīḥ al-Qāsim also translates from Arabic to Hebrew. The fact that he edited and translated an anthology of Hebrew poets and also his decision to render an anthology of the Israeli-Jewish poet Ronni Somek demonstrates that not only is he connected to Hebrew literature, but he also assumes the role of culling and selecting modern Hebrew poetry.[13]

One of the most salient features of Israeli-Arab authors who write in Hebrew is that most of them are Christian or Druze, rather than Muslim. Ethnic identity is still an issue, especially with the tensions between Muslims and the other two communities – the Druze and the Christians – fanned by both the Lebanon War in 1982 and the growth of the Islamic movement throughout the Middle East. In other words, the group of Arab authors who write in Hebrew is not homogeneous. Clearly the Druze are more integrated in Israeli society, primarily as a result of their compulsory service in the Israeli army, which has a social, political and cultural impact manifested in the relatively large number of Druze who write in both languages, Na'īm 'Arāidī being foremost among them. This group is exposed to the Hebrew language in the army and often in many other realms. The exposure to Hebrew of these writers and of many in the Arab population – whether through university education where the language of instruction is Hebrew or through the media – all accelerate the process of integration into the life of Israeli-Jewish culture.

Another interesting phenomenon is the literary genres chosen for writing in Hebrew. Israeli-Arab authors use Hebrew to write in three genres – poetry, novels and short stories – as well as literary criticism and articles. But indisputably the most popular genre in Hebrew for Israeli-Arab writers is poetry. This strikes me as evidence of their internalization of the Hebrew language, as the writing of poetry is the most personal medium for the artist. Recall that when Jewish writers lived in Spain during the Golden Age of the medieval period, they used Arabic for all genres except one: their poetry was generally written in Hebrew, not Arabic. And in modern Israel, although not in great numbers, there are several writers who write poetry in Hebrew as well as in Arabic. Among these, the two most prominent poets since the 1970s have been Anton Shammās and Na'īm 'Arāidī.[14]

Israeli Arabs who write in Hebrew can be divided into two general categories: those who wrote from the birth of the state of Israel until the late 1960s; and those who have been writing since then. There is a sharp delineation between these two periods. In the first, we know of two Arab writers who wrote in Hebrew, 'Aṭāllāh Manṣūr (1934–) and Rāshid Ḥusayn (1936–77); while in the second period there are many writers, most prominently Na'īm 'Arāidī and Anton Shammās. In the first period, mainly prose was written, while in the second period, both prose and poetry were written in Hebrew. These two features are important, as they help us define the social, political, economic and cultural relations between Jews and Arabs during the periods, and the correlation with processes of Israelization and/or Palestinization undergone by Arab citizens of Israel. The fact that in the first 20 years Arab authors in Israel did not write in Hebrew (with the few exceptions noted above) points not to the Israelization of Arabs in Israel, but to the fact that efforts to relate Arab society to Jewish society in Israel were private rather than collective. The linkage took place primarily in the fields of journalism and fiction, especially Arabic newspapers and journals that appeared in the 1950s, whether sponsored by the Israeli-Jewish establishment such as *al-Mirṣād*, *al-Yawm*, *Ḥaqīqat al-Amr* or *al-Anbā'*, or by the Israeli Communist Party – *al-Ittiḥād* and *al-Jadīd*. In both types of periodicals, Arabs and Jews all wrote in Arabic. In between, attempts were made (some successful and others not) to found independent or quasi-independent newspapers and journals in the 1950s, such as *al-Wasīṭ* and *al-Mujtama'*.

'Aṭāllāh Manṣūr was the only Arab writer who published a narrative text in Hebrew during the first period, namely, his novel *Be-Or Ḥadash* (1966), issued by a minor publishing house.[15] To understand the background to the Hebrew writing of 'Aṭāllāh Manṣūr, a brief sketch of his life would be useful. Manṣūr, born in the village of Jish in 1934, completed high school in 1949, and moved to Kibbutz Sha'ar Ha'Amakim where he lived for a year when he was seventeen. He then worked as a journalist for the anti-establishment weekly *Ha'Olam HaZeh* (1954–56) and subsequently wrote for the daily *Ha-aretz* for many years. In 1983, Manṣūr was one of the founders of the Arab newspaper *al-Ṣinnāra,* and is a member of the editorial board to this day.[16] This thumbnail sketch indicates not just Manṣūr's rich background in the Hebrew and then the Arab press – and the shift in his perspective and emphasis from the Jewish to the Arab sector, i.e., from

Hebrew to Arabic – but also his cultural and social background. In this context, the sociological aspect of cultural consumption should be noted. Israeli Arabs in the 1950s were limited consumers of culture, and the Arab world was to a large extent closed to them, but this situation entirely changed in the 1970s. The very fact that Manṣūr as a young man chose to live in Jewish society reflects a flaunting of convention that not many dared to in Arab society. Manṣūr notes that he was not the first Israeli-Arab intellectual to publish in Hebrew, but was preceded by Rāshid Ḥusayn, who wrote Hebrew poetry and even translated poetry from Hebrew to Arabic, as well as Ṣabrī Jiryis, who wrote a book in Hebrew about the Arabs in Israel.[17] In this article, Manṣūr also illuminates the complex subject of an Arab writing in Hebrew in Israel, as he reflects upon his personal motivations for doing so. Manṣūr is aware of the strangeness of his having written in Hebrew during that period. He relates it to the cultural, social and political situation of the Arabs in Israel, who found themselves between a rock and a hard place. On the one hand, they were called traitors by the Arab states for not abandoning their land and, on the other hand, the Israeli Government viewed them as fifth columnists. This difficult and delicate situation is reflected in the literature of the Israeli Arabs. Manṣūr asserts that when he wrote his first novel in Arabic, *Wabaqiyat Samīra* (1962)[18] – published by the Histadrut – he was harshly condemned by the Hebrew press and accused of hostility toward Israel and the Jews. He then decided to write a novel in Hebrew with only one motivation: vengeance. He wanted to take revenge on the most important Israeli-Jewish ideal of the time: the kibbutz. Thus, he wrote in Hebrew out of anger and a desire to humiliate this ideal. To his amazement and bewilderment, the Hebrew novel not only failed to anger the Jewish critics, they generally heaped praise upon it. Manṣūr suggests two possible explanations for the good reviews. The first was that the literary critics represented liberal views and therefore they praised this novel, while his first book, *Wabaqiyat Samīra*, written in Arabic, was reviewed by the so-called experts on Arab affairs, who saw their role as censors of the enemy. The second reason for the praise was that his Jewish readers were amazed and impressed that a gentile could use Hebrew as a literary medium.[19]

The issue of Israeli Arabs writing in Hebrew and Arabic had already come up in the 1960s. ʻAṭāllāh Manṣūr had been one significant representative, but there were other Arab writers who published fiction, articles and even scholarly research in Hebrew. It does not really matter whether Manṣūr, who wrote this article in 1992 – 40 years after the appearance of his first book in Arabic and 36 years after his first Hebrew book – was actually motivated by revenge or not. It casts light on the distress felt by Israeli Arabs and the writers among them in particular, and thus his own choice of Hebrew. This may be a rationalization of something that happened a long time ago, and it may be that the relatively large number of books written in Hebrew by Arabs since the 1970s led him to this explanation of his choice of Hebrew. But if this were true, it is hard to understand why Manṣūr continued to write for the Hebrew press for so many years: he had freedom of choice and for whatever reason he chose to be a journalist in Hebrew, just as he chose in recent years to write for the Arab press and to use Hebrew for his scholarly articles about Israeli Arabs.[20] However, it is hard to disagree with Manṣūr who concludes with the words: 'I do not claim that Israel today enjoys a bi-educational culture or is a binational state, but it is also not a Jewish state in an absolute way.'[21]

The reasons presented so far for the use of Hebrew by Arab intellectuals of the older generation during the first 20 years of the state of Israel were political, social and cultural. These reasons reflected the difficult situation of the Arabs in Israel until the military regime was lifted in 1966. The turning point in attitudes toward Israeli Arabs by the Arab world, and particularly the Palestinians, took place after the 1967 war, in the late 1960s and early 1970s. Have the circumstances and atmosphere changed since the early 1970s? Are these changes sufficient to explain the trend evident from the early 1970s in which Arab writers – not in large numbers, but a phenomenon that cannot be ignored – engage in bilingual writing in Arabic and Hebrew, though under no circumstances writing only in Hebrew?

The writers who were active from the early 1970s on and who can be called writers of the second period contribute to three central spheres of writing: the media, fiction and translations. They include both veteran authors and poets such as Emile Ḥabībī, Samīḥ al-Qāsim, Sālim Jubrān, and 'Aṭāllāh Manṣūr, as well as young writers such as Nazīh Khayr, Na'īm 'Arāidī, Anton Shammās, Salmān Maṣālḥa, Sihām Dāūd and Asad 'Azzī. In other words, in the second period, we include veteran writers who had also written and published in the first period, and younger writers who started out only in the second.

For all, the question arises: what are the factors leading to their writing in Hebrew, and do these differ from the external and internal factors in the first 20 years of the state of Israel? The political considerations remain, but have markedly changed. There has been a political transformation following the confrontations between Israel and the Arab and Palestinian world in 1967, 1973, the Lebanon War of 1982, the intifāḍa that erupted in

1987, the Declaration of Principles with the Palestinians in 1993, the peace treaty with the Jordanians in 1994, and the attempts at a peace agreement with Syria and Lebanon. All have profoundly influenced the overall relations between Israel and its neighbours and also the web of relations between Jews and Arabs within the state of Israel, as Israeli Arabs take an increasingly active role in the peace process, especially in the context of the Palestinian Authority headed by Yasser Arafat. There has also been a marked transformation in the media between the first two decades of the state and the most recent 25 years. Changes have occurred in all the media, especially newspapers and journals, not only quantitatively but also in terms of their greater variety and openness. As for the electronic media, television did not even exist during the first era, having been introduced to Israel in 1968, but its great intensity in the 1980s and 1990s, the fact that there are three television channels in Israel today, as well as the option of tuning in to radio and television broadcasts from various Arab states, all expose Israeli Arabs to what is going on in the Arab and Muslim world. As for education, there is no question that education in Israel, both in the Jewish and Arab sectors, have undergone a metamorphosis since the 1970s. Until then, among Israeli Arabs there were only a small number of writers as well as readers of journals and newspapers, and hence the number of Arab intellectuals who had more than an elementary school education was limited. The dramatic increase in education of Israeli citizens, including the Arabs, in the past 25 years has brought about changes in employment and media-consumption patterns, and has increased the number of girls in school, the education of the writers and their readers, and the level of periodicals. The opening of the borders in 1967 changed the constellation of relations between Israeli Arabs and their kin in the Arab world and the Palestinian diasporas especially. These political, social, economic and cultural ties gathered momentum during the years of the intifāḍa and the peace process between Israel and the Palestinians, and here, too, Israeli Arabs can and do play an active role. This cooperation with Israeli society did not overlook the literary sphere, as noted in the first chapter, as well as the general relationship between the Jewish and Arab sectors in Israel. During the first period, most of the Arab population in Israel was rural, with approximately 150,000 inhabitants. Today, the Arab minority in Israel is over 800,000 strong, some living in Arab cities such as Nazareth, Shfaram and Umm al-Fahim as well as the mixed cities of Haifa, Ramle, Lydda and Jaffa. All this is significant on the socioeconomic and educational–cultural plane. There are more links between the two populations in the second period, and these are reflected in the literature of Israeli

Arabs – which we examine in other chapters of this book – as well as in Israeli-Hebrew literature.

This complex of factors exacerbated the tension between the Arab population and the Hebrew language, culture and way of life. There is a clear demarcation between the two periods, and we find in more recent years a greater knowledge of Hebrew among Arabic speakers. More and more Arab writers, such as Sihām Dāūd and Na'īm 'Arāidī, acquired their high-school education in Jewish schools, and some, such as Na'īm 'Arāidī and Anton Shammās, also did their university training in Hebrew in Israel. The effect is that Arab writers in Israel have not only a greater command of Hebrew but also a much more complex understanding of Jewish reality. Thus we see more Arab writers translating literary texts from Hebrew into Arabic, with some striking examples such as Anton Shammās in the 1970s and 1980s, and Samīḥ al-Qāsim and Nazīh Khayr in the 1980s.[22] Anton Shammās, like other Arab writers such as Na'īm 'Arāidī and Salmān Maṣālḥa, also translated stories, poems and novels from modern Arabic into Hebrew, mainly in the late 1980s and early 1990s.[23]

Other than Na'īm 'Arāidī, the only example, to the best of my knowledge, of an Israeli-Arab writer who began writing in Hebrew and then switched to bilingual writing is that of Sihām Dāūd. This poet was born in Ramle (1952–) and moved to Haifa, becoming known not just for her poetry in Arabic, but also because she had studied in a Jewish, Hebrew-speaking school in Ramle. Dāūd recounts her first steps in writing in Hebrew: 'Hebrew and Arabic are both part of my culture. At first I wrote in Hebrew, as I went to a Jewish school in Ramle.'[24] In this, Sihām Dāūd differs from most of her colleagues in the second period, most of whom began their literary careers in Arabic, from which they switched into Hebrew. Common to all is that not one abandoned writing in Arabic, but added writing in Hebrew. Anton Shammās is to some extent an exception as he not only wrote his most recent works in Hebrew, but afterwards he did not return to writing in Arabic . . . unlike Na'īm 'Arāidī, who took pains to write in Arabic and be involved in the Arab literary world as well.[25] This bilingual writing characterizes Arab writers in the second period, primarily those in fiction and translations. For some of these writers there sometimes appears to be a confusion or blurring of the differences between writing and translation, especially for 'Arāidī, Shammās, Dāūd and Nazīh Khayr. The latter writes not just for newspapers and journals, but also translates together with Samīḥ al-Qāsim, especially from Hebrew to Arabic, and publishes anthologies separately.[26]

The Arab writers in Israel in the second period were born at about the time of Israeli independence or soon after. This period was a decisive one in shaping the writers and others in their adolescence and young adulthood. Thus young writers such as ʻArāidī, Dāūd and Shammās were influenced by worldwide Arab and Israeli works and ideologies of the mid 1960s and afterwards. An analysis of the possible factors of influence raises several complex possibilities. The first were the political, social and cultural realities of the Arab world in the mid-1960s. Most Arab states had already achieved independence and were preoccupied with state-building. The glorification of Nasserism was past its prime, processes of urbanization in the Arab world had gathered momentum, and the turning points of the 1960s and 1970s were the confrontations of the Arab world with Israel: the trauma that gripped the Arab world in 1967, or the 1973 war and its restoration of pride to Arabs as grasped by the Arab states. Clearly, Israeli Arabs did not remain indifferent to the political–military events or the outcomes of the 1967 and 1973 wars.[27]

The second significant factor was the impact of Hebrew and Arabic literature on this group of Israeli-Arab writers. We need to remember that Hebrew literature in the 1960s took a giant step forward and to some extent abandoned its recruitment for the cause of the collective that had existed before Israeli independence and until the late 1950s. Writers such as Amos Oz, Abraham B. Yehoshua, Amalia Kahana-Carmon, Pinḥas Sadeh, Joshua Kenaz and others enriched and varied the literary inventory in the 1960s.[28] As for world literature in the late 1960s, the influence of the major literatures in the United States and Europe diminished, while the literature of South America, until then considered marginal, burst upon the scene, thanks in large measure to the Columbian writer Gabriel García Márquez (1928–) and his novel *One Hundred Years of Solitude*.[29] As for Arabic literature or, to be precise, modern Arabic literatures, it flourished in the 1960s, especially prose, with the novel, novella and short story reaching one of its peaks, if not the peak, in the history of modern Arab literature. This was led primarily by Egypt with writers such as Najīb Maḥfūẓ (1911–), Fatḥī Ghānim (1924–99), and ʻAbd al-Ḥakīm Qāsim (1935–90). In Lebanon, there was Laylā Baʻlabakkī (1938–); and in Syria, Zakariyyā Tāmir (1931–) and Ḥannā Mīna (1924–) were the outstanding writers. From Iraq, we can cite Fū'ād al-Takarlī (1922–) and Muḥammad Khuḍayyir (1940–). In Sudan, al-Ṭayyib Ṣāliḥ (1929–) and Ibrāhīm Isḥāq Ibrāhīm (1946–) tower over the others. The influence of al-Ṭayyib Ṣāliḥ on Arab writers in Israel such as Zakī Darwīsh (1944–), Muḥammad ʻAlī Ṭāha (1941–) and Riyāḍ Baydas (1960–) was profound from the late 1960s on. Other prominent Arab writers since the 1960s such as Laylā al-'Uthman (1945–) and Sharīfa al-Shamlān (1947–) came from Saudi Arabia, Kuwait and the Gulf states; while from the Maghrib came Muḥammad Zifzāf (1945–), Muḥammad Barrāda (1938–) and others.[30] In short, the literary and cultural activity of the Arab world in the 1960s was at a zenith, and ripples of it reached Israel as well. We must keep in mind, however, that until 1967, books from Arab countries almost never reached Israel. This situation changed drastically in the wake of the 1967 war, when Israeli-Arab writers were exposed to more newspapers, journals and books, and could meet with Arab and especially Palestinian writers. The influence of modern Arab literatures on Israeli-Arab authors is important throughout the history of Israel, but more so as of the late 1950s, although this influence should not be overstated.

As for the influence of Hebrew writing on local Arab literature, we cannot make a claim for a significant impact either on the Arabs writing in Arabic or on those writing in both Arabic and Hebrew.[31] Young Arab writers did, however, use literature in Hebrew translation to gain access to writing from around the world. In other words, Hebrew was influential as a bridge to other cultures, although language is never just a mediator, but functions as a cultural world with its own codes and indicators. Anton Shammās describes well the process in which Arab writers drew sustenance from both Arab and Hebrew literature:

> Today the younger generation of writers and poets is trying to capitalize on the achievements of the generations that preceded it. But while discovering its ties to the culture of the region, it is also leaping beyond the fence, overcoming the barrier of the Hebrew language, and trying to reach other areas. Poets such as Sihām Dāūd and Na'īm 'Arāidī belong to this generation. The fact that I also belong to this generation seems to liberate me from the obligation of evaluating it and taking a stand. But I believe that the uniqueness of this generation is that it draws from two worlds; knowledge of the Hebrew language brings it into contact, both through Hebrew literature and world literature translated into Hebrew, with unfamiliar mappings of experience, and knowledge of Hebrew confronts it with the latest achievements of modern Arabic literature.[32]

In the second period, at least four writers stand out: Na'īm 'Arāidī, Anton Shammās, Sihām Dāūd and Nazīh Khayr. A survey of the other writers in this group reveals that Sihām Daūd is the only Arab woman to write in both languages. Efforts to understand why these authors chose to write also in Hebrew indicate that they did it less out of a desire 'to strike the Achilles heel'[33] and more out of a desire to be integrated in Israeli culture and its emerging identity, each author for his or her own reasons. As for the Achilles heel theory of Hannan Hever, this is clearly applicable only to Anton Shammās, to whom we shall return. In the following pages, we will look at two key writers: Na'īm 'Arāidī and Anton Shammās. There are two main reasons for this choice: First, these are the two most prolific writers in Hebrew (in addition to their publications in Arabic, of course). And, second, each has made a singular contribution to the translation of writing from Hebrew to Arabic, and vice versa. But besides these common features, there is a fundamental difference between the two and their manner of writing.

Na'īm 'Arāidī began his writing career in Arabic at a rather early stage, in poetry and research, then tried his hand at Hebrew writing in 1972, and has ever since continued to publish in Hebrew, especially poetry and fiction, as well as in Arabic. Interestingly, 'Arāidī preferred to write his first novel in Hebrew (*Tevila Katlanit*, 1992), while he writes poetry and stories in both Arabic and Hebrew. In general, 'Arāidī is more aware of his choice, with all his doubts, misgivings and reservations, in comparison with Anton Shammās, in response to whom he wrote: 'I don't know if I, who write in Hebrew, am writing Hebrew literature. But I do know that I am not writing Arab literature in Hebrew. And I believe that this possibility exists, since I do write Hebrew literature in Hebrew.'[34] 'Arāidī does not attempt to gloss over the difficult dilemma he faces. On the contrary, he is fully aware of it and struggles with it in a way that leaves him with both options – two languages and two worlds. 'Arāidī is aware that his choice of writing in Hebrew does not relegate Arabic to the background, marginalizing it so that it would not serve him for lectures, poetry, and nonfiction. He consciously chooses the division, entering and leaving the world of Hebrew not diminished, but enriched. He understands that the choice of two languages for his fiction and nonfiction is not just a matter of bilingualism, but is a choice that is bicultural, binational and bi-identity, and he makes this choice in the clear understanding that he is not forsaking his mother tongue. If he had chosen simply to write Hebrew literature, then he would stop writing in his mother tongue.

'Arāidī arrives at the same conclusion as Shammās concerning the limitations of the Arabic language and culture and the situation of the Arabs in Israel. He speaks openly about the fossilized state of Arab society in Israel, and the dogmatism that dominates it, in sharp contrast with the openness, freedom and flexibility of the Hebrew language and the absence of dogmatism of the Jewish religion. Shammās, though he well understands this, does not mention it as a factor in his choice of the Hebrew language as his preferred language of creativity. Instead, he points to the political, social, economic and cultural situation of Arabs in Israel, as Israel is at war with some of the Arab world and the Palestinians in particular. As this situation is in flux, and there are peace agreements with some Arab countries and the Oslo Agreement with the Palestinians, this reason is eliminated, and thus the argument is undermined. Interestingly, both 'Arāidī and Shammās, each citing different reasons, reach the same conclusion – that there is no hope of creating a high quality literature among Israeli Arabs. This is also the common opinion among educated Israeli Arabs. It is a view that is not shared, however, by many critics from the West and from the Arab states, who sometimes take great interest in Arab literature written in Israel. Their interest is not just politically motivated, but based also on the high quality of some Arab writing in Israel, in both poetry (Samīḥ al-Qāsim, Sihām Dāūd, Michel Ḥaddād, Muḥammad 'Alī Ṭāha) and prose (Emile Ḥabībī, Zakī Darwīsh). I am not trying here to defend Arabic literature written in Israel, but to assert that the statements by 'Arāidī and Shammās are fundamentally in error when one considers the Arabic literature written today and the small numbers of Arabs who live in Israel writing it. The best proof of the incorrectness of their view is the fact that both 'Arāidī and Shammās translate poetry and prose by Israeli-Arab authors and poets such as Zakī Darwīsh, Muḥammad Naffā' and Sihām Daūd, and above all, the extraordinary works of Emile Ḥabībī.[35]

'Arāidī and Shammās have each entered the canon of modern Israeli literature. It is interesting to examine the reaction of the Hebrew critics to their entry, and some would use the term 'invasion'. Be that as it may, their presence has certainly provoked debate about the nature of their literary activity, not only from Hebrew critics in Israel, but also from Arab critics, over the question of whether or not their works are Hebrew literature. Clearly, their literature, written in Israel, is Israeli literature; it is similarly legitimate, however, to consider the works of the two authors who write in Arabic as either Palestinian or Israeli literature. At any rate, the Hebrew critics addressed the issue of Arab authors writing in Hebrew, most viewing their work as part of modern Hebrew literature, while others dismissed this view. Although Hebrew critics have addressed this question for a long time, the works of Anton Shammās, more than any other writer, have focused attention on this issue, not so much his Hebrew poems, but publication of his Hebrew novel *Arabeskot* [arabesques] in 1986.[36] This was a turning-point not just for Shammās and the other Arabs who write in Hebrew, but for Jewish and Arab critics altogether.

The central thesis of this chapter is that one writer only, indeed, one novel only of one writer, brought about the revolution, raising the problematic issue of Arab authors writing in Hebrew and exposing it to broad daylight, indeed, exposing it to criticism and serious debate. An examination of the complete opus of Anton Shammās indicates that until now, he has published only one book in Arabic, *Asīr Yaqẓatī wa Nawmī* [prisoner of my wakefulness and my sleep] (1974), which was the very first book he published, although two poetry books in Hebrew had already appeared and he had translated five books mainly of poetry from Hebrew into Arabic and three books from Arabic into Hebrew.[37] This impressive literary output by Shammās is quite different from the literary output of his colleague 'Arāidī, although they are similar in quantity. First and most important, more than half the books published by 'Arāidī are in Arabic. And, second, 'Arāidī published studies in Arabic and Hebrew about both Arab and Hebrew literature.[38] Both writers are active in the Hebrew literary community, while 'Arāidī – as opposed to Shammās – does not neglect his audience of readers in Arabic. And yet the reactions in the press and among Hebrew critics to Shammās have been much more intense, charged and agitated than to 'Arāidī. Why is this so? Is 'Arāidī's literary activity considered more legitimate because he is a Druze who served in the Israeli army? Or because Hebrew critics feel threatened by the quality of the writing by Shammās in Hebrew? Why is Shammās perceived by a wide range of critics and journalists to be a fig leaf for coexistence and cooperation between Arabs and Jews? Whatever the answers, the reactions of the Hebrew press to the Hebrew works of Shammās, initially to his poetry collections (*Krikha Kasha*, 1974; and *Shetaḥ Hefker*, 1979), were above and beyond what other Arab writers who write in Hebrew had ever received in Israel, encompassing newspapers and periodicals from the entire political and literary spectrum.[39] But this criticism of the Shammās *oeuvre* in poetry was only a preamble to the flood of reactions that met publication of his novel *Arabeskot*. In a sense, this novel shattered the standards and conventional wisdom of criticism inside and outside Israel, by Jews and by Arabs, and in Hebrew, Arabic and English.

Hebrew criticism, which drew the literary map in the 1980s and early 1990s, related to the works of Shammās, and specifically to his novel *Arabeskot*, as part of the total literary output of Hebrew writing by Jewish authors including Yoel Hoffmann, Youval Shimoni, Orly Castel-Bloom, and others. For example, the Hebrew critic Avraham Balaban writes:

> One of the salient features of modern [Hebrew] literature is the shattering of accepted literary and cultural dichotomies, and the challenging of

> the principles of hegemony that accompany it. Arabeskot is typical of this new writing direction in this as well. What could be more post-modernist than the text of an Arab-Palestinian-Christian that describes the conquest of his village by the 'Jewish army', a text written in spit-and-polish Hebrew and constructed like a mask upon a mask upon a mask.[40]

The question of the place of the novel *Arabeskot* in modern Hebrew literature is also addressed by Hannan Hever, who claims that:

> A double provocation was thrown into the Israeli arena with the appearance of *Arabeskot*, the Hebrew novel by Shammās that cleverly served to undermine several of the most accepted criteria that define the limits of Hebrew literature. To address this complex issue of cultural identity, Shammās exposed the Israeli duplicity over the vague and loose distinction between Israeli and Jew. These trends were strikingly confirmed by the fact that, for example, some found it hard to accept this as a novel that belongs organically to Hebrew literature.[41]

Dan Laor, one of the prominent scholars of modern Hebrew literature, treats the novel *Arabeskot* as a 'normal' book, barely dealing with the fact that the author is an Arab, and views the novel as a failure from a literary artistic point of view, opening his article as follows:

> The failure of Anton Shammās in the writing of the novel *Arabeskot* can be attributed, first and foremost, to the fact that the author lacked the determination, artistic maturity, and perseverance for writing a novel that focuses entirely on the unknown world of the Galilean village of his birth, Fassuta. This statement is made recognizing that the encounter between an author like Shammās and materials taken from his nearby childhood surroundings created an extraordinary opportunity for artistic exposure of a unique and unfamiliar geographic, social, and historical reality, that while existing on the periphery of Israeli reality, can singularly illuminate its centre.[42]

Literary critics, in addressing the use of Hebrew by Shammās, saw this novel as a throwing down of the gauntlet to the acceptance of non-Jewish writers in modern Hebrew literature. The author, poet and translator Aharon Amir, who praises the work profusely, makes the following observation about the language of the writing:

> It is sufficient for me to note that this is a multifaceted work, laden with talent, and from the point of view of language and style, it is a multifaceted diamond, glittering, polished to perfection. I did not

> hesitate to tell the author himself that in my opinion, he returns to Hebrew writing the honor that it lost to a great extent in the past decade, as it became permeated with the haphazard, sloppy style of pen-pushers who are poseurs, arrogant, superficial, smart alecks, raucous, show-offs. What Shammās does for Hebrew literature can be compared, in truth, to what was done for English literature in this century by English-writing authors born in India, Poland, the West Indies, or Russia: Just as this can be compared to the work of writers from the cultural periphery of France – in northern or equatorial Africa, Egypt, the Antilles, Lebanon, Belgium, or Romania – to contemporary French literature, without which these literatures would be far poorer and more boring than they are.[43]

Not only does Aharon Amir not perceive any danger to Hebrew language and literature by an author who is not Jewish writing in Hebrew, but he praises the Hebrew of Shammās, something which put other Jewish critics off, though they could not fail but be impressed by the level and quality of the language. These critics, moreover, refused to include the works of Shammās or of any Arab writer into the Hebrew corpus of modern Israeli literature. Obviously, the considerations of those who are pro and con this matter are not purely artistic or literary, but often political, rooted in the relations between the Jewish majority in Israel that writes in Hebrew (not all of them, by the way), and the Arab minority that writes in Arabic (and not all either). Some critics suggest that by writing in Hebrew, Shammās is deliberately defying Israeli linguistic–cultural conventions and mounting a challenge to the dominant Zionist discourse to include Israeli-Arab culture within it. This then is clearly a post-Zionist and postmodern throwing down of the gauntlet.

The debate about this subject has not been confined to the literary merits of the Hebrew writing by those who are not Jewish, but is inextricably bound up with the question of majority and minority relations, private and collective identity, which we shall soon address. But this debate would fall short if we failed to examine the reaction of Arab critics, especially those outside the borders of Israel. We have already noted that the Arab critics have not viewed favourably – to put it mildly – the writing in Hebrew of Israeli Arabs, and therefore their attitude was always aggressive and expressed in crass, insulting terms such as charging these writers with betrayal of Arab culture. But the case of Anton Shammās is exceptional in this regard. Criticism in Arabic to the novel *Arabeskot* was based on a reading of the French translation, and we shall present two striking examples. The first is by the Lebanese poet and critic Sharbal Dāghir, who lives in Paris, and appeared in the journal *al-Nāqid* that was published in London. The critic praises the novel from an artistic point of view, but condemns the choice made by Shammās to write in Hebrew because the reader cannot ignore the fact that the language of the novel is Hebrew, noting the grumbling of Israelis that Shammās writes in Hebrew, as well as the problem of writing in the language of the conqueror. The critic himself wavers between praise and censure and asks:

> Is it possible that Shammās, by using Hebrew, is provoking the rival in his own home with his very own weapons? It is possible, but this provocation seems to take the form of a demand to recognize the other in him. Shammās has the right and the freedom to write in any language he wants, and we have the right and the freedom to raise these sensitivities, especially since language – as we and others have learned – is the fundamental basis in shaping national identity.[44]

The second criticism was written by Yumnā al-ʻĪd, a prominent Arab critic, who analyses the novel *Arabeskot* in her long and comprehensive article also based on the French translation of the book. In this article, she applies the structuralist approach to *Arabeskot*, and deals with poetics, thematics and ideology in a general way. As far as the poetics of the work is concerned, al-ʻĪd praises the structure of the novel, the depiction of the characters and the treatment of time and place. But she has incisive criticism in two areas: the Christian dimension, which she feels is all-encompassing at the expense of the Palestinian element, and the writing of the novel in Hebrew. She attacks Shammās on this latter point, and in her didactic criticism claims:

> It's strange, Anton Shammās in Israel, or so he says, but he wants to learn the language of this country. Hence he is beginning to write in Hebrew. And the Hebrew writing is the writing of a novel that creates its own authority, i.e., from a foreign land, and from its own time, it shapes the biography of the family (or the biography of the relationships among a group of Christians) and makes from the original that it creates an original for the narrator to relate, to write.[45]

As noted, the criticism in Hebrew and Arabic often dealt at length with the question why the novel *Arabeskot* was written in Hebrew and not in Arabic. And, indeed, why *was* the novel written in Hebrew and not Arabic? And no less important, why was this novel translated into English, French and Dutch, inter alia, but not into Arabic? This is clearly not Arabic literature written in Hebrew letters, as Anton Shammās could claim. Note what Shammās himself has to say:

> One needs a lot of chutzpa to write Hebrew prose. And to have perfect chutzpa, one must work hard to hone one's tools. In retrospect, the poems were my small battles with the language. To command and to grapple with the angel of the Hebrew language. Prose is the true battleground. Here all the possible forms of nakedness are exposed. I came to the language with a particular baggage and I did not forget my language. But when I wrote this book, I did forget my language, or otherwise I would have written it in my language. This forgetting is a kind of salute to the language, homage that I give the Hebrew language – I tried to treat the language with great cautiousness, with respect, like an Arab elephant in a china shop (without breaking anything), trying to preserve inside the new language all the side baggage that I brought from my other culture, from the other side, from a world that doesn't even exist for some Arabs. It's a kind of double redemption of a slice of life that has now vanished. When legend disintegrates and recedes, from beyond the horizon the new language appears, the one my father tried to command and knew inside that he would have to bind the mouth of the Arabic language beast in order to conquer the Hebrew language. Now I return the honor and write in Hebrew.[46]

To the best of my understanding, the novel *Arabeskot* was written in Hebrew and not in Arabic because Shammās, who was active in the Hebrew literary world from the 1970s until the mid 1980s, saw it as natural that he would continue to write in the language in which he had published his two previous poetry books. Moreover, at the time Shammās decided to write in Hebrew, this was not perceived as writing in the language of the other, as opposed to the Maghrib writers who wrote in French and lived in France, such as Ṭāhir Ben Jallūn, or the Mahjar writers in the American diasporas who write in the local language. But what is common to these two groups of writers is that they wrote outside their homeland, their country, their land, and there was a complete split between the writers and their home territory. They preferred to write in their new cultural language that represented not just the language of the dominant majority, but of the 'higher' culture, the more 'advanced' and 'modern' world. Therefore, it would not be unreasonable to assume that the combination of these reasons is what motivated Shammās to write his novel in Hebrew, a language in which he swims like a fish. And he also made wonderful use of the Hebrew language in all its levels and nuances, thus delivering a double message to readers and critics. The first: I, Anton Shammās, an Arab, am writing

Hebrew that is not only no worse than your Hebrew, but even better. And the other message: Whether you like it or not, I am part of your literature, your culture, and you; and this is my place at this stage of my life, my education, and my literary work.

As for the unwillingness of Shammās to have his novel translated into Arabic or to do it himself (as he is one of the top translators in Israel from Hebrew into Arabic), he rejects this, at least at this stage, for precisely one of the reasons that led him to write the novel in Hebrew in the first place. One of the main reasons that Shammās wrote *Arabeskot* in Hebrew was the freedom in Israeli-Jewish society – more than Israeli-Arab society – to criticize not just the other, but also itself. In this novel, Shammās offers some rather harsh criticism not just of Jewish society in Israel, but also of Arab society inside and outside Israel, and he was not willing to criticize his society in its own language. Perhaps in another time and place Shammās will change his mind and allow the translation of his novel into the language of his people. In this context, we refer to the words of Shammās in the aforementioned interview:

> I write in Hebrew about the village. I'm not sure what story would emerge had it been written in Arabic. I would certainly have been more cautious had I written in Arabic about the village. The Hebrew language paradoxically seems to give me security. I would not have had this freedom had I written in Arabic, because what would my aunt and uncle have said? This is a conscious act of camouflage. I use Hebrew as camouflage cover. But all this is in my mind. The younger generation in the village will read it all [anyway], know what is true and what not, and will undoubtedly pursue me until my dying day.[47]

Another subject that we dealt with here, as in other chapters of this book, is that of identity. This subject is relevant for Israeli Arabs in general, for writers in general, and especially for Israeli-Arab writers, and the case of Anton Shammās is particularly fascinating. Shammās understood that his debate over identity epitomized the debate over the identity of Arabs and Jews in Israel. The dialogues between him and Abraham B. Yehoshua and the reactions of writers from all shades of the political spectrum only clarified and sharpened the nuances of the problem of identity, which is an existential problem of the individual, of Israeli Arabs, and of the Jewish community in Israel, as raised by the case of Shammās.[48] A short time after *Arabeskot* appeared, Shammās wrote an article that continued the debate not just with Abraham B. Yehoshua and others, but with himself, in which he describes the trap in which he finds himself:

> Israel defines itself as a Jewish state (or as a state for the Jewish people) and demands that its Arab citizens invest their citizenship with content, but when they do, the state clarifies in no uncertain terms that this was meant to be a social partnership only, that they have to search elsewhere for the political content of their identity (i.e., national belonging – to the Palestinian nation), and when they do search for their national identity elsewhere, they are at once accused of undermining the foundation of the state, and one who undermines the foundation of the state cannot possibly be recognized as an 'Israeli', and so it goes, a perfect catch.[49]

Three years later, when he was outside Israel in the United States, at some distance of time and space, Shammās related both to the subject of having written *Arabeskot* in Hebrew and the problem of identity and definition of the Israeli Arabs:

> In articles about *Arabeskot*, people didn't always know how to define me. 'An Israeli author?' they would ask. Not exactly, I would respond, even though this is what I called myself for years. 'An Arab?' Also not. I chose the impossible combination of 'an Israeli-Palestinian', and this was an act of defiance against them all, even against myself: de-Judaization and de-Zionization of the Jewish state by bestowing Israeli, national meaning on the word 'Israel', and at the same time, emphasis of the Palestinian as an ethnic dimension equivalent to Jewish. And this was somewhat of a self-fulfilling prophecy in our day: Just as Israel exists, so too Palestine will exist. And it held something of the fleeting and innocuous despair of the Israeli idea that I wanted to define in my battles with the windmills of the literary world over the years. And it held something of the desire to deal with bilingual translation – the identity of the Galilean Arab translated to Israeli-Arabic, and then translated to Palestinian in Hebrew letters, and finally to Israeli-Palestinian, in spite of it all and thanks to the Hebrew.[50]

In this chapter we saw that the special situation of Israeli Arabs is reflected in their literature. This situation is even more striking for the group of Israeli-Arab writers who write in both Hebrew and Arabic. We found that there are no Israeli Arabs who publish only in Hebrew, but that most publish in Arabic and a minority publish in both languages. These authors who write in both languages generally publish Hebrew work which is not translated into Arabic, and Arabic work that is not translated into Hebrew. There is one striking exception of an Arab author who wrote a text in Arabic and later rewrote it – rather than translated it – into Hebrew, namely, the novella by Salmān Nāṭūr (1949–) *Yamshūna 'alā al-Rīḥ* (1991) in Arabic, or *Holkhim 'al Ha-Ruaḥ* (1992) in Hebrew [walking on the wind].[51] Most of the writers in this group began their literary careers in Arabic and sooner or later also began to write in Hebrew. A few of the writers began to publish first in Hebrew (Na'īm 'Arāidī). The motivations of these authors to add writing in Hebrew are varied, but common to all is the awareness that their choice of using Hebrew plunges them into Israeli reality and, at the same time, perpetuates their peculiar difference. A distinction is made here about the identity of Israeli-Arab writers by both Israeli-Jewish critics and Arab critics inside and outside Israel. Writers with a defined ideology – national, nationalist, communist or socialist, for example – are perceived and defined as Palestinian writers (Emile Ḥabībī, Samīḥ al-Qāsim, Tawfīq Zayyād), even when they write in Hebrew. However, Israeli-Arab writers without a defined ideology (Na'īm 'Arāidī, Anton Shammās, Maḥmūd 'Abbāsī) who write in Hebrew are perceived as Israeli-Arab or even Israeli writers. What's more, Israeli-Arab authors perceived as Palestinian writers in all senses, such as Emile Ḥabībī and Samīḥ al-Qāsim, do not hesitate to write articles, criticism and even fiction in Hebrew, but nothing detracts from their identification as 'Palestinian'. Because of their special position, their nationalist identity as an Arab or Palestinian can be called into question only infrequently. This happened with Emile Ḥabībī when he accepted the Israel Prize for Literature in 1992, greatly agitating the literary and non-literary world in Israel and the Arab countries and exposing Ḥabībī to scathing criticism, as we shall see at the conclusion of this book.

We have seen that bilingual authorship is not unique to Arab writers, but exists in other nations. The uniqueness and sensitivity of Israeli-Arab authors who write in Hebrew stems from their special situation: a minority writing in the language of the majority which is a minority in the Middle East. Moreover, the Jewish majority in Israel is in ongoing conflict not just with some of the Arab world but also with various components of the Palestinian community. It is possible that Israel's peace agreements with some of the Arab states, the Declaration of Principles, and its peace contacts with Syria and Lebanon, will neutralize some of the accusations flung at Israeli-Arab writers who write in Hebrew. And it is possible that these writers and others will not continue to write in Hebrew if peace comes to the region; or perhaps the opposite is true: peace in the region could relieve the resistance to writing in Hebrew felt by most Arabs inside and outside Israel. This would indicate not only an acceptance of Israel in the Middle East, but acceptance of these Israeli-Arab authors who write in Arabic or Hebrew, or both together.

Two additional points should be mentioned as part of this discussion.

One is related to the question of writing in the territory defined as Israel, which is not an Arab state, although it is their homeland. Furthermore, the Arab minority in Israel writes in the language of the majority, which differs from the situation of modern Maghrib literature, where some Arab writers consciously choose to write in French, the language of the former conquering power. The French, however, have a state of their own, although they ruled parts of the Maghrib from the nineteenth through the middle of the twentieth century. Thus, from the point of view of the French-writing Maghrib authors who live in their own state, the language is perhaps that of the other, the conqueror, but it is perceived as the language of the 'great culture' – French culture. Moreover, the best Maghrib writers, including those with nationalist and patriotic sentiments, write French, speak French and often prefer to live in France, at least part of the time. This is a serious dilemma not just from the cultural perspective, but primarily from the nationalist and ethical perspective.

The second point, related to the first, concerns modernity. If we accept the words of the Moroccan poet and translator al-Muʿṭī Q̱abbāl that bilingualism is the doorway to modernity, this would explain the longing to write in Hebrew of some Israeli-Arab authors, as it reflects their desire to enter the process of modernization.

It is not clear whether the writing in Hebrew of Israeli-Arab authors, and hence their identification with the language and culture of the majority, stamp the authors with the mark of Cain or bring them honour and pride. Israeli Arabs have certainly felt a sense of pride with regard to *Arabeskot* by Anton Shammās and its successful incorporation into modern Hebrew literature. The fact that the book was translated into European languages from the Hebrew does not dim their pride, or at least this is accepted as a fact of secondary importance. The creators of this corpus define themselves as Palestinian Arab Israelis, and some will add Druze when required. It is possibly less important how Jewish and Arab critics define them, and more important how these writers define themselves, and if they really distinguish between their writing in Hebrew and their writing in Arabic. Since the same subjects come up in their writing in both languages, the poetics of the writing do not matter, although the target audience does change. And as we saw with regard to Salmān Nāṭūr, the change in target audience, the writer's appeal to the specific reader and not the general reader, also changes the rules of the game, not just in shaping the characters and the style of writing, but primarily in the message conveyed and the treatment of sensitive subjects related to the image of both nations.

NOTES

1. Joshua Blau, *Dikduk Ha'Aravit-Yehudit Shel Yemei HaBeinayim*, 2nd edn, Jerusalem, Magnes, 1979–80, p. 14.
2. For more about this cultural context, see Rina Drori, *Reshit HaMaga'im Shel HaSifrut HaYehudit 'im HaSifrut Ha'Aravit BaMe-ah Ha'Asirit*, Tel Aviv, HaKibbutz HaMeuḥad and Tel-Aviv University, 1988.
3. On the formation of the various diasporas of the Mahjar group, see Robin C. Ostle, 'The Romantic Poets', in Muhammad Mustafa Badawi (ed.), *The Cambridge History of Arabic Literature, Modern Arabic Literature*, Cambridge, Cambridge University Press, 1992, pp. 95–110. Cornelis Nijland, 'Love and Beyond in Mahjar Literature', in Roger Allen, Hilary Kilpatrick and Ed de Moor (eds), *Love and Sexuality in Modern Arabic Literature*, London, Saqi Books, 1995, pp. 46–55.
4. On the life and work of Jubrān Khalīl Jubrān, see Ghazi Fū'ād Barākis, *Jubrān Khalīl Jubrān fī Dirāsa Taḥlīliyya Tarkībiyya l'Adabihi wa Rasmihi wa Shakhṣihi*, Beirut, Dār al-Kitāb al-Lubnānī, 1981; Tawfīq Ṣā'igh, *Iḍā'ā Jadīda 'alā Jubrān*, Beirut, al-Dār al-Sharqiyya li'l-Ṭibā'a wa'l-Nashr, 1966; Anṭwān al-Qawwāl, *Jubrān Khalīl Jubrān*, Beirut, Dār Amwāj li'l-Ṭibā'a wa'l-Nashr, 1993; Cornelis Nijland, *Michail Nuaymah, Promotor of the Arabic Literary Revival*, Leiden, Brill, 1975; Badawi, *Modern Arabic Literature*, pp. 96–8; Roger Allen (ed.), *Modern Arabic Literature*, New York, Ungar Publishing Company, 1987, pp. 169–76.
5. On modern Maghrib literatures, see 'Abd al-Khālifa Rakībī, *al-Qiṣṣa al-Qaṣīra fī al-Adab al-Jazā'irī al-Mu'āṣir*, Cairo, Dār al-Kitāb al-'Arabī li'l-Ṭibā'a wa'l-Nashr, 1969; Najīb al-'Awafī, *Muqārabat al-Wāqi' fī al-Qiṣṣa al-Qaṣīra al-Maghribiyya, min al-Ta'sīs ilā al-Tajnīs*, Beirut, Casablanca, al-Markaz al-Thaqāfī al-'Arabī, 1987; Muḥammad 'Azzām, *Ittijāhāt al-Qiṣṣa al-Mu'āṣira fī al-Maghrib, Dirāsa*, Damascus, Manshūrāt Ittiḥād al-Kuttāb al-'Arab, 1987; and Sayyid Ḥāmid al-Nassāj, *al-Adab al-'Arabī fī al-Maghrib al-Aqṣā*, Cairo, al-Hay'a al-Miṣriyya al-'Āmma li'l-Kitāb, 1985.
6. Ami Elad-Bouskila and Erez Biton (eds), *Le Maghreb, Littérature et Culture (Special Issue), Apirion*, 28 (1993), pp. 11–12.
7. On the writing of Jabrā Ibrāhīm Jabrā in English, primarily his poetry, see 'Abd al-Wāḥid Lu'lū, 'Ṣūrat Jabrā fī Shabābihi, Shi'r bi'l Inklīziyya', *al-Nāqid*, 10 (April 1989), pp. 26–31.
8. Salma Khadra Jayyusi, *Anthology of Modern Palestinian Literature*, New York, Columbia University Press, 1992, pp. 333–66.
9. For more information, see ibid., pp. 727–8 and also the book edited by Joanna Kadi, *Food for our Grandmothers: Writing by Arab-American and Arab-Canadian Feminists*, Boston, South End Press, 1994, pp. 279–80.
10. The better known works of Afnān al-Qāsim are, among his novels: *al-'Ajūz*, Baghdad, Wizārat al-I'lām wa'Ittiḥād al-Kuttāb wa'l-Ṣuḥufiyyīn al-Filasṭiniyyīn, 1974; among his short stories: *Kutub wa'Asfār*, Cairo, al-Hay'a al-Miṣriyya al-'Āmma li'l-Kitāb, 1990; among his plays: *Umm al-Jamī'*, Beirut, 'Ālam al-Kutub, 1989; and in the field of criticism: *Mas'alat al-Shi'r wa'l-Malḥama al-Darwīshiyya, Maḥmūd Darwīsh fī Madīḥ al-Ẓill al-'Ālī, Dirāsa Sūsyū-Bunyawiyya*, Beirut, 'Ālam al-Kutub, 1987.
11. Ami Elad [-Bouskila], 'Sifrutam Shel Ha'Aravim BeYisrael (1948–93)', in Ami Elad [-Bouskila] (ed.), *HaMizraḥ HeḤadash*, special issue devoted to the literature of Israeli Arabs, *Sifrutam Shel 'Arviyei Yisrael*, 35 (1993), pp. 1–4.
12. Emile Ḥabībī, 'K'mo Petza'', *Politika*, 21 (1988), pp. 6–21. In an anthology that

appeared in Arabic called *Mukhtārāt min al-Qiṣṣa al-Qaṣīra fī 18 Baladan 'Arabiyyan* [selections of short stories from 18 Arab countries], Cairo, Markaz al-Ahrām li'l-Tarjama wa'l-Nashr, 1993, pp. 239–51, a footnote in Arabic notes: 'This chapter was first written by the author [Emile Ḥabībī] in Hebrew in response to a request by the monthly *Politika* and appeared in its special issue "Arabs in Israel – An Inside Look – Mid-1988"; the Arabic-language version was translated by the author himself, who also made additions to the text' (ibid., p. 240).

13. Samīḥ al-Qāsim and Nazīh Khayr (eds and trans.), *al-Dhākira al-Zarqā'*, Tel-Aviv, Mifras, 1991; Samīḥ al-Qāsim, *Yāsmīn, MeShirei Ronni Somek*, Haifa, Beit al-Karma, 1995.
14. Anton Shammās, *Krikha Kasha*, Tel-Aviv, Sifriyat HaPo'alim, 1974; *Shetaḥ Hefker, Shirim*, Tel-Aviv, HaKibbutz HaMeuḥad, 1979; Na'īm 'Araīdī, *Eikh Efshar Le–Ehov*, Tel-Aviv, 'Eked 1972; *Ḥemla U-Faḥad*, Tel-Aviv, 'Eked, 1974–75; *Ḥazarti El HaKafr, Shirim*, Tel-Aviv, 'Am 'Oved, 1986. To this list can be added poets such as Asad 'Azzī, *LeMargelot HaGoral HaMar*, Haifa, Renaissance, 1976; *'Onat HaLeḥishot*, Haifa, Renaissance, 1978; Asad 'Azzī and Fāḍil 'Alī, *Shirei Reḥov*, Daliyat al-Karmil, Milim Publishing House, 1979; Fū'ād Ḥusayn, *Yom Shīshī*, Tel-Aviv, Sa'ar, 1990; *Si'aḥ Psagot*, Haifa, Dfus HaVadi, 1995; Maḥmūd Zaydān, *Ketovet BaḤalal*, Tel-Aviv, 'Eked, 1992. Fārūq Mawāsī wrote his poem 'Shnayim' in Hebrew, *Ha'Etzvonim Shelo Hūvnū, Shirim* (trans. Roge Tavor), Kafer Qar', al-Shafaq, 1989, pp. 79–81.
15. 'Aṭāllāh Manṣūr, *Be-Or Ḥadash*, Tel-Aviv, Karni, 1966. This book was translated into English as *In a New Light*, London, Vallentine Mitchell, 1969.
16. Shmuel Moreh and Maḥmūd 'Abbāsī, *Tarāj'im wa-Āthār fī al-Adab al-'Arabī fī Isrā'il 1948–1986*, 3rd edn, Shfaram, Dar al-Mashriq li'l-Tarjama wa'l-Ṭibā'a wa'l-Nashr, 1987, pp. 218–19
17. 'Aṭāllāh Manṣūr, "Arab Yaktubūn bil-'Ibriyya: al-Wuṣūl ilā al-Jār', *Bulletin of the Israeli Academic Center in Cairo*, 16 (1992), p. 65. Rāshid Ḥusayn published his book *Ḥayim Naḥmān Biyālīk, Nukhba min Shi'rihi wa-Nathrihi*, Jerusalem, Hebrew University, 1966; Ṣabrī Jiryis published *The Arabs in Israel*, Haifa, self-published, 1966.
18. 'Aṭāllāh Manṣūr, *Wabaqiyat Samīra*, Tel-Aviv, Dār al-Nashr al-'Arabī, 1962.
19. Manṣūr, ' 'Arab Yaktubūn bil-'Ibriyya', *Bulletin*, p. 65.
20. Uzi Benziman and 'Aṭāllāh Manṣūr, *Dayarei Mishneh, 'Arviyei Yisrael Ma'amadam VehaMediniyut Klapeihem*, Jerusalem, Keter, 1992.
21. Manṣūr, "Arab Yaktubūn bil-'Ibriyya', *Bulletin*, p. 63.
22. Anton Shammās translated into Arabic the poems of David Avidan in his book, *Idhā'a min Qamar Iṣṭinā'ī*, Tel-Aviv, David Avidan the Thirtieth Century, 1982, and edited and translated the anthology *Ṣayd al-Ghazāla*, Shfaram, Dār al-Mashriq, 1984. Samīḥ al-Qāsim and Nazīh Khayr translated into Arabic and edited the anthology, *al-Dhākira al-Zarqā'*, Tel-Aviv, Mifras, 1991. Samīḥ al-Qāsim translated into Arabic a selection of poems by Ronni Somek under the title *Yāsmīn, Qaṣā'id*, Haifa, Beit al-Karma, 1995.
23. Na'īm 'Araīdī edited and translated some of the works in Arabic as well as Hebrew texts that appeared in his anthology 'Ḥayalim Shel Mayim', Tel-Aviv, Sifrei Ma'ariv and Sifrei Hasidra HaPetuḥa, 1988. He also edited and translated poems by Adonis, *Teḥiliyot*, Tel-Aviv, Kadim, 1989. In the 1970s Salmān Maṣālḥa translated into Hebrew the novel by Saḥar Khalīfa, *HaTzabar* [al-Ṣubbār], Jerusalem, Galileo, 1978; and in the late 1980s, the book by Maḥmūd Darwīsh, *Zekher LaShikheḥa* [dhākira li'l-nisyān], Jerusalem and Tel-Aviv, Schocken, 1989.

24. In an interview with Sihām Dāūd in the Jerusalem weekly newspaper *Yerushalayim*, (19 February 1990).
25. By Anton Shammās in Hebrew: *HaShakran Hakhī Gadol Ba'Olam*, Jerusalem, Keter, 1982; and *'Arabeskot*, Tel-Aviv, 'Am 'Oved, 1986. By Na'īm 'Arāidī in Hebrew: *Eikh Efshar Le-Ehov*, Tel-Aviv, Traklin-'Eked, 1972; *HaNozlim HaMenagnim BeYitzirat Uri Tzvi Greenberg*, Tel-Aviv, 'Eked, 1980; *Ulai Zo Ahava*, Tel-Aviv, Ma'ariv, 1983; *Ḥazarti el HaKefar, Shirim*, Tel-Aviv, 'Am 'Oved, 1986; *BeḤamisha Memadim*, Tel-Aviv, Poalim, 1991; and *Tevila Katlanit*, Tel-Aviv, Bitan, 1992. By Na'īm 'Arāidī in Arabic: *Qaṣā'id Karmiliyya fī al-'Ishq al-Baḥrī*, Shfaram, Dār al-Mashriq li'l-Tarjama wa'l-Ṭibā'a wa'l-Nashr, 1984; *Masīrat al-Ibdā', Dirāsāt Naqdiyya Taḥlīliyya fī al-Adab al-Filasṭīnī al-Mu'āṣir*, Haifa and Shfaram, Maktabat kull Shay', Dār al-Mashriq li'l-Tarjama wa'l-Ṭibā'a wa'l-Nashr, 1988; and *Maḥaṭṭāt 'alā Ṭarīq al-Ibdā', Dirāsāt Naqdiyya fī al-Adab al-Filasṭīnī al-Mu'āṣir*, Haifa, Maktabat kull Shay', 1992.
26. Nazīh Khayr (ed.), *Mifgash Ve'Imut BaYetzira Ha'Aravit Veha'Ivrit*, Haifa, Dfus al-Karma, 1993. This book includes texts in Arabic and Hebrew and also translations from and into both languages, which is not always noted in the text and raises questions about the original language in which it was written. Interestingly, the Arab and Jewish writers who appear in this anthology in the original or in translation also appear in anthologies edited by Nazīh Khayr, Samīḥ al-Qāsim, and others.
27. Aharon Layish, 'Kavim U-Megamot Aḥarei Milḥemet Sheshet HaYamim', in Aharon Layish (ed.), *Ha'Aravim BeYisrael, Retzifut U-Temura*, Jerusalem, Magnes Press, 1981, pp. 240–7.
28. Gershon Shaked, *HaSiporet Ha'Ivrit 1880–1980, BeḤevlei HaZeman*, vol. 4, Tel-Aviv/Jerusalem, HaKibbutz HaMeūḥad and Keter, 1993, pp. 97–188.
29. Gabriel García Márquez, *One Hundred Years of Solitude* (trans. Gregory Rabassa), London, Penguin, 1970.
30. For broad surveys of the modern Arabic literatures of the Mashriq and the Maghrib from the 1960s, see: In English: Ami Elad [-Bouskila] (ed.), *Writer, Culture, Text, Studies in Modern Arabic Literature*, Fredericton, York Press, 1993; Ami Elad [-Bouskila], *The Village Novel in Modern Egyptian Literature*, Berlin, Klaus Schwarz Verlag, 1994; 'Ali Gad, *Form and Technique in the Egyptian Novel 1912-1971*, London, Ithaca Press, 1983; Sabry Hafez, 'The Egyptian Novel in the Sixties', *Journal of Arabic Literature*, VII (1976), pp. 68–84; Roger Allen, *The Arabic Novel, Historical and Critical Introduction*, Manchester, University of Manchester, 1982; and Muhammad Mustafa Badawi (ed.), *Modern Arabic Literature: The Cambridge History of Arabic Literature*, Cambridge, Cambridge University Press, 1992. In Arabic: 'Abd al-Raḥmān Abū-'Awf, *al-Baḥth 'an Ṭarīq Jadīd li'l-Qiṣṣa al-Qaṣīra al-Miṣriyya, Dirāsa Naqdiyya*, Cairo, al-Hay'a al-Miṣriyya al-'Āmma li'l-ta'līf wa'l-Nashr, 1971; Sayyid Ḥāmid al-Nassāj, *Bānūrāmā al-Riwāya al-'Arabiyya al-Ḥadītha*, Cairo, Dār al-Ma'ārif, 1980; and al-Sa'īd al-Waraqī, *Itijāhāt al-Riwāya al-'Arabiyya al-Mu'āṣira*, Cairo, al-Hay'a al-Miṣriyya al-'Āmma li'l-Kitāb, 1982.
31. In this context, it is interesting to note the possible influence of Hebrew poetry on Arabic poetry in Israel. For an analysis of the influence of the poetry of Bialik on the work of Maḥmūd Darwīsh, see the study of Jamāl Aḥmad al-Rifā'ī, *Athar al-Thaqāfa al-'Ibriyya fī al-Shi'r al-Filasṭīnī al-Mu'āṣir, Dirāsa fī Shi'r Maḥmūd Darwīsh*, Cairo, Dār al-Thaqāfa al-Jadīda, 1994.
32. Anton Shammās, 'HaSifrut Ha'Aravit BeYisrael Le-Ahar 1967', *Skirot*, Tel-Aviv

University (June 1976), no. 2, p. 7.

33. Hannan Hever, 'Lehakot Ba'Akevo Shel Akhiles', *Alpayim*, 1 (June 1989), pp. 186–93; Hahnan Hever, "Ivrit Be'Ito Shel 'Aravi, Shisha Prakim 'Al *Arabeskot* Me-et Anton Shammās', *Te-oriya U-Vikoret*, 1 (Summer 1991), pp. 23–38. For an entirely different point of view, see Reuven Snir, 'Petza' MePtza'av: HaSifrut Ha'Aravit HaFalastinit BeYisrael', *Alpayim*, 2 (1990), pp. 244–68.
34. Na'īm 'Arāidī, 'Sifrut 'Ivrit, Ma Na'amt', *Moznayim*, 65: 4 (January 1991), p. 41.
35. Emile Ḥabībī, *al-Waqā'i' al-Gharība fī Ikhitfā' Sa'īd Abī al-Naḥs al-Mutashā'il*, 3rd edn, Jerusalem, Manshūrāt Ṣālāḥ al-Dīn, 1977; for the Hebrew version, see *Ha-Opsimist: HaKhronika HaMufla-ah Shel He'almut Sa'id Abū al-Naḥs al-Mutasha'il* (trans. Anton Shammās), Jerusalem, Mifras, 1984. Also, *Ikhṭayya*, Nicosia, Kitāb al-Karmel 1, 1985; for the Hebrew version, see *Ikhṭayya* (trans. Anton Shammās), Tel-Aviv, 'Am 'Oved, 1988. The stories by Ḥabībī, 'Levasof Paraḥ HaShaked', 'Rūbābīkā', and 'Kinat HaSartan', were translated by Na'īm 'Arāidī in the anthology he edited, *Ḥayalim Shel Mayim*, pp. 57–71. And Emile Ḥabībī, *Sarāyā bint al-Ghūl, Khurrāfiyya*, Haifa, Dār Arābesk, 1991; for the Hebrew version, see *Saraya, Bat HaShed HaRa', Khurafiyya* (trans. Anton Shammās) Tel-Aviv, HaSifriya HaḤadasha, HaKibbutz HaMeūḥad, 1993.
36. This appeared in English translation as Anton Shammas, *Arabesques* (trans. Vivian Eden), New York, Harper & Row, 1988.
37. Moreh and 'Abbāsī, *Tarājim wa-Āthār*, pp. 122–3.
38. Ibid., pp. 155–6.
39. Ibid., pp. 123–4.
40. Avraham Balaban, ''HaGal HeḤadish' Neged 'HaGal HeḤadash'', *Yediot Aḥaronot* (5 June 1992), pp. 34–5.
41. Hever, *Alpayim*, 1, p. 191. For a full discussion of the novel *Arabeskot*, see Hever's article,"Ivrit Be'Ito Shel 'Aravi, Shisha Prakim 'Al *Arabeskot* Me-et Anston Shammas', *Te-oriya U-Vikoret*, 1 (1991), pp. 23–38.
42. Dan Laor, 'HaFasuta-im: HaSipur Shelo Nigmar', *Ha-aretz* (30 May 1986), pp. B6, B7.
43. Aharon Amir, 'Ge'ula VeHitbolelut', *Be-Eretz Yisrael* (October 1986), p. 9.
44. Sharbal Dāghir, 'Arābisk Filasṭīniyya', *al-Nāqid*, 2 (August 1988), p. 75.
45. Yumnā al-'Īd, *Taqniyyāt al-Sard al-Riwā'ī fī ḍaw al-Manhaj al-Bunyawī*, Beirut, Dār al-Fārābī, 1990, p. 149.
46. 'Milim SheMenasot Laga'at', an interview conducted by Dalia 'Amit with Anton Shammās, 1988.
47. Ibid.
48. On the debate between Anton Shammās and Abraham B. Yehoshua, and those who joined the debate, see: Anton Shammās, 'Avram Ḥozer LaGola?' *'Iton 77*, 72–3 (6 February 1986), pp. 21–2; 'Ashmat HaBabushka', *Politika*, 5–6 (February–March 1986), pp. 44–5; 'Rosh HaShana LaYehudim', *Ha'Ir*, 13 (September 1985), pp. 13–18; 'Kitsh 22, O: Gevul HaTarbut', *'Iton 77*, 84–5 (January–February 1987), pp. 24–6; and Abraham B. Yehoshua, 'Im Ata Nishar – Ata Mi'ut', *Kol Ha'Ir*, (31 January 1986), pp. 42–3. The latter article also appeared under the title 'Abraham B. Yehoshua: Teshuva Le-Anton', *Ha'Ir* (31 January 1986), pp. 22–3. See also Herzl and Balfour Ḥakak, 'Shammas Eino Makir BeMedina Yehudit', *Moznayim*, 5–6 (November–December 1986), p. 80; Michal Schwartz, "Al Ashmat Alef Bet Yehoshua VehaBabushka Shel

Shammās', *Derekh HaNitzotz* (5 February 1986), pp. 6–7; and B. Michael, 'Kosot Ru-aḥ, Pitzpon Ve-Anton', *Ha-aretz* (17 January 1986), p. 9.

49. Shammās, *'Iton 77*, 84–5 (January–February) p. 25.

50. Anton Shammās, 'Yitzu Zemani Shel Ḥafatzim Nilvim', *Ha-aretz*, Sefarim (13 June 1989), p. 11.

51. Salmān Nāṭūr, *Yamshūn 'alā al-Rīḥ*, Nazareth, Markaz Yāfā li'l-Abḥāth, 1991. *Holkhim 'Al HaRu-aḥ*, Beit Berl, HaMerkaz LeḤeker HaḤevra Ha'Aravit BeYisrael, 1992. For a detailed article about both these works, see Mattityahu Peled, 'Hashpa'at HaKoreh BeGirsa-ot Holkhim 'Al HaRu-aḥ Me-et Salmān Nāṭūr', *HaMizraḥ HeḤadash*, 35 (1993), pp. 115–28.

3

Between Interlaced Worlds

Riyāḍ Baydas and the Arabic Short Story in Israel

In Chapter 2 we examined the issue of bilingual writing among a small number of Arab writers in Israel. This chapter is devoted to one writer only: Riyāḍ Baydas. From the point of view of major Palestinian writers, a separate chapter should be devoted to each of the following Palestinians: Emile Ḥabībī, Maḥmūd Darwīsh, Jabrā Ibrāhīm Jabrā and Samīḥ al-Qāsim. However, as noted in the Introduction, some chapters, including this one, appeared originally as articles. Therefore, having one entire chapter devoted to a writer who is not in the front ranks of modern Palestinian writers, though definitely prominent among the younger generation, should not be construed as overstating his role or the quality of his narrative works.

This chapter examines the world of Riyāḍ Baydas, one of the outstanding authors among young Arabs writing in Israel, through his works published in the decade 1980–90.[1] Born in 1960, Baydas belongs to the third generation of Arab short-story writers in Israel. He was born into a literary climate and tradition that had already been shaped by two generations: first that of Emile Ḥabībī (1921–96), Najwā Q'awār Faraḥ (1923–), and Ḥannā Ibrāhīm (1927–);[2] and second the generation of the writers Muḥammad 'Alī Ṭāha (1941–) and Zakī Darwīsh (1944–).[3]

The literary climate is important to a writer not only in establishing stature but also in determining significant issues such as where one writes, for whom one writes, where the work is published and the subject of one's writing, as noted previously. Such questions are critical for every writer, and particularly for the Israeli-Arab writer, whose literature is that of a national minority. I would like to examine these questions in the context of the uniqueness of Palestinian literature in Israel, a literature whose very terms of reference are controversial.

One of the issues we examined in the first chapter related to the audience of the Arab writer in Israel. From the late 1960s and particularly the early 1970s, Israeli-Arab writers began to focus on the readers, critics and publishers in the large centres of Arab culture: Cairo, Beirut and Casablanca. Palestinian-Israeli writers began to address not just the local audience, but also and perhaps primarily readers outside Israel, appearing in newspapers and journals in the Arab world.

One notable example of an Israeli-Arab author published outside Israel is Riyāḍ Baydas. His first two books were published in Jerusalem (1980, 1985), his third in Cyprus (1987), and his fourth in Casablanca (1988).[4] Most articles and short stories written by Baydas appear in Israeli-Arab journals, but they have also been published in Arab countries and Arab centres in Europe and Cyprus.[5]

THE THEMATIC WORLD OF RIYĀḌ BAYDAS

Riyāḍ Baydas, an Arab-Palestinian writer who lives in Israel, derives his subject matter from Israeli reality – both Arab and Jewish – and from universal themes not necessarily set in this time or region. Baydas began his literary activity in earnest in the late 1970s, and is the most prolific short-story writer among Arab writers in Israel of his generation. His writing bears the imprint of three main spheres of influence: first, the culture, predominantly modern, of non-Palestinian Arab writers such as the Sudanese writer al-Ṭayyib Ṣāliḥ (1929–), the Syrian writer Ḥannā Mīna (1924–) and the Saudi writer ʻAbd al-Raḥmān Munīf (1933–); second, the influence of other Palestinian writers, especially Israelis, such as Emile Ḥabībī, Maḥmūd Darwīsh, Muḥammad Naffāʻ and Zakī Darwīsh; and, third, the influence of non-Arab writers – either Israelis writing in Hebrew (Hanoch Levin) or South American storytellers (García Márquez and Borges), or Europeans (Kafka, Camus and Joyce).[6] The openness of Baydas to local and world literature enriches his internal world and brings a diversity to both the themes and the techniques of his writing.

Baydas draws his themes from the current situation in Israel; they are not novel and have already been addressed by other Israeli-Arab writers. The uniqueness of Baydas, however, is his treatment of these subjects – their intensity and the sometimes unconventional poetic wrappings. Baydas deals with a variety of themes, but to several he ascribes particular importance: Arab–Jewish relations, alienation, isolation, persecution, the situation of the refugees and the status of women.

An examination of the writing of Riyāḍ Baydas reveals that the Arab–Jewish theme is of greatest interest to him. The possibility of a connection between Arab and Jew, or the image of the Arab versus the image of the Jew, have been dealt with before by Arab writers in Israel, mostly prior to the mid 1960s, but since then literary interest in this subject has significantly waned.[7] Baydas addresses this web of relations, and hence it is of interest to observe how he describes his characters, primarily the Arab, who is within the writer's natural purview. The image of the Arab in the writing of Baydas is not stereotypical, monolithic, or common, but rather comprises a range of characters drawn primarily from one stratum of Arab society – village life. Baydas depicts different types of Arabs, sometimes distinguishing between an Israeli Arab and an Arab from the occupied territories, but, in the final analysis, all Arabs are drawn in a positive light, with isolated exceptions that we shall soon mention. Often, the author does not explicitly identify a character as Arab, but the atmosphere and the dialogue make this unequivocally clear.[8] Arab figures are drawn from several angles, most prominently: the young Arab, the Arab in relation to the Jew, the link between the Israeli Arab and the Arab from the territories, the Arab from the territories and the 'bad' Arab.

In his stories Baydas often depicts young Arab men, usually educated, who are grappling with the political, social and economic difficulties of life in Israel. This young Arab bears some resemblance to Baydas, explicit or implied. He may also be clearly defined, even though in many senses he is meant to symbolize the collective, and thus he sometimes has the cardboard quality of slogans. One of the cardinal features of this figure is that he is persecuted. This is the sensitive intellectual for whom the nightmare and the dream are interwoven, who lives with a sense of being pursued by the 'forces of darkness' – the army, the police and the security services. This sense of persecution is so exaggerated that even the innocent act of holding a rose is perceived as a violation of the law.[9] Often this young man has no name, i.e., he is an anonymous and even archetypal figure, not even explicitly labelled an Arab. He is usually portrayed as sensitive and refined, in stark contrast with the security police (the Jews) who are brutal, crude and insensitive in their behaviour towards him.[10]

But Baydas offers a complex set of relationships between the Arab and the surrounding Jewish society, not merely confrontation with the 'forces of darkness'. These relations occur on two levels: interactions with Jewish women and day-to-day encounters, especially on the bus. In the former, the young educated Arab develops an intimate and emotional relationship, often with a Jewish prostitute. In the story 'Hadhayān' [delusion], a young

Arab satisfies his needs with Ruth the prostitute, but he also develops a relationship with her. Ruth, it turns out, is a war widow who has fallen into prostitution. The narrator's attitude is that of a man to a woman, the nationalist issues never arising between them. He knows clearly, however, that their relationship cannot continue and he ends it, even though he is aware of the dishonesty of this behaviour toward her.[11]

Another relationship based on feelings between a young Arab and a Jewish woman appears in the story 'Bākiran, fī Had'at al-Ṣabāḥ' [early in the calm of the morning], in which Baydas takes a universal, humanist approach. The hero, a young Arab named Riyāḍ, is a journalist living with his Arab girlfriend in a room rented from Rachel, an Iraqi-born Jew. (The phenomenon of an unmarried Arab couple living together in itself defies the norms of acceptable behaviour in Arab society in Israel.) Drawn to Rachel's unusual story, Riyāḍ sacrifices his relationship with his Arab girlfriend. When Rachel is on her deathbed, Riyāḍ promises her he will write a book about her life, but, for various reasons, he does not keep his promise.[12] On another level, this story reveals contact between a young Arab and the surrounding Jewish society. Much of this interaction, it is interesting to note, takes place on bus rides. Whether by bus or another journey, Baydas intimates a transition between worlds, a crossing of social and internal boundaries, a situation of being on the threshold (liminality).[13]

This phenomenon can be seen in a harsh confrontation in 'al-Bu'ra' [the focus][14] – one of his more outspoken stories concerning relations between Arabs and Jews. Here the author polarizes to an extreme the differences between 'him' and 'them'. The young Arab (again nameless) is portrayed as sensitive, proud, humanitarian, decent, strong and articulate – able to hold his own against three Jews. Additional messages in this story are that Jews perceive Arabs as an undifferentiated mass, not distinguishing between Israeli Arabs and Arabs from the territories; and if they do distinguish, Jews may even regard Israeli Arabs as more threatening than Arabs from the territories. And the Jews do not understand how Israeli Arabs get along with the Jewish residents of Israel.[15]

As noted, most of the Arabs in the stories by Baydas are positive figures in Palestinian society, but some negative types do appear and can be classified into three groups: those who are on the take from the Israeli Government, those who abandon their homeland and emigrate, and members of the Christian priesthood. Among those on the take are Arabs who hold key posts in the Arab sector, such as the mayors of local councils and *mukhtārs* [village chiefs]. Ever since the beginning of the Arab short story (and other literary genres) in Israel, these leaders, especially the *mukhtārs*, have been the object of intense criticism for serving the powers-that-be and seeking only personal gain. They are perceived as collaborators and sometimes even as traitors.[16] In keeping with this tradition, Baydas censures a mayor in his story 'al-Awrāq lā taṭīr 'Āliyan fī al-Faḍā'' [the papers don't fly away high in space], describing him as 'tall, with an immense body, a large head, small legs, and a big voice',[17] thus disparaging him by distorting his physical appearance.

The second category of Arab that Baydas castigates are those who abandon the homeland and emigrate, especially to the United States. The most outstanding story here is 'Muḥāwala Jadīda liTanaffus al-Ṣu'adā'' [a new attempt to breathe freely],[18] in which Baydas condemns the phenomenon of emigration that has spread through some parts of Arab society in Israel. He describes Fū'ād, a well-respected teacher with a family, who emigrates primarily because he is drawn to the material comforts in 'the land of Uncle Sam' (rather than the 'United States' or 'America'). The diaspora is presented as a cold, alien and materialistic land, in stark contrast with the homeland suffused with the fragrance of *za'tar* and olives, where honour and the family are the essence. The author's conclusion is unequivocal: Fū'ād must return to his homeland, not just for himself, but also for his children. Interestingly, the author presents Fū'ād's wife as blinded by money and an obstacle to his return.

Even men of the cloth taste the rod of censure from Baydas. He does not criticize Christianity (his own religion) *per se*, but rather the clergy, in this case the archbishop who makes an appearance in 'al-Jū' wa'l-Jabal' [hunger and the mountain], and who, paradoxically, is in league with the devil. The proud father of the narrator contemptuously rejects advice from the religious man as dishonourable, even though it might ease his financial strain.[19] A Christian presented in a positive light appears in 'al-Jarād' [the locusts]. This is a proud Arab who clings to his land and unites the townspeople in defeating the locusts. Incidentally, this figure of a town hero is exceptional in the stories of Baydas, though common in other modern Arab literature.[20]

Stories by Baydas also reflect the phenomenon of closing ranks among Israeli Arabs in spite of their differences, in conformity with the tradition of other Palestinian writing.[21] Nonetheless, Baydas does not hesitate to criticize Arab society in Israel. This criticism focuses on preserving the values and norms which seem to have become *passé*. The most notable example of this is his allegorical story 'al-I'dām' [the execution].[22] Here, Baydas reproaches Israeli-Arab society for opposing all change. He goes even further and looks at the issue of pride in Arab society, a concept ostensibly taboo, but Baydas, in impressive fashion, uses irony to criticize it. Cleverly, he airs his views through an old man, who reveals that the emperor is naked, although it costs the old man his life.

Baydas breaks ranks on other issues as well, even some in national consensus among Israeli Arabs. In 'Shadharāt' [particles],[23] Baydas depicts a new model of an Arab, a successful businessman who lives well with his conscience despite his low level of morality. Baydas criticizes the lip-service he pays to solidarity with his Palestinian brethren in the territories, condemning the purely verbal identification with Palestinians under occupation, especially during the intifāḍa.

The relationship between Israeli Arabs and Arabs in the territories, and the image of Arabs in the territories among Israeli Arabs and Jews are among the most important and sensitive subjects that Baydas addresses. With the exception noted above, the sense of common destiny of all Palestinians and the identification of Israeli Arabs with Palestinians in the territories are absolute. Baydas does not differ here from other Israeli-Arab writers, who repeatedly emphasize solidarity with Palestinians in the territories, even though they are aware of the differences between them. This bond between Israeli Arabs and their Palestinian kin, whether in the occupied territories or in Lebanon or Syria, began after the 1948 war and intensified after the 1967 war. It appears in much of the writing of Israeli Arabs and of Palestinians across the border, and is most fully and comprehensively expressed in the genre of the short story.[24] Baydas continues this tradition and the stories he has written at various times constitute a corpus that deals directly or indirectly with the Arabs in the territories.[25] He describes this bond among Palestinians on both the individual and the collective levels, and also presents it from the point of view of a Jew. In 'al-Lawḥa' [the picture],[26] he describes a poor boy selling pictures in the Old City of Jerusalem. The narrator buys a picture, not because he likes it but out of a sense of their common fate, as this boy evokes memories of himself after the 1948 war. The wife of the narrator is unaware of his thoughts and surprisingly insensitive.[27] The strong identification of the author with the Palestinians in the territories leads him to idealize their image, especially during the intifāḍa. In 'Ḥajar 'alā Ṣamt al-Qabr' [a stone on the silence of the grave], Baydas depicts a released prisoner who grew up in a refugee camp as a totally positive human being: not only did prison not break his spirit, it even strengthened him and led him to believe that the army of oppression will some day disappear.[28]

Baydas elucidates the status of women in Arab society and the changes that have taken place from several angles. He does not use one prototype of a woman, but a selection of characters. Most are young, educated and diverge from conventional norms in Arab society. There is Sanā' in the novella *al-Maslak* [the way], a mother of three who lives with 'Abdallāh, a teacher. Another type is represented by Lu'lu' in 'al-Nās' [the people],[29] an educated and wise young woman who believes in freedom and who puts in their place any men who interpret this incorrectly as an invitation to sexual relations. In 'Bākiran, fī Had'at al-Ṣabāḥ' [early in the calm of the morning], we learn about the phenomenon of an unmarried couple living together: Riyāḍ the journalist rents a room (apparently in Haifa) together with his Arab girlfriend (at least she appears to be Arab in the story, although this is not explicitly stated). The women who populate the works of Baydas generally defy conventions and challenge the norms of traditional Arab society. What we see here are processes of modernization of Arab society in Israel, which lives in a reciprocal relationship with the surrounding Jewish society and is influenced by it, whether consciously or while denying it.

ARAB SOCIETY IN TRANSITION

Abolition of the military rule in the mid 1960s, the flood of villagers to the cities to find work and the introduction of compulsory education expedited the process of modernization among the Arab population, which is primarily rural. This produced a host of problems in social issues and values, which are reflected in the writing of Baydas. One example is the change in attitude toward land. Baydas depicts Arabs, mostly from the younger generation, who assert that there is no longer any point in agriculture, as one can no longer make a living from it in modern times.[30] Land as a pivotal issue in Arab society comes up repeatedly in the writing of Baydas, framed in his ambivalence. On the one hand, it is acknowledged that times are changing and land as a source of livelihood is losing its power to white collar or clerical jobs. On the other, land has become a national and even mythic symbol, and cleaving to it is a measure of the powerful bond of Palestinians to their homeland. An extreme example of clinging to the land can be found in the story 'al-'Āi'dūn' [those who return],[31] which takes place on 30 March 1976, a date since known as Land Day because of the violent events that day surrounding Arab resistance to the appropriation of land by the Israeli Government. Aḥmad, who witnesses the confiscation of his father's land, cannot remain silent and gives his life in defence of the land. Slogans like 'Bi'l-Rūḥ Bi'ldam Nafdīki yā Arḍanā' [in spirit and in blood we shall redeem you, our land] or 'Yā Arḍanā yā 'Irḍanā' [O our land,

O our honour] faithfully convey the inseverable bond of Arabs with their land[32] and the sanctity ascribed to the land, which bestows courage and spiritual strength on its defenders, and for which Arabs are willing to give their lives. Therefore, when an outside party (such as the Israeli Government) seeks to purchase or take control of Arab land, or when Kahanists call for the uprooting of Arabs from their lands, the result is a closing of ranks and ever more determined clinging to it.[33]

Baydas's stories portray the difficult problems with which the Arab population is grappling: works education and modernization in general. Expressions such as 'We haven't stopped being Arabs. At least drink our coffee!' in the novella *al-Maslak*[34] coexist with expressions to the contrary: In 'Qiṣṣa bilā 'Unwān' [story without a title], the narrator tells his aunt that people haven't eaten bulgur for a long time because 'it's gone out of style'.[35]

Education is undoubtedly a key factor in accelerating the process of change and deepening the rift within Arab society in Israel and in the Arab countries. The attitude toward education depicted in these stories is ambivalent. On the one hand, there is acknowledgement of the importance of education for economic security and social advancement, and Baydas portrays both fathers and mothers struggling to afford an education for their children. In 'al-Ṭafra' [the jump],[36] Fahd the floor-washer had once excelled in school, but the family's financial straits forced him to abandon his studies and get a job. He doesn't want his son Yūsuf to share the same fate so Fahd works hard and makes great sacrifices to pay for his children's education. In 'al-Qiṭṭa, al-Ḥafīda, al-Jadda wa'l-Umm' [the cat, the granddaughter, the grandmother and the mother],[37] a mother works day and night to pay for her daughter's education so that the daughter can achieve more than the mother did. On the other hand, education is also viewed as one root of the alienation of educated people from their culture. Thus in the story 'Kalb Ibn Kalb' [dog son of a dog],[38] one son goes abroad to study, using part of his property to finance his education, while the other son uses his property to build a house. The father writes to the educated son, who does not even bother to reply to his father's letters (for reasons that are unclear). After several attempts, the father reviles him as 'a dog son of a dog'. In 'Kūlāj Qaṣaṣī, al-Indhār mā qabla al-Akhīr, Khuṭūṭ Bayḍā' 'alā Ufuq Aswad' [a story collage, the next to the last warning, white threads on a black horizon],[39] education is criticized from another angle, this time the negative effect of the university on its students.

But while Arab society in Israel is undergoing a process of change, some traditional patterns abide, folk beliefs foremost among them.[40] One such belief in spirits and devils is described in 'Yawm min al-Ayyām' [one day],[41] in which Umm Mikhā'il uses the chain of her cross to protect her from those who would do her all manner of harm. Another type of folk belief is related to magic and sorcery. The story 'Ma Ḥadatha li-Kitāb al-Jadd Nā'if' [what happened to the book of Grandfather Nā'if][42] is about the book of magic and sorcery with which Grandfather Nā'if tries unsuccessfully to heal the women of the village. The grandson develops a respect for these methods, and when the book is lost after the death of the grandfather, the grandson begins to search for it. The story approaches these old beliefs not with haughtiness or disdain, but respectfully. Sometimes the author makes use of folktales, and anchors them in current reality. Thus in 'Kayfa Ṣār al-Khityār Aḥmad al-'Alam Shābban?', a story his old grandfather told him in his youth about a terrible monster is engraved in the memory of the narrator. In the current incarnation, the monster appears as Kahane who wants to persuade the Arabs of Umm al-Faḥm to abandon their land.

As indicated, Baydas draws upon folk beliefs not just from Muslim, but also from Christian tradition. There are not many Christian elements in his work, and these are mainly the mention of a cross, the crucifixion, or the Virgin Mary.[43] Baydas's attitude toward Christianity is illuminating, betraying a rift between the community of believers and the senior priesthood. He does not withhold censure from religious leaders on political and social matters, and two illustrations of this come to mind. The first is the father of the protagonist in 'Ashlā' min Ḥayāt Rajul Aḥabba Warda Ṣaghīra' [remnants from the life of a man who liked a small rose], who strongly rejects the efforts of the archbishop to curry favour with the English, stating, 'If the grandfather of the Messiah were English, I wouldn't believe him.'[44] Secondly, in 'Yawm min al-Ayyām', we see that social equality is a higher priority for Baydas than religion. Through an old woman, Umm Mikhā'il, he not only criticizes religious leaders, in this case the archbishop, but he does so mockingly. This woman describes how wealthy families invite the archbishop to their homes, but that if poor families invite him, it's not certain 'whether his new car could get into this dust-filled neighbourhood?!'[45] Later in the story, the author states with conviction that Christianity and the servants of religion do not take the side of the poor, and only through Communism can the poor expect any help.[46] In the preceding two examples, Baydas is more critical of religious leaders than of religion itself. A similar critique has been expressed by the Christian Lebanese Mahjar author and poet Jubrān Khalīl Jubrān against the church and its clergy. Baydas is no exception among Palestinian authors in Israel: Muslim and Druze writers in Israel have also attacked the religious establishment and its representatives,[47] and this phenomenon is rather common in modern Arab literatures in general.[48]

Baydas brings the picture of poverty and neglect to new depths in his descriptions of refugee camps in the territories, juxtaposing the abject poverty to the pride and sense of warmth among the families. He does not devote much space to the refugee condition, but he clearly regards it as a crucial issue. The theme of refugees appears frequently in Palestinian writing, particularly in the Palestinian short story of the 1950s and 1960s, with some decline in the 1970s and 1980s. Baydas treats the theme of refugees on two levels. The first is the difficult experience of being uprooted in 1948, which he draws in grim terms: the expulsion of Arabs from Jaffa ('Marthiyat al-Ḥanīn al-'Amīq' [the lament of deep longing])[49] or from Haifa ('Ma Ḥadatha li-Kitāb al-Jadd Nā'if') and a stark description of becoming a refugee: 'family names with their roots and branches, details, leaders, land-owners, land deeds, those who left or were expelled by force, photographs of natural regions that were completely erased from the map, names of villages that were wiped out'.[50] On the second level, Baydas addresses the relationship between the dispersed refugees and Arabs who live in Israel. He places great emphasis on this bond, consciously and deliberately, noting the relationship between the narrator and his grandmother who lives in Jordan ('Ma Ḥadatha li-Kitāb al-Jadd Nā'if'), or with some of his grandfather's family who fled to Lebanon. The experience of being a refugee is what links the narrator in 'al-Lawḥa' with the boy selling pictures in the Old City, evoking memories of his childhood and the wanderings of his family.

POETICS, STYLE AND WRITING TECHNIQUE

A look at the four collections of stories by Baydas discussed in this chapter reveals a change in themes as well as in style and poetics. This is not a radical change, and in many ways indicates continuity and a natural progression.

In the first collection (*al-Jū' wa'l-Jabal*), the themes that Baydas addresses are circumscribed, limited mainly to problems between Arab citizens and Jewish authorities. He treats the same subjects differently in his second collection (*al-Maslak*), and adds the themes of education, employment, livelihood and problems of the young educated Arab. Baydas's treatment of these is brought to an extreme in his third collection (*al-Rīḥ* [the wind]), when he writes about problems of employment, changes in Arab society, the generation gap, loneliness and actual events such as provocations by Kahane. The fourth collection (*Takhṭīṭāt Awwaliyya* [early sketches]) – all stories written during the intifāḍa – deals with Jewish–Arab relations, problems in the occupied territories and family affairs. The criticism heaped by Baydas on both Arab and Jewish societies here becomes more severe, and is also evident in stories published after the fourth collection.

Regarding style, structure and technique, the writing in all four collections is unequivocally realistic, as the subject matter is drawn from current events and society. Yet in all four collections, especially in the first, there are romantic and even sentimental tales. In the second book, the characters are more defined and complex, but they are less so in the fourth book, perhaps because the political turbulence at the time evoked strong feelings that led to the depiction of more shallow characters.

As for the use of language, Baydas wrote most of the dialogue in literary Arabic [*fuṣḥā*], but he introduced more colloquial Arabic [*'āmmiyya*] with each subsequent book. He also increased his use of an omniscient author, parables, intertextuality and other literary devices that enrich and vary the writing.

One of the difficult problems in modern Arabic literature is the need to decide in what language to write the dialogue – literary or colloquial Arabic. There is no clear mandate about this in the Palestinian short story, except for writers like Muḥammad Naffā', who writes all dialogue in the colloquial Arabic of the local dialect of Beit Jann. Dialogue (and monologue) are key elements in the works of Riyāḍ Baydas. Most of his work is written in literary Arabic, and there is no significant difference here between his early and later stories. The literary Arabic is classic but not overblown, as conveyed by the translation of the following excerpt from 'al-Ṣamt al-Dāmī fī Iḥdā al-Layālī al-Bārida'. This dialogue takes place between Jewish soldiers and Nājī, an Arab labourer:

> Alā t'arifu inna al-yawm yawm 'īd?
> Balā!
> Idhan, limādhā ta'akhkharta fī makān al-'amal?
> Hādhihi awāmir al-masu'ūl!
> Awāmirnā kadhālika lā tukhālaf.
> Lam aqṣud hādhā!
> Mādhā taḍummu ila ṣadrika?
> Akyās fīhā khubz wa-bandūra wa-baṣal.

In English translation:

> 'Do you not know that today is a feast?'
> 'Certainly!'
> 'Why then were you delayed at work?'
> 'Those were the orders of the supervisor!'
> 'Our orders must also be obeyed.'
> 'It was not my intention to disobey!'
> 'What do you hold against your chest?'
> 'Bags of bread, tomatoes, and onions.'[51]

Another example of dialogue translated from literary Arabic is from 'Bisāṭ al-Rīḥ' [the wings of the wind] in the fourth collection of stories. This scene takes place between a Jewish cab driver and his Israeli-Arab passenger:

> Na'rifu ba'ḍanā al-ba'ḍ. Hādhā kull mā fī al-'amr. Fī'l-qarya ya'rifu'l al-wāḥid al-'ākhar, ḥattā lam yakun ṣadīquhu.
>
> Ibtasama bi'imti'āḍ wā'alqā naẓra khāṭifa min al-shubbāk, thumma iltafata nāḥiyatī wahuwa yaqūlu: Lākin baladakum laysat qarya . . .
>
> Qāṭa'tuhu: wa-laysat madīna kadhalika . . .
>
> Qāla mustafsiran: Hal ta'rifu Ḥilmī? Ji'tu 'indahu, fahuwa al-ballāṭ alladhī sayuballiṭu baytī al-jadīd. Wa-biṣu'ūba wajadtu baytahu. Ji'tu ma'a raqam al-bayt, faḍaḥika al-nās 'alayya. Wa-ḥīn qultu lahum ḥilmī al-ballāṭ 'arafūhu bisur'a.
>
> Ḍaḥiktu wa-anā aqūlu māziḥan: Kullnā Ḥilmī!

And in English translation:

> 'We all know one another. That is the point. In the village, each one knows the other, even if the other is not one's friend.'
>
> He smiled in annoyance and glanced quickly out the window, then turned to me and said, 'But your place is not a village . . .'
>
> I interrupted him, 'Yet not a city . . . '
>
> He asked, 'Do you know Ḥilmī? I came to see him because he is a tiler who will tile my new home, and I had difficulty finding his residence. I brought with me the number of the house and the people laughed at me, and when I said to them 'Ḥilmī the tiler', they knew him at once.
>
> I laughed and said in jest, 'We are all Ḥilmī!'[52]

In the dialogues of the first collection (*al-Jū' wa'l-Jabal*), colloquial Arabic was not used at all, while in the second collection (*al-Maslak*), it was used only once in the story 'al-Qiṭṭa' [the cat]. The granddaughter appeals to her grandmother to tell her a bedtime story: She uses a word in colloquial Arabic, but then continues in literary speech: 'Dakhīlek, Iḥkī lī Qiṣṣa' [C'mon, relate to me a story].[53]

In the third collection (*al-Rīḥ*), Baydas uses colloquial Arabic extensively. In stories such as 'Kayfa ṣār al-Khityār Aḥmad al-'Alam Shābban?' (pp. 21, 28) and 'al-Kalimāt al-Maksūra' [the broken words] (pp. 42, 45), the author integrates a bit of colloquial Arabic into the dialogues. But in 'Kalima Wāḥida Bass' [only one word] in this collection, the use of colloquial Arabic is extensive, possibly deriving from the situation in which simple folk are talking inside a cab. Note, for example, the following dialogue:

> Sa'ala al-sā'iq wa-huwa yanẓuru ilā ashjār al-ṣanawbar allatī tantashiru 'alā aṭrāf al-ṭarīq:
> – Esh tishtghel?
> – Fī tazfīt al-suṭūḥ.
> Wa-māla al-sā'iq wa-huwa yaḥīdu 'an iḥdā ḥufar al-shāri', thumma iltafata ilā al-rākib al-amāmī wa-huwa yabtasimu bi-tawaddud:
> – Esh yikallif tazfīt saṭḥ?
> Wa-ash'ala aḥad al-rukkāb sīgāra aḍāfat jawwan thaqīlan ākhar 'alā al-jaww al-'āmm.
> Qāla al-rākib: Ḥasab al-saṭḥ.
> Ḥawālī?
> – Ṣa'b al-taqdīr heik.
> – Anā biddi azaffit al-saṭḥ. Wa waqaddesh al-takālīf?
> – Lāzem ashūf qabl mā aqūl!
> – Mānta shāyef al-zift fi kull maḥall ḥawālyy

In English translation:

> 'What kind of work are you in?' asked the driver as he glanced at the pine trees at the sides of the road.
> 'Tarring roofs.'
> The driver leaned over as he circled a ditch in the road, and then turned to the passenger in the front seat with a friendly smile: 'And how much does it cost to tar a roof?'
> One passenger lit a cigarette, which added to the generally oppressive mood.
> 'Depends on the roof.'
> 'Give or take?'
> 'Hard to estimate.'
> 'I want to tar my roof. So how much?'
> 'I have to see it first!'
> 'But you see tar everywhere. About how much?'[54]

In other stories in the third collection Baydas uses an interesting device that has been used elsewhere in modern Arabic literature: The dialogue is written in literary Arabic, but words from colloquial Arabic are integrated for extreme or surprising behaviour.[55] For example in the story 'al-Ziyāra' [the visit], when Badī'a, Yūsuf's sister, is surprised by the neighbour, she stammers, 'Eish . . . Biddāk . . . ', [what do you want].[56] This also occurs in the fourth collection of Baydas (*Takhṭīṭāt Awwaliyya*). For example, in the story 'al-Ṭayarān' [the flight], the conversation in the coffee house takes place in literary Arabic, but when it gets rowdy, we hear one person involved in the argument say, 'Ya'nī Inta Shāyif' [Do you see what I mean].[57] In 'Ḥikāyat al-Dīk al-Faṣīḥ' [the story of the silver-tongued rooster],[58] the dialogue between the father and son – in hostility, suspicion and resentment – is written in a mixture of literary and colloquial Arabic.

A close look at the texts reveals that Baydas consistently refrains from using Hebrew words, except for terms that have no equivalent in Arabic and are commonly used in the Arab sector,[59] such as *mashkanta* [mortgage], *kupat ḥolim* [Sick Fund], *kipa* [skullcap] and *goyim* [non-Jews].[60] Baydas makes special use of the Hebrew words *'aravī* [Arab] and *'arabūsh* [Arab in the pejorative]. The latter appears to illustrate the harsh, crude, insulting and arrogant attitude of soldiers or religious Jews.[61] Baydas also consistently avoids non-Arabic words, with one exception that is justified in terms of the plot and atmosphere of the story: In 'Qiṣṣa bilā 'Unwān', one of his later works, Taghrīd, a young woman born and educated in the United States, comes to visit her aunt and calls her 'Aunt' (in English). Taghrīd occasionally embellishes her speech with English words such as 'stereotype' and 'air-conditioning' and even the hero of the story falls into it once and says 'self-service'.[62] The exclusive use of Arabic by Baydas is a matter of ideology, as is his use of parables and sayings common to Arab society in Israel, such as 'al-mu'akhkhar Khayrun' [every delay is to the good] or 'ḍarabanī wa-bakā sabaqani wa-ishtakā' [he hit me and cried, he caught me and complained].[63]

Most of the stories by Baydas take place in Israel. The setting is frequently Baydas's hometown of Shfaram, even if he doesn't always mention it by name, or the city of Haifa. For Baydas, Shfaram symbolizes permanence and rootedness, many of his heroes living, working and dying there, while Haifa symbolizes the big city which one visits. Many Arab authors, especially Palestinians, use Haifa as a setting for their plots. Emile Ḥabībī, one of the foremost Arab authors, sets much of his writing in Haifa, especially his novels. Baydas, despite his great love for Haifa and his intimate knowledge of its highways, byways and coffee houses, does not forget that this is a mixed city with a large presence of Jews. Thus, his attitude toward Haifa is a mixture of love, fear and rejection. We find evidence of this complex attitude in his novella *al-Maslak*, when Zakariyya takes a bus to visit his friend 'Abdallāh: 'The bus first proceeds slowly, then quickly, then it crosses the broad, clean streets of the Hadar section, dropping people off on both sides of the streets like a wave that lifts on both sides and freezes in the middle. Zakariyya looked at the Carmel and the tall buildings set upon it like tigers ready to pounce with a roar and claw him.'[64]

Other locales mentioned in stories by Baydas include Israeli towns such as Nazareth, Jaffa, Furaidis, Tamra and Umm al-Faḥm; and, in the occupied territories, mainly Hebron, East Jerusalem and the refugee camps. This reflects his ideology of the bond between Israeli Arabs and Palestinians in the territories, and the absolute identification with them and their suffering before and after the intifāḍa. Apropos places, most Baydas stories are played out in a confined space such as a bus, cab, or plane, hence the number of characters is limited and their world and outlook are more simple and accessible to the reader. One example is the story 'Kalima Wāḥida Bass',[65] in which waiting for a shared cab to Haifa and then scrambling for seats in it allows the author to describe the changes that have transpired in the village. In earlier times, it would have been inconceivable that a teenager – even had he waited on line and it was his turn to enter the cab – would have dared quarrel with his elders. The taxi with its passengers is a microcosm of society. In the passengers' conversation the reader hears negative attitudes toward modernization, full awareness of the activities of Israel in Lebanon, and also attitudes toward work in the village during a period of economic instability in Israel.

A varied cast of characters populates the short stories of Riyāḍ Baydas, and they fall into several distinct categories. First, there is a clear difference between Jewish and Arab characters: The Jew is generally described in negative terms and the Arab more positively. But Arab figures in his stories are not homogeneous, though they are more vital and convincing and less stereotyped and superficial than the Jewish figures. Several stock personae reappear in his writing. One is the figure of the mother, with some autobiographical reference to the author, and another is the old Arab (be it the traditional figure whom Baydas does not respect or the activist who takes part in the Palestinian struggle). However, the central figure who reappears in many pieces is that of the young Arab.

The young man in Baydas's fiction is usually well-educated, sensitive and introspective, leads a modest, often ascetic, life, and is persecuted by the authorities. He quite naturally calls to mind the image of the author. The figure is usually nameless and the fact that he is an Israeli Arab is not even made explicit, but can be inferred. He is young, orphaned and poor, oppressed by existential problems on the one hand, and by philosophical issues on the other.[66] On the personal level, he is engaged in an eternal search for meaning in his life and on the national level, he suffers from the absence of a real homeland. He holds the Arab countries responsible for this and points an accusing finger at their leaders[67] (in this he represents the Palestinian younger generation which is disillusioned by pan-Arabism). Indeed, he accuses the leaders of being traitors to the Palestinian cause. For him, the treachery of 1977 (Sadat's visit to Israel) was more serious than the results of the wars of 1948 and 1967. His love for the homeland becomes an obsession and the solution that he longs for can materialize only through unity, which will lead the Palestinians to a homeland since 'the homeland is us' [the Arabs].[68] In this context the stories by Baydas generally have more than a touch of pessimism and sometimes even nihilism, but, somewhat surprisingly and not in keeping with the natural progression of the plot, they often have a happy end. This phenomenon is characteristic not just of Baydas but of many Arab writers in Israel.

The search for meaning among Palestinian Arabs without a homeland who live in Israel is often conveyed during his frequent visits to Haifa. Baydas, who lives in the town of Shfaram both in reality and in his writing, frequently travels to Haifa, a city that embodies the Palestinian tragedy. This city where Jews and Arabs live together is viewed by Baydas as a place to visit or work, but never to live. Baydas chooses to live in his own environment, i.e., where only Arabs live. Haifa and Shfaram represent two poles in his life: local Arab society and Jewish society, as well as the ideology of pan-Arabism and the aspiration for social justice. Poverty and neglect are an axis around which he builds the painful and trying story of daily life in Arab society. Baydas describes the burdensome reality of the many educated young people in Arab society in Israel, he among them. He sees around him young teachers, writers and labourers, different faces of the same person. He characterizes them, as he characterizes himself, with great loneliness that sometimes borders on romanticism. There is a paradox here: great loneliness within a society that is permeated by the strength and security of family ties. This loneliness reaches an extreme in the figure of Zakariyyā in the novella *al-Maslak*.[69]

Baydas persistently expresses his ideas in his writing, even when this entails the direct intervention of the author in the story, marring its credibility and artistic value. Sometimes he uses the stratagem of the omniscient author and tries to avoid direct statements and too much interference. These literary shortcomings are more noticeable in his description of characters than of situations or atmosphere. The lack of credibility is conspicuous when Jews confront Arabs in his stories, especially when the Jewish characters are nameless. When the Jews have names, they are much more convincing. One exception is the story 'al-Bu'ra' in which all three Jewish characters are named, but still not credible. Indeed, they are one-dimensional and stereotypically negative characters. And on the subject of names, Baydas uses his own first name 'Riyāḍ' on only two occasions: in the novella *al-Maslak* when Zakariyyā asks to visit his friend Riyāḍ who has fallen in love with Paris, and in the story 'Bākiran, fī Had'at al-Ṣabāḥ', when Riyāḍ the journalist is portrayed as a human and sensitive person who sacrifices some of his relationship with his life partner on behalf of the ideals in which he believes.[70]

In general, Baydas is a young author writing in the circumstances unique to Palestinian writers in Israel. The tradition of prose and poetry of the previous generation (Ḥabībī, al-Qāsim, Naffā', Ṭāha, Zakī Darwīsh) allowed his writing to grow and develop. In it, he balances diverse elements: Muslims and Christians (note that Baydas does not address relations among Muslims, Christians and Druze, nor does he examine Islamic fundamentalism in Arab society in Israel); and the influence of European writing (Joyce, Kafka) with South Americans (Borges, García Márquez), Jewish Israelis (Yehoshua, Oz, Grossman, Hanoch Levin), Arabs (al-Ṭayyib Ṣāliḥ, 'Abd al-Raḥmān Munīf, Ḥannā Mīna), and other Palestinians (Jabrā, Kanafānī, Zakī Darwīsh, Ḥabībī). His general education and broad perspectives have given him access to varied writing techniques. Although his writing is essentially realistic, he does not adhere to one style, and allegory, surrealism and fantasy can also be found there. In this and in his use of local subject matter, he is not unlike other Arab short-story writers in Israel. Baydas's writing and sensitive style have unique features, but he remains essentially within the tradition, making important contributions to the development of the local Arab short story. Many stories are suffused by a great lyricism, and some are 'atmosphere pieces'. His personal world stands at the core of his writing and his characters are generally Arab. Nevertheless his writing shows great awareness of Israeli-Jewish society. This is evinced not only by the Jewish characters in his stories, but also by his articles about Israeli-Jewish writers that have appeared in Palestinian literary journals such as *al-Jadīd* and Palestinian ideological journals such as *Shu'ūn Filasṭīniyya* and *Balsam*.[71] The most prominent figure in his stories is the sensitive, introspective hero who is searching for his place as part of a minority within Israel, which is a minority in the Middle East. This figure, which bears clear autobiographical features, radiates a sense of persecution and fear of the authorities that brings to mind a world further from Middle Eastern reality, like that of Kafka. This world is characterized by restlessness and disquiet that derive from life in a homeland where there is a state from which one feels estranged and searching for one's roots. The criticism that Baydas levels against the majority society is sharp and sometimes even brazen, and stems not just from a well-formed ideology, but also from a personal existential anxiety based on daily life. And though this figure often bears the stamp of orphanhood, poverty, sorrow and death, his optimism emerges and blossoms in some stories, especially in their endings, which testify to a positive approach to life despite, and perhaps even because of, the hardship.

Despite the great importance that he ascribes to writing for local periodicals, Baydas has gone beyond local borders and published in journals in Arab countries and Europe. He is thus part of the dynamic process among Arab writers in Israel who, since the late 1960s, and more so from the early 1970s, have addressed audiences of readers beyond the borders of Israel.

NOTES

1. Riyāḍ Baydas was born in 1960 in Shfaram, a town in the Galilee, where he attended high school before studying comparative literature at Haifa University. To date, he has published seven collections of short stories as well as stories that appeared in journals and newspapers (*al-Ittiḥād*, *al-Jadīd*, *al-Karmil*, *al-Sharq*, *al-Kātib*, *al-Ma'rifa*, *al-Nāqid*). Some of his stories have been translated into Hebrew, French and English.
2. For a discussion of these writers and their work, see: Maḥmūd 'Abbāsī, 'Hitpatḥut HaRoman VehaSipur HaKatzar BaSifrut Ha'Aravit BaShanim 1948–1976', PhD thesis, Jerusalem, 1983, pp. 28–43, 100–2; Shmuel Moreh and Maḥmūd 'Abbāsī, *Tarājim wa-Āthār fī al-Adab al-'Arabī fī Isrā'īl 1948–1986*, Shfaram, Dār al-Mashriq li'l-Tarjama wa'l-Ṭibā'a wa'l-Nashr, 1987, pp. 8–9, 50–1, 174–5, 208–11; Avraham Yinnon, 'Kama Nos'ei Moked BaSifrut Shel 'Arviyei Yisrael', *HaMizraḥ HeḤadash*, 15 (1965), p. 80; Shmuel Moreh, 'HaSifrut BaSafa Ha'Aravit BeMedinat Yisrael', *HaMizraḥ HeḤadash*, 9 (1958) pp. 26–31, 36–8; Sasson Somekh, 'Batim Gevohim, Karim: Demut HaShakhen HaYehudi BeYetziratam Shel Sofrim 'Aravim MeḤaifa VehaGalil', *Mifgash*, 4–5 (Winter 1986), pp. 21–3; and Shimon Ballas, *HaSifrut Ha'Aravit BeTsel HaMilḥama*, Tel-Aviv, 'Am 'Oved, 1978, pp. 34–6, 65–70, 330–2; and Maḥmūd Ghanāyim, *al-Madār al-Ṣa'b, Riḥlat al-Qiṣṣa al-Filasṭīniyya fī al-Isrā'īl*, Kafr Qar', Dār al-Hudā, 1995, pp. 59–105, 149–83, 239–72.
3. For a discussion of these writers and their work, see: 'Abbāsī, *Hitpatḥut HaRoman VehaSipur HaKatzar*, pp. 137–41, 150–1; Maḥmūd 'Abbāsī, 'al-Qiṣṣa al-Qaṣīra ba'd Ḥazīrān 67', *Filasṭīn al-Thawra* (2 August 1986), pp. 48–59; Moreh and 'Abbāsī, *Tarājim wa-Āthār*, pp. 85–6, 139–41, 235; Somekh, 'Batim Gevohim', *Mifgash*, pp. 23–5; Nabīh al-Qāsim, *Dirāsāt fī al-Qiṣṣa al-Maḥalliyya*, Acre, Dār al-Aswār, 1979, pp. 109–82; Anton Shammās, 'HaSifrut Ha'Aravit BeYisrael Le-Aḥar 1967', *Skirot*, 2, (June 1976), pp. 2–7; Ghanāyim, *al-Madār al-Ṣa'b*, pp. 185–222.
4. Riyāḍ Baydas, *al-Jū' wa'l-Jabal*, Jerusalem, Dār Ṣalāḥ al-Dīn, 1980; *al-Maslak*,

Majmū'at Qiṣaṣ Qaṣīra, Jerusalem, Intermīdiyā, 1985; *al-Rīḥ*, Nicosia, Dār al-Ṣumūd al-'Arabī, 1987; *Takhṭīṭāt Awwaliyya*, Casablanca, Dār Tūbqāl li'l-Nashr, 1988.

5. Some examples of Baydas' stories and articles published in Israeli journals: 'Sartr wa'l-Adab', *al-Sharq*, 2 (April–June 1980), pp. 45–52; 'al-Ṭafra', *Liqā'*, 9 (spring 1986), pp. 56–60; 'Mastūra wa'l-Ḥamdu lillāh', *al-Ittiḥād* (2 January 1987), p. 5; 'al-Ziyāra', *al-Jadīd*, 2 (February 1987), pp. 71–82. His works were also published in Arabic journals outside Israel, such as 'Mā bayn al-Mawt wa'l-Ghubār zara'anī al-Ward al-Aḥmar', *al-Kātib*, 23–4 (December 1982), pp. 53–7. His works published in Europe and Cyprus include the story 'Ḥikāyat al-Dīk al-Fasīḥ' in the Arabic periodical *al-Nāqid*, 3, published in London (September 1988), pp. 55–7, and his story 'al-Rīḥ' in the Palestinian journal *al-Karmil*, 26 (1987), pp. 130–3.
6. The Arab writers cited here are close to Baydas and he has internalized some of their styles and contents. By way of very brief illustration, let me first mention the great influence on him of the Sudanese writer al-Ṭayyib Ṣāliḥ. The stories 'Nakhlā 'alā Jadwal' and 'Dawmat wad Ḥāmid' (al-Ṭayyib Ṣāliḥ, *Dawmat wad Ḥāmid, Sab' Qiṣaṣ*, 3rd edn, Beirut, Dār al-'Awda, 1970, pp. 7–18, 33–52) have clearly inspired Baydas in his story 'Khuyūṭ al-'Anākib' (*al-Maslak*, pp. 71–7). For example, Baydas writes in this story, 'During that period I would eat only mutton or venison and drink goat's milk' (ibid., p. 73), as compared with the lines in al-Ṭayyib Ṣāliḥ: 'In my youth I would eat half a sheep for breakfast and for supper I would drink the milk of five cows . . . ' (*Dawmat wad Ḥāmid*, p. 43). Also, it is hard to ignore the similarity between the opening line of the first chapter of the novella *al-Maslak* by Baydas: 'Innahu al-taghayyur' – [Thus the change] (*al-Maslak*, p. 111) and the opening line of a book by 'Abd al-Raḥmān Munīf: 'Innahu al-qaḥṭ, al-qaḥṭ marra ukhrā' [Thus the drought, again the drought!] (*al-Nihāyāt*, 3rd edn, Beirut, Dār al-Ādāb, 1982, p. 5). Another example are the books in the room of Zakariyyā and 'Abdallah (two main characters in the novella *al-Maslak*) that include works by Ḥannā Mīna, al-Ṭayyib Ṣāliḥ, Emile Ḥabībī, Borges, and others (ibid., pp. 138, 142). Finally, there is the Kafkaesque and Hanoch Levin-like atmosphere in a number of stories by Baydas and in the thoughts and behaviour of some of his characters (*al-Maslak*, 'Mawṭa' Qadam', 'al-Rīḥ', 'al–Ṣawt', 'al-Khanjar').
7. Somekh, 'Batim Gevohim', *Mifgash*, pp. 21–5.
8. Baydas, 'Kitābat Dībājat Risāla liKāfūr', *al-Jū' wa'l-Jabal*, pp. 52–65; 'Ashlā' min Ḥayāt Rajul Aḥabba Warda Ṣaghīra', *al-Jū' wa'l-Jabal*, pp. 65–72; 'Hadhayān', *al-Jadīd*, 11–12 (November–December 1989), pp. 80–1; 'Qiṣṣa bilā 'Unwān', *al-Aswār*, 6 (winter 1990), pp. 214–27.
9. Baydas, 'Ashlā' min Ḥayāt Rajul Aḥabba Warda Ṣaghīra', *al-Jū' wa'l-Jabal*, pp. 65–72. Compare this with similar expressions by Emile Ḥabībī about a sense of persecution and the Arab under constant suspicion, especially in his two novels: *al-Waqā'i' al-Gharība fī Ikhtifā' Sa'īd Abī al-Naḥs al-Mutashā'il*, 3rd edn, Jerusalem, Manshūrāt Ṣalāḥ al-Dīn, 1977, translated into Hebrew by Anton Shammās as *HaOpsimist: HaKhronika HaMufla-ah Shel He'almut Sa'id Abū al-Naḥs al-Mutashā'il*, Jerusalem, Mifras, 1984; and *Ikhṭayya*, Nicosia, Mu'assasat Bīsān Press, 1985, translated into Hebrew by Anton Shammās, Tel-Aviv, 'Am 'Oved, Proza Aḥeret, 1988.
10. Baydas, 'al-'Atama wa'l-Madīna', *al-Jaw' wa'l-Jabal*, pp. 35–8. These qualities of the persecuted Arab contrast dramatically with the crassness of the security forces, as in the works of Ḥabībī, especially the novels *al-Waqā'i'* and *Ikhṭayya*.
11. Baydas, 'Hadhayān', *al-Jadīd* pp. 80–1.

12. Baydas, 'Bākiran, fi Had'at al-Ṣabāḥ', *al-Jadīd*, 2 (February 1990), pp. 25–9.
13. On the subject of the borderline hero, his journey and search, see my article 'Maḥfūz's Za'balāwi: Six Stations of a Quest', *International Journal of Middle East Studies*, 26 (1994), pp. 631–44.
14. Baydas, 'al-Bu'ra', *Takhṭīṭāt Awwaliyya*, pp. 9–18.
15. Ibid.
16. Yinnon, 'Kama Nos'ei Moked', *Hamizraḥ HeḤadash*, pp. 74–5; 'Abbāsī, *Hitpatḥut HaRoman VehaSipur HaKatzar*, pp. 176–80.
17. Baydas, *al-Awrāq la Taṭīr 'Āliyan fi al-Faḍā'*, *al-Rīḥ*, p. 95.
18. Baydas, 'Muḥāwala Jadīda liTanaffus al-Ṣu'adā', pp. 27–33.
19. Baydas, *al-Jū' wa'l-Jabal*, p. 75.
20. Such as 'Abd al-Hādī, the hero of the novel *al-Arḍ* (1954) by the Egyptian writer 'Abd al-Raḥmān Sharqāwī, or Ḥusein 'Alī, hero of the novel *al-Jabal* (1958) by the Egyptian writer Fatḥī Ghānim, or Maḥjūb, hero of the novels *Mawsim al-Hijra ilā al-Shamāl* (1966) and *'Urs al-Zayn* (1967) by the Sudanese writer al-Ṭayyib Ṣāliḥ. It should be noted that these heroes are rooted in the ancient Arab epics such as the stories of 'Antara and Abū Zayd al-Hilālī.
21. The motif of closing ranks appears in other works of Baydas such as the story 'al-'Āidūn', *al-Maslak*, pp. 17–25 and in other Palestinian short stories such as 'Hazīmat al-Shāṭir Ḥasan', by Akram Haniyya, *Ṭuqūs liYawm Ākhar*, Nicosia, Mu'assasat Bīsān Press, 1986, pp. 85–9.
22. Baydas, 'Kūlāj Qaṣaṣī, al-I'dām', *al-Ittiḥād* (22 December 1989), p. 4.
23. Baydas, 'Shadharāt', *al-Ittiḥād* (27 December 1988), p. 4.
24. Samīra 'Azzām, "Ām Ākhar', *al-Ẓill al-Kabīr*, Beirut, Dār al-'Awda, 1982, pp. 67–77; Emile Ḥabībī, 'Bawwābat Mandelbāwm', *Sudāsiyyat al-Ayyām al-Sitta wa-Qiṣaṣ Ukhrā*, Haifa, Maktabat al-Ittiḥād al-Ta'āwuniyya, n.d., pp. 11–19; Qayṣar Karkabī, 'Sittī', *al-Bi'r al-Mashūra wa-Qiṣaṣ Ukhrā*, Tel-Aviv, Dār al-Nashr al-'Arabī, 1969, pp. 101–5; Salīm Khūrī, "Awdat Umm 'Ādil', *al-Widā' al-Akhīr*, Tel-Aviv, Maṭba'at Dūkmā, 1961, pp. 5–8; Muḥammad 'Alī Ṭāha, 'al-Khaṭṭ al-Wahmī', *Salāman wa-Taḥiyya*, Acre, Dār al-Jalīl, 1969, pp. 23–7.
25. Baydas, 'al-Ṣāmt al-Dāmī fī Iḥdā al-Layālī al-Bārida', 'Tawahhujāt al-Shams al-Thā'ira', 'Kitābat Dībājat Risāla liKāfūr', 'al-Lawḥa', *al-Jū' wa'l-Jabal*, pp. 7–12, 13–19, 52–65, 93–100, 'al-Maslak' in the collection *al-Maslak*, pp. 111–81; 'al-Ziyāra', *al-Rīḥ*, pp. 67–86; 'al-Bu'ra', 'Mashhad: Liqā' Khātif', 'al-Ṭayrān', 'Ḥajar 'alā Qabr al-Ṣamt', 'Wajhān li-Rās Wāḥid', *Takhṭīṭāt Awwaliyya*, pp. 9–18, 19–20, 25–7, 29–38; 'Shadharāt', *al-Ittiḥād* (27 December 1988), p. 4.
26. Baydas, *al-Jū' wa'l-Jabal*, pp. 93–100.
27. Baydas blames the woman in other stories as well, such as 'Muḥāwala Jadīda liTanaffus al-Ṣu'adā'', where the woman's pursuit of wealth is what prevents the family from returning to its country.
28. Baydas, *Takhṭīṭāt Awwaliyya*, p. 31.
29. Baydas, *al-Sharq*, 3 (July–September 1979), pp. 93–7.
30. Baydas, *al-Maslak*, pp. 137–50.
31. Ibid., pp. 17–45.
32. Ibid., p. 19.
33. Baydas, 'Kayfa ṣār al-Khityār Aḥmad al-'Alam Shābban?', *al-Rīḥ*, pp. 19–28.
34. Baydas, *al-Maslak*, p. 120.

35. Baydas, *al-Aswār*, 6 (winter 1990), p. 220.
36. Baydas, *al-Rīḥ*, pp. 99–107.
37. Baydas, *al-Maslak*, pp. 89–93.
38. Baydas, *Takhṭīṭāt Awwaliyya*, pp. 21–4.
39. Baydas, *al-Ittiḥād* (17 November 1989), p. 4.
40. Baydas, *al-Maslak*, pp. 79–88.
41. Ibid., pp. 95–110.
42. Ibid., pp. 35–48.
43. Baydas, 'Ashlā' min Ḥayāt Rajul Aḥabba Warda Ṣaghīra', *al-Jū' wa'l-Jabal*, p. 71; 'Suqūṭ al-Laylak', *al-Jū' wa'l-Jabal*, p. 115; 'Khuyūṭ al-'Anākib', *al-Maslak*, p. 73; 'al-Maslak' in *al-Maslak*, p. 118.
44. Baydas, *al-Jū' wa'l-Jabal*, p. 75.
45. Baydas, *al-Maslak*, p. 95.
46. Ibid., p. 98.
47. Muṣṭafā Murrār, *al-Khayma al-Mathqūba*, Tel-Aviv, Dār al-Nashr al-'Arabī, 1970, pp. 107–21; Muḥammad 'Alī Ṭāha, *Salāman wa-Taḥiyya*, pp. 13–22; Zakī Darwīsh, *Shitā' al-Ghurba wa-qiṣaṣ Ukhrā*, Jerusalem, Majallat al-Sharq, 1970, pp. 83–91; Muḥammad Naffā', 'Mudhakkirāt Lāji'', *al-Jadīd*, 1 (January 1965), pp. 37–40.
48. Ṭāha Ḥusayn, *al-Ayyām*, Cairo, Dār al-Ma'ārif, 1974, vol. 1, p. 62; Tawfīq al-Ḥakīm, *Yawmiyyāt Nā'ib fī al-Aryāf*, Cairo, al-Dār al-Namūdhajiyya, n.d., pp. 112–15; 'Abd al-Raḥmān al-Sharqāwī, *al-Arḍ*, 3rd edn, Cairo, Dār al-Kitāb li'l-Ṭibā'a wa'l-Nashr, 1968, pp. 64, 73, 75–7; Muḥammad Khalīl Qāsim, *al-Shamandūra*, Cairo, Dār al-Kitāb li'l-Ṭibā'a wa'l-Nashr, 1968, pp. 97–102; Muḥammad Yūsuf al-Qa'īd, *Yaḥduth fī Miṣr al-ān*, 2nd edn, Beirut, Dār Ibn Rushd, 1979, p. 69. (For the English translation of some of these novels, see the Bibliography.)
49. Baydas, *al-Jū' wa'l-Jabal*, pp. 20–30.
50. Baydas, 'al-Rīḥ', *al-Rīḥ*, p. 143.
51. Baydas, *al-Jū' wa'l-Jabal*, p. 10.
52. Baydas, *Takhṭīṭāt Awwaliyya*, p. 52.
53. Baydas, *al-Maslak*, p. 92.
54. Baydas, *al-Rīḥ*, p. 53.
55. See my article, 'Varieties of Language Usage in Dialogue in the Modern Egyptian Village Novel', in S. Ballas and S. Snir (eds), *Studies in Canonical and Popular Arabic Literature*, Toronto, York Press, 1998, pp. 77–86.
56. Baydas, *al-Rīḥ*, p. 71.
57. Baydas, *Takhṭīṭāt Awwaliyya*, p. 26.
58. Ibid., pp. 39–43.
59. On the use of Hebrew among Arab writers in Israel, see Hannan Hever, 'Lehakot Ba'Akevo Shel Akhiles', *Alpayim*, 1 (June 1989)', pp. 186–93; Reuven Snir, 'Petza' MePetza'av: HaSifrut Ha'ravit HaPalestinit BeYisrael', *Alpaim*, 2 (1990), pp. 244–68; Na'īm 'Arāidī, 'Sifrut 'Ivrit Ma Na'amt', *Moznayim*, 65, 4 (January 1991), pp. 42–3.
60. Baydas, *al-Maslak*, p. 108; *al-Rīḥ*, p. 6; *Takhṭīṭāt Awwaliyya*, pp. 9, 10.
61. Baydas, *al-Jū' wa'l-Jabal*, p. 10; *Takhṭīṭāt Awwaliyya*, pp. 12, 13.
62. Baydas, *al-Aswār*, 6 (winter 1990), pp. 219, 221, 223.
63. Baydas, *al-Maslak*, p. 117; *al-Aswār*, 6 (winter 1990), p. 217.
64. Baydas, *al-Maslak*, pp. 130–1.
65. Baydas, *al-Rīḥ*, pp. 49–66.

66. Baydas, *al-Jū' wa'l-Jabal*, pp. 72–85.
67. Ibid., pp. 107–9.
68. Ibid., p. 111, and cf. Akram Haniyya, 'Hazīmat al-Shāṭir Ḥasan', *Ṭuqūs li Yawm Ākhar*, pp. 85–9.
69. Baydas, *al-Maslak*, p. 130.
70. Ibid., pp. 147–8, *al-Jadīd* (February 1990), pp. 25–9.
71. Riyāḍ Baydas, 'al-'Arabī al-Bashi' fī Riwāyat 'Amos 'Oz, 'Ulba Sawdā', Dirāsa Naqdiyya'', *al-Jadīd*, 6 (June 1987), pp. 33–8; 'Ẓāhirat Ḥanoch Levin', *Shu'ūn Filāsṭīniyya*, 206 (May 1990), pp. 83–96; 'al-Kātib al-Yahūdī Sāmī Mikhā'il, Muḥāwalat Muḥākamat al-Maḍī wa'l-Ḥaḍir', *Shu'ūn Filāstīniyya*, 196 (July 1989), pp. 76–87; 'Shabtai, Inghilāq al-Makān wa'l-Ikhtiyār al-Baṭi'', *Shu'ūn Filāsṭīniyya*, 199 (October 1989), pp. 66–79; 'al-'Arabī fī Adab al-Aṭfāl al-'Ibrī', *Shu'ūn Filāsṭīniyya*, 181 (April 1988), pp. 102–3; 'al-Anā fī Muwājahāt al-'Ālam', *Shu'ūn Filāsṭīniyya*, 184 (July 1988), pp. 99–101; 'Dafīd Grosman, min al-Usṭūra ilā al-Wāqi'', *Shu'ūn Filāsṭīniyya*, 190 (December 1988), pp. 62–73; 'Zaman al-Iḥtilāl al-Aṣfar', *Balsam* 101 (January 1988), pp. 104–6.

4

Stones for the Homeland
Palestinian Literature of the Intifāḍa (1987–90)

This chapter examines the response of Palestinian literature to the intifāḍa during the first three years, as reflected in the contents of *al-Kātib*, the leading journal in the West Bank and the Gaza Strip. The period ends with the Gulf War in January 1991, regarded as a watershed not just for literature but for the intifāḍa itself.

The beginning of the Palestinian uprising in the West Bank and the Gaza Strip is commonly placed at 9 December 1987. While this date does mark the outbreak of violent resistance to Israeli occupation, leaflets of the Islamic Jihād place the beginning at 6 October 1987, two months earlier. The Islamic Jihād movement has reasons of pride for moving up the beginning of the intifāḍa, as the earlier date marks the escape of Jihād members from Israeli prison. One might hark back to the Yom Kippur War in 1973, which was followed by waves of disturbances of all types, reaching a peak with the outbreak of the uprising. Or the claim could be made that the roots of the intifāḍa are in 1948 with the founding of the state of Israel, or even that its seeds were planted at the turn of the century with the beginning of the national conflict between the Palestinian and Jewish national communities, or, more recently, with the Lebanon War of 1982. Thus, the literature of the intifāḍa, like the intifāḍa itself, can be placed on a continuum of parameters in a given situation of time and place.

The intifāḍa literature written by Palestinians and other Arabs was canonical, unlike the Hebrew literature written about the intifāḍa, which was marginal. Palestinian literature is composed of four main genres: poetry, plays, short stories and novels. It addresses the reader consciously and directly, with a deliberate appeal to emotion. This literature is an immediate response to events, direct and blatant, with poetry comprising the major part of it. The large quantity of Palestinian poetry written during the intifāḍa – as before it – can be traced back to the tradition of Arab oral poetry in the pre-Islamic period, and perhaps also to a universal truth that writing poetry is more direct, immediate and accessible than writing prose. But the output of prose in Palestinian intifāḍa literature slowly increased, markedly so by the end of the first year of the intifāḍa. This trend was evident in the quantity of works – short stories and novels – published in the West Bank and the Gaza Strip, in the centres of Palestinian culture in the various diasporas, particularly in Cyprus, and also in publications by Israeli Arabs.

Palestinian literature of the intifāḍa continues to be replete with slogans and stereotypes, even if the outpouring of works that characterized the first year of the intifāḍa ultimately diminished to a trickle. Perhaps the reason for this is the cooling of the initial fervour of the early period. In the second period, especially in prose, the writing is more muted and authors seem to prefer novels on Palestinian themes set in previous eras. Examples are *Ayyām lā Tunsā* [days that will not be forgotten] (1988) by Jamāl Bannūra (1953–) and *Layl al-Banafsaj* [night of the violet] by As'ad al-As'ad (1947–).[1]

Another corpus of writing characteristic of the second year of the intifāḍa includes poetry, journals and stories written in the jails, prisons and detention camps of the West Bank and the Gaza Strip. These works are less valuable for their artistic merit and more as documents of distress and of personal and national aspirations. Examples are the poems by al-Mutawakkil Ṭāha in the Anṣār detention camp and the journal by Dr 'Abd al-Sattār Qāsim, *Ayyām fī Mu'taqal al-Naqab* [days in the Negev detention camp] (1989).[2]

Research about intifāḍa literature is woefully lacking. Although there is tremendous interest in Arab countries about life in the territories during the intifāḍa, and a plethora of Palestinian writing, works of literary criticism are sparse. With the exception of short and not particularly profound articles, there are no comprehensive studies about the literature of the intifāḍa. In my view, this inattention is rooted not only in the low level of intifāḍa literature or in the need for a perspective of distance, but primarily in the state of scholarship about modern Palestinian literature: unlike the fields of history and politics, Western and Arab scholarship of Palestinian literature has not been given due attention, despite the lip-service paid to the Palestinian issue. Scholarship about Hebrew intifāḍa literature is no better. To the best of my knowledge, no systematic and comprehensive research has yet been published in Israel about how Israeli-Arab literature has come to grips with the events of the intifāḍa.

THE STATUS OF PALESTINIAN PERIODICALS DURING THE INTIFĀḌA

A separate issue is the role played by Palestinian periodicals in the territories, in Israel and in the various Palestinian diasporas. In the early months, literature about the intifāḍa was given top priority in Palestinian periodicals, whether predominantly literary journals (*al-Kātib*, *al-Karmil*) or not (*Filasṭīn al-Thawra*, *Balsam*). This was the case in general for newspapers published in the Arab world and Arab centres of culture outside Arab countries such as London, Paris and Nicosia.

From the end of the second year, the centrality of the intifāḍa in Palestinian literature decreased. The intifāḍa was pushed even further to the sidelines when Iraq occupied Kuwait and it was completely marginalized during the war that erupted in January 1991 between the coalition armies and Iraq. Palestinian and Arafat's open support for Iraq and the opposition of most Arab states to the measures taken by the Iraqi ruler contributed to this. Literature is certainly not cut off from reality, and key events such as the Gulf War had an impact on the quantity and themes of intifāḍa literature. One expression of this can be found in the Palestinian journal *al-Kātib*.

al-Kātib [the writer] was a monthly that has been published in East Jerusalem since November 1979. It is affiliated to the Association of Palestinian Writers in the Territories (the West Bank and the Gaza Strip), though it is not its official organ. As'ad al-As'ad, editor of the journal, is former Secretary-General of the Association, many of whose prominent members publish in *al-Kātib*. As suggested by its subtitle – 'For humanistic culture and progress' – this journal is not fundamentally literary; it is ideologically left-wing and it assumes a communist perspective on political subjects related to the Palestinian issue, economic and social problems of the territories, and international political and economic matters. Nevertheless, this is the main journal in the territories for literary writing, and hence is the subject of this chapter in its effort to explore literature in the territories during the intifāḍa period.[3]

al-Kātib appears in a format of 96 medium-sized pages. The journal was temporarily expanded to incorporate a supplement, '*al-Kātib* Supplement for Thought and Questions of Peace and Socialism': articles in translation about communism and socialism in the world and perestroika in the eastern bloc.[4]

al-Kātib was the leading journal in the territories. Other journals appear there, also not primarily literary, but more limited in scope and influence.

Palestinian journals in the territories, and *al-Kātib* in particular, had an impact far beyond that of a regular journal, simply because they were the foremost medium of communication in the absence of local television or radio stations at the time. The electronic media to which Palestinians in the territories were exposed during the period under review were primarily television and radio broadcasts from Jordan, Israel, Syria and Lebanon.

al-Kātib was published in metropolitan Jerusalem. During the period surveyed, it sold for five shekels a copy. A year's subscription for individuals cost $30 locally, $60 in Europe and $75 in other countries. For institutions, subscription rates were $50 locally, $100 in Europe and $150 in other countries. Total circulation was approximately 2,000 copies. According to the editor, *al-Kātib* has about 500 subscribers from individuals and institutions in the territories, Israel, Arab countries, Europe, the United States, and Latin America. Most copies are sold in the West Bank, East Jerusalem, the Gaza Strip, inside Israel, in several Arab countries and Europe. The main audience of *al-Kātib* is in the territories and Israel, primarily the Palestinian intelligentsia, but it appeals to additional sectors because of its varied contents, which extend beyond literature.

There are ideological ties between *al-Kātib* and Palestinian journals outside the territories, especially the journal *al-Jadīd* and the daily newspaper *al-Ittiḥād*, both of which belong to the Israeli Communist Party. This connection is reflected in the exchange of information, writing and mutual interviews. Indeed, according to the editor of *al-Kātib*, communist journals, such as *al-Thaqāfa al-Jadīda* of the Iraqi communist Party and *al-Ṭarīq al-Jadīd* of the Lebanese Communist Party, served as a model for him.

Palestinian journals and newspapers, like their Arab counterparts, have a tradition with roots in the nineteenth century. Some of these journals, especially those in Egypt and Lebanon, are literature proper, while others are a mix of culture, society and politics. *al-Kātib* encompasses many facets, and therefore its influence exceeds that of a literary journal. The world view of its editor is directed to specific audiences, primarily the Palestinian left within and outside the territories. Palestinian literature has a special impact in Palestinian society by virtue of the fact that it serves political interests. The political involvement of Palestinian writing is unusual even in the political–literary landscape of Arab countries. Thus there is a correlation between the literary and the non-literary materials that appear in *al-Kātib* during the period under review: both sought to serve and promote Palestinian interests.

al-Kātib operated in the milieu of literary journals in East Jerusalem and the West Bank, such as *al-Fajr*, *al-Jadīd* and *al-Bayādir al-Adabī*, political journals such as *al-Bayādir al-Siyāsī* and *al-Usbū' al-Jadīd*, and the religious journal *Hudā al-Islām*, published in Jerusalem. Daily newspapers also appear – *al-Quds*, *al-Fajr*, *al-Sha'b*, *al-Nahār* – and weeklies such as *al-Tali'a*, *al-Ṣadā* and *al-Manār*. *al-Kātib* was the only journal in the territories that contains both literary and non-literary contents such as economics and politics. Thus it is not surprising that *al-Kātib* serves as a fertile source for scholars of Palestinian society – literature as well as economics and politics – during and prior to the intifāḍa.

During the period under review, literary material comprised approximately one-third of the journal material, with non-literary material taking up the remaining two-thirds or so. These proportions vary from issue to issue, as does the allocation of space to various content categories. Poetry appeared in every issue. Articles of criticism appeared fairly regularly about specific Palestinian poetry or prose, or general phenomena in Palestinian literature such as the woman in intifāḍa poetry,[5] Palestinian poetry in the territories from 1967 to 1988,[6] the Palestinian novel in the late 1980s,[7] and intifāḍa poetry in the territories.[8] Some space, though not much, was allocated to Arabic literature in general and regional literature in particular. No plays were published, but from time to time articles appeared about the theatre. Infrequently, there were pieces about the plastic arts, most of these related to the intifāḍa. One article was published about Palestinian film, and several pieces focused on the field of folklore. A column entitled 'Aṣdā Adabiyya' [literary echoes] provided information about publications and cultural events.

Most pieces were written by Palestinians from the territories. Short stories and poems also appeared by Israeli Palestinians, by Palestinians born in the territories or Israel who now live elsewhere (Arab or other countries), by non-Palestinian Arabs, and by international literary figures in translation.

An analysis of the writing of Palestinians who live in the territories with others who live elsewhere reveals some interesting differences. The writing of the former deals primarily with the Palestinian experience of living under occupation: descriptions of the routine of Palestinian life in the city, the village and refugee camps and their hardships due to harassment by the army – crude and humiliating treatment, night searches, interrogations, detention and clashes with soldiers. Only a small fraction of the articles do not deal with the Palestinian–Israeli conflict. Prose examples of this are the stories by Jamāl Zakī 'Abd al-Jabbār al-Qawāsmih[9] that expose, unusually, negative aspects of Palestinian society – attitudes toward women or children with disabilities; and works by the folk poet Mūsā Ḥāfiẓ,[10] that give sincere and direct expression to the feelings of the common man – the peasant and the labourer – without recourse to the histrionics or heroism characteristic of most of the poetry published here.

Social problems are discussed in prose works only, but in a way that is totally marginal to the story line. Social problems do surface here and there, such as economic distress, class differences between the thin stratum of the wealthy and the impoverished masses, and the plight of the young Arab woman in a society that is not liberal.[11] The generation gap is expressed only minimally and blandly in stories where the parents are unaware of the patriotic efforts of their children, but always draw pleasure and encouragement from them.[12]

Virtually all the stories and poems are at the service of the national cause, although it is sometimes hard to determine if the poem is addressing a more general and perhaps apolitical issue or the struggle against the occupation. This becomes clearer when there are descriptions of clashes with the army or the appearance of key words such as 'intifāḍa', 'casualties', 'children', 'stones', 'children of the stones', names of Arab towns or detention camps, etc.[13]

The artistic level of the writing is not high. This should not be attributed, in my opinion, to the pressures and constraints of reality or the desire to give unmediated expression to the turbulent emotions they arouse. Nonetheless, the stories in which the nationalist theme is not the main axis (such as those of al-Qawāsmih, mentioned above) are, in my view, more successful from a literary point of view.

Regarding translations, only one prose work by a non-Arab writer appeared during this period – a French story written during the Second World War about the struggle against the Nazi conquest.[14] On the other hand, much space was devoted to poems translated from other languages. Here three periods can be discerned. In the 13 months between January 1988 and January 1989, poets from abroad appeared in more than half the issues – seven of the 13 under study. This was followed by a hiatus of about a year and a half, and then the reappearance of poems in translation in October and December 1990. Some of these poems were composed in the 1970s, and many have a socialist or revolutionary communist bent, as well as a universal approach. There is no specific locale or time, and no reference to the Palestinian problem or the intifāḍa. While most of the poems in the first period reflect a revolutionary fighting spirit, they become more 'moderate' in the third period, expressing a world view rather than an active struggle. Note, for example, the poem 'Laysa Jayyidan bimā fīhi al-Kifāya' [it's not enough] by the Jamaican Alan Thomas, who advocates the liberation not only of various oppressed peoples, but of women as well.[15]

THE MAIN THEMES IN INTIFĀḌA WRITING

The main themes in Palestinian and/or Arabic literature – prose and poetry – that appeared during the period surveyed are varied. Palestinian society is generally depicted as patriotic, united, in solidarity, free of internal bickering, cherishing the values of national and personal pride, suffering and survival, elevating the burdens of its struggle and glorifying its casualties. Expressions offensive to the image of the Palestinian are rare and marginal.[16] There are no expressions of weakness, confusion, doubts or ideological division (the one exception being a minor and unexplained reference to political difference, but even this is used to emphasize rising above the quarrel).[17] There is no trace of Palestinian collaboration with Israeli authorities, conflict or violence within Palestinian society over such collaboration, or internal power struggles.

However in the third year, cracks in the solidarity appear, often caused by wealthy individuals: a rich factory owner refuses to transport the body of a martyr lest the Israelis close down his factory; a wealthy sycophant supplies cocaine to soldiers bivouacked on the roof of his house; the son of a well-to-do family tries to lord it over his friends by lies, hypocrisy and bribery, and exploits their patriotic struggle for his selfish needs; a woman is apathetic in the face of other women uniting to rescue someone apprehended by the soldiers; wealthy Palestinians exploit the plight of a young woman who had been raped by a Jew, forcing her to work without wages; young people utter derogatory remarks about a young woman because of her inferior social status, and an Arab man tries to force a kiss on her.[18]

References to qualities that might compromise the heroic image – materialism, pettiness, embarrassment, perplexity, aimlessness, depression – are rare. One such example appears in the poem 'Tafṣīl liḤāla min Jahannam' [a detailed report of hell], written in the detention camp Anṣār-3, in which al-Mutawakkil Ṭāha describes the experiences that he and others underwent, including petty quarrels or frequent and extreme mood swings among the detainees.[19]

The strength of the oppressed Palestinian nation is presented in a dualism of weak-powerful. Although moral and mental fortitude is depicted – the people's courage, endurance, and unflagging belief in future victory – their weakness as a nation is also shown, in persecution, humiliation, torture and suffering.

Some works are didactic, describing and prescribing a mental revolution for Palestinians. Sometimes Palestinians are presented as unaware of their own power, as capable of greatness and achieving all their goals if only they realized their power. This appears in a symbolic story by Fāṭimā Khalīl Ḥamad in which a Palestinian named Nāhiḍ [one who gets to his feet or is revived] is amazed to see the wadi swallow up the Israelis who came to expropriate the land, until he realizes that the miracle is of his own doing.[20]

Confidence in the moral justice of the Palestinian cause is absolute and practically no other points of view are expressed. One seeming exception is the story 'Jasad al-Shahīd' [the body of the martyr] by Ibrāhīm al-'Alam, in which a woman says: 'I used to think that the young boys were provoking the soldiers, but after they shot 'Iṣām, may he rest in peace, I realized that the soldiers are provoking our sons, and the young boys respond to defend their honor.'[21] The conceivable aggression of Palestinians against Israelis is intimated here, hence their culpability for the Israeli reaction. Palestinian aggression is presented as the product of volatile young spirits – the antics of the young, rather than a political statement – but this interpretation is not really offered as valid and is uttered, not surprisingly, by a woman. Moreover, she continues: 'My son 'Azīz was right when he said, "Did we provoke them when they came from Europe and Russia and established farms beside our villages, or when they began to harass us, killing our herds and burning our produce at night, or when they forced us to leave at gunpoint?"' In other words, the root of Israeli aggression is the original sin of Jewish settlement in the land of Israel. This story is unusual in that it sets back the source of the Palestinian–Israeli conflict to before the 1967 War. Though several stories mention the loss of the homeland in 1948 or the hope of return to it, this is the only one in which the events of 1948 are used as moral justification for the struggle for greater Palestine.[22]

Blemishes in the idyllic image described above appear toward the third year of the intifāḍa and thereafter. Examples can be found in the writing of Maḥmūd Shuqayr, an East Jerusalem Palestinian who was expelled to Jordan in 1974. In his story 'Liqā'' [encounter] published in August 1989, Shuqayr expresses his sense of loneliness and despair in exile. In 'Riḥla ilā al-Madīna' [journey to the city] by 'Umar Abū-'Iqāb, written in February and published in April 1990, there is a description of the anti-hero – a village youth, a failure in the eyes of his teacher, his father and himself, who, after an interrogation and beating by soldiers, daydreams of how he will gain esteem and even become a *shahīd* [martyr] if he dies. Glorification of the *shahīd* and the boy's symbols are played down in this story, and it is not clear if the author intended to be self-critical and chip away at myths.[23]

At the end of the third year of the intifāḍa, the very short symbolic stories by Taysīr 'Abd al-'Azīz express tiredness, breaking points, apathy, hypocrisy, and the falling short of high standards.[24] In the poem 'Taḍārīs 'alā Ḥā'iṭ al-Zaman' [bas-reliefs on the wall of time] by Fayṣal Muḥammad Ṣāliḥ, there is a wavering between hope and despair: 'In my hands the bells of hope ring at my door, approaching-receding.' The poet also cites pain, exile, obstacles and a broken spirit, and ends by wondering if the light will shine or the apathetic powerlessness will grow: 'Will the light awaken in us' or 'And that does it for the Arabs!' – an ironic expression acknowledging defeat and destruction.[25]

In general there is little evidence of organized activism or obedience to leadership beyond the sense of solidarity and ideological consensus. There are only a few exceptions to this, such as the villagers leaving jugs of water outside their doors in support of the veiled youth who have clashed with the army, or the mobilization of neighbours to build a shack for a family whose home was destroyed.[26]

There are only isolated instances of military organizing. Mention is made of civil defence forces composed of young people who patrol in Bethlehem, or of organizations like the Unified National Command, the Popular Committees, 'shock troops' who enforce the strikes, and organized groups of youth who engage the army in violent action.[27] Censorship presumably prevented greater attention to this subject.

The Arab countries are not generally accorded favourable mention: Jordan is perceived as alienated from the Palestinians and in league with Israel and the United States. Egypt too is criticized.[28] There are also references to the Arab world – especially the oil-producing states – as having degenerated to a state of moral bankruptcy in their pursuit of materialism and their efforts to imitate the West. One striking example is the self-lacerating poem 'Simfoniyyat al-Arḍ' [symphony of the land] by the Kuwaiti poet Su'ād al-Ṣabāḥ, in which she says that the intifāḍa

> . . . turned the roulette tables and the wine on us
> pulled the ground out from under our feet
> instantly swept out the names of all the leaders
> sealed in wax the dens of politics . . .
> extracted the teeth of all the preachers
> spilled oil on the beard of all the caliphs
> and threw them into the fires of hell.[29]

In his poem 'Māta Ṣamtan' [died in silence], 'Abd al-Qādir al-'Izza, speaking through the dead victim, says:

> A servant of the West expropriated all my sleep from me . . .
> my lords poured milk over bananas and drank them in a drunken stupor
> Thus, my God, we died – at the hand of an enemy not of us, and an enemy who is of us!
> One slaughters a she-camel for a feast in which he will choose his whores
> and the other shoots with a merciful hand and then cries over the victims
> I died from the silence of the Arab women and the Arab leaders.[30]

The West and the United States are mentioned negatively, especially in the early days of the intifāḍa, although this diminishes over time. References to world sympathy multiply, not as material aid but in terms of moral support, and this comes mostly from people rather than governments.[31]

Characters in the stories are generally stereotyped. Sometimes they do not even have a name and the author simply refers to them as 'the boy', 'the girl', 'the young person', 'the man', 'the woman'. There is almost never a physical description and no in-depth exploration of their souls. They are often one-dimensional, lacking complexity and development. This is another manifestation of the writers' obsession with the nationalist cause, yet critics of this writing give it broad support, finding no fault with it.[32]

Although the readership of this journal is adult, children often feature in its fiction. Indeed, many stories give the impression of having been written for children or adolescents, either because children are the heroes of the tales, or because of their simplistic style (embarrassing to readers accustomed to another kind of literature), or because of the blatant didacticism and moralizing.

The writing is certainly a reflection of how writers perceive their society, and this comes through clearly in the content. The boy symbolizes the Palestinian people – its innocence and powerlessness – as Palestinian writers pour into him their longing for renewal, boundless energy, and dauntless bravado. The figure of 'Ḥanẓala' exemplifies this, a cartoon character created by the Palestinian Nājī al-'Alī which often appeared in his caricatures to symbolize the Palestinian people. Ḥanẓala [the colocynth (bitter apple) in Arabic], who symbolizes the sad and bitter fate of the Palestinians, has grown beyond the trademark of its creator and become the symbol of the Palestinian people, just as 'Srulik', created by Dosh, represents the Israeli. Ḥanẓala appears in cartoons as an overgrown baby, his back to the observer and his head bowed, signifying sadness, poverty, powerlessness;

he is under the control of others and gives the impression that he is reconciled to his fate.[33]

In an interview, Sīdī Ḥarkash (the pseudonym of the poet Ya'qūb 'Isma'īl) was asked to compare the figure of Sīdī Ḥarkash – a popular poet whose name he adopted – with the cartoon character Ḥanẓala. They are one and the same, he said, except that 'ḥarkash' means vitality and fervour in Arabic, and thus the time has come for Ḥanẓala to face the world, i.e., to throw off his passivity.[34]

The child appears in the writing in realistic scenes – as a victim of soldiers' cruelty, a symbol respected and admired by the entire world, or the essence of the fighting spirit of the Palestinian people: a baby throws a dummy at a soldier conducting a house search, a young girl belligerently rejects a soldier who tries to pat her head, a girl perched on the ruins of her demolished home gives the V for victory into the foreign lens aimed at her.[35]

The boy in these stories is not afraid of the conqueror. He is innocent, pure, uncorrupt and instinctively opposes the oppressor. The only story of a frightened child is 'al-Aṭfāl Yarfuḍūna al-Ḥalwā' [the children turn down the sweets] by Qāsim Manṣūr, about the son of well-to-do parents of the upper class, who takes no part in the lower-class struggle but exploits it in an effort to dominate, while he tries to save his own skin and manages to weasel out of taking part in the uprising. However, as the title of the story suggests, this act of corruption is an exception.[36]

Children are those from whom one should learn: In the story 'Ḥijāra 'alā Jabīn al-Waṭan' [stones on the brow of the homeland] by the Israeli-Arab writer Nabīl 'Awda from Nazareth, the old man who was driven out in 1948 remarks: 'The stone thrown by my grandson brought me out of my cave, the cave of loss, of dispersion, of fear that paralyzes the human will . . . Now I understand what foreignness is . . . My grandson understood it more quickly than I did . . . Our grandchildren are the ships that will carry us to a safe harbor.'[37]

While the strength of the children is their symbolic purity and they rebuff the occupation despite their physical weakness, the young men fill a more practical role. At first they appear primarily in clashes with the army after demonstrations or stone-throwing. Later they turn into more effective fighters and the backbone of the struggle, organizing into gangs and devising strategies against the army and the settlers. It is usually the young people who are killed and become *shahīds*. They know no fear and relish confrontation with the army, even though it may cost them their lives. The young man says to his mother: 'If I am hurt, do not be sorry; be happy', and she does not let him down.[38] When this is the ethos, it is not surprising that the conventional problems of youth are not addressed, and young love is peripheral to intifāḍa exploits.[39]

The activity of the children, the young men and the women underscores the key roles they play in the intifāḍa and, by contrast, the passivity of the adult men. The man is generally the father of the family, engaged in hard labour all day and returning home at night. He takes no part in the national struggle, but is a passive observer who sometimes finds himself involved despite himself, as for example when the soldiers demand that he erase the political graffiti outside his home or clear the road of stones thrown there, and he submissively obeys. He does not know of the deeds of his children who actively participate in the struggle. In one story, the scene in the home of a young man killed in the intifāḍa is described. While the mother is weeping with her woman friends, the men conceal their sorrow and talk politics 'as if they are at a rally'. Here, the role of the man is summed up as 'men's talk', useless as the women's tears.[40]

One exception is the story 'Abū-Muḥammad' by Nawāl al-As'ad, in which the hero is a labourer who feels that his manhood has been tarnished in his wife's eyes because of the helplessness of the Arabs *vis-à-vis* the Israelis. He ends up trying to rescue friends who carried out an action against an army camp . . . and loses his life. Interestingly, it was a woman who wrote the only story that appeared in this journal in which grown men, rather than children or young men, engage in violent activity against the occupation. Although the hero of the story does not participate in the planning and execution of the action in which his friend takes part, the assumption is that the hero is no different from his friends.[41]

In the first year of the intifāḍa, one finds almost no women in the writing, and when a woman does appear, she is generally marginal to events, as the partner of the man – the husband, the fiancé, or the boyfriend. One exception is the story 'Ḥayāt Unthā' [the life of a woman] by Jamāl Zakī 'Abd al-Jabbār al-Qawāsmih that is not related to the intifāḍa, but deals with the inferior status of women in Arab society, which has not yet forsaken its traditional patriarchal structure and is still in the process of liberating itself from rigid patterns.[42]

In the second year of the intifāḍa, the woman takes centre stage, especially in the stories. First, the woman appears as the mother – of the *shahīd* and later of the wounded and the detainee. The mother of the *shahīd* appears in mourning – lamenting her fallen son, or refusing to acknowledge his death – symbolic in and of itself. A bereaved mother frequently visits the grave of her son and brings him fruit from her garden. Elsewhere, a mother in mourning prepares a cup of tea every day for her *shahīd* son.[43] Such behaviour – mourning or failure to acknowledge reality – is not attributed to men (with the exception of old men, as we shall later see).

In the second half of the period under review, the passive stance disappears and women begin to participate more vigorously, even carrying out men's roles. They take an active part in anti-occupation activity, watching for the appearance of soldiers, sounding the alarm with their *zaghārīd* [a high trilling call sounded by women on joyous occasions], the special voice of women.[44]

While the man is submissive and obedient, the woman allows herself to respond more actively to the soldiers and to express her nationalist longings, as she knows the soldiers will not harm a woman. Women use feminine guile to extricate young men from soldiers who have arrested them. In one case, the women streak a girl's face with red paint and, in a feigned storm of emotion, they drag over the doctor to help the seemingly sick child, while the soldiers, flustered at the sight of the hysterical emotions, do not interfere. On another occasion, they gather for a demonstration on International Woman's Day, the men protecting them from the rear against the soldiers. The innovation here is both the nature of the activity and the consciousness that motivates it, although the women do not venture into 'male turf' in the full sense of the word.

The height of the woman as activist is a story in which two young women, separately, organize and lead young men in demonstrations against the army. Both are arrested and put in jail[45] – a place for proving one's manhood – 'jail is for men', as the saying goes. One wonders if this story is a reflection of reality.

Dr Ilhām Abū-Ghazāla, a lecturer at Bir-Zeit University and an author in her own right, sees the intifāḍa as a phenomenon that paved the way for a substantive change in the status of Arab women, who have taken an active role not just in fiction, but in reality itself. In an article about a story by Nāhida Nazzāl, Abū-Ghazāla writes, 'The creation of a text by a woman is a phenomenon that may truly characterize the intifāḍa, as women have long left their voices inside their minds and not put them down on paper for the public at large.'[46]

Interestingly, the writing of the six women among the writers under review – five authors and one poet – does not deal with 'feminist' subjects, nor are women their main characters, even when they appear in the writing.

Elderly characters appear infrequently, even in the second half of the period surveyed. The folk poet Mūsā Ḥāfiẓ of the Jenin refugee camp draws upon the figures of old people he has known, using them to symbolize the helplessness and passivity of the Palestinian people. In one case, an eccentric, possibly crazy, man (resembling a child in his innocent faith) believes in the possibility of turning back the clock. In the introduction to his poem 'Abū Ḥashīsh', Ḥāfiẓ gives a thumbnail sketch of his main character:

> A real person, flesh and blood, who lives in the camp and has believed for forty years that time stopped when he left his village, that the sheep and cattle he abandoned are still alive. His daily task is to gather weeds from the Jezreel Valley and, without pay, to feed the sheep and cattle in the camp. He never shaves or changes his clothes, and firmly refuses to sleep in the UNWRA units [the U.N. welfare agency]. Finally, they find him dead in the cowshed beside a pile of weeds.

The poem, addressed to Abū Ḥashīsh, opens with the 'friendly' insult 'May your home be destroyed, Abū Ḥashīsh' and ends with the wish 'May your home be built, Abū Ḥashīsh': i.e., the dream of the crazy man will ultimately come true.[47] In another work, a lonely old man, blind and forgotten, who has never known laughter or happiness, symbolizes the Palestinian people, wretched refugees. In the poem 'Abū-Nabbūt', the writer again prefaces the poem with a short life-history of the protagonist:

> 'Abū-Nabbūt died at the age of eighty-five, blind and forsaken. He lived in a small, round mud hut, without light or ventilation, with a small palm tree opposite. Every morning one of the porters in the camp would transport him on a wooden cart to the town where he would beg, and return him in the evening to his home. Occasionally the children of the camp would steal food from their homes and sell it to Abū-Nabbūt for a few pennies. When Abū-Nabbūt died, nobody knew until his friend came to take him to town and found the body.[48]

The poet says to him, 'When the angels come to interrogate you in the grave, say: "I am a refugee" and be silent.'[49] The suffering of the Palestinian speaks in his name and ensures him a just reward.

In the story 'Ḥijāra 'alā Jabīn al-Waṭan' by Nabīl 'Awda of Nazareth, the persona of the old man appears again, a weak refugee lamenting the loss of his home, and bursts into tears. But inspired by pictures of children throwing stones at soldiers, the old man throws off his passivity and declares that his grandson had more wisdom than he by throwing stones, which shaped his character. In the symbolic ending to the story, the old man stands and asks for stones to throw. In this story, the stone-throwing of the child is equated with courage and the ability to see reality, while the stone-throwing of the old man is a form of craziness born out of desperation and the feeling that there is nothing to lose, and he comes across as a pathetic figure. To his credit is only his recognition of the value of his grandchildren who are unwilling to bow their heads as he has done. He declares, 'Our grandchildren are the ship sailing us to the shore. They are the future.'[50]

In contrast, the old man in the story 'Ammū Fā'iz' [Uncle Fā'iz], by 'Abd al-Raḥmān 'Abbād, is a proud and self-confident figure who sets an example of nationalist pride for his children and grandchildren in his refusal to kowtow to a British jailer while under arrest in the British Mandate period. Although this had happened when he was a youth, his spirit has remained as stalwart as it had once been, and when the boy-narrator asks him, 'Why did you refuse to say "Yes, sir" to the sergeant?', he replies, 'It is inconceivable to say "Yes, sir" to a jailer [because] he denies me my freedom.'[51]

The religious elements in the writing generally indicate that the writers are 'secular' (with all the reservations of being 'secular' in a society where Islam is dominant). This is evidenced by the absence of declarations of a strong belief in God, in his prophet Muḥammad, in the Koran, in reward and punishment, in the resurrection of the dead and the after-life; by the use of symbols and concepts of a religion that the writer was not born to (Christianity) or of several religions (usually Islam and Christianity, though sometimes reference to ancient mythologies may appear); and by the expression of thoughts or phrasing that a truly religious person would regard as heretical. Conceivably the reason for introducing these elements into secular poetry is the desire to endow the struggle with an historical–metaphysical quality and to ensure divine support for victory.

Christian and Muslim poets alike make use of Christian symbols in their writing. The crucified Jesus symbolizes the suffering of the Palestinian people; his resurrection and return symbolize the victory of the Palestinian people.[52] In her poem 'Simfoniyyat al-Arḍ', Su'ād al-Ṣabāḥ integrates the Christian and Shi'ite motifs of the messiah who will return to earth:

> Leave your doors open . . .
> because the messiah whose coming is awaited may appear
> and perhaps among them [the children of the intifāḍa] will appear
> the face of 'Alī
> or 'Umar [two revered caliphs of the Muslims].[53]

Sometimes there are expressions of mild complaint and heresy toward God, as in the poem 'Māta Ṣamtan' by 'Abd al-Qādir al-'Izza, in which he instructs the *shahīd* that he need not fear the afterlife when he gives an account of his deeds on earth. He has him state ironically to God and the angels:

> Have you heard about the plastic bullet?
> . . . It yearns toward the young one. It causes no harm!
> It rips open the guts, which use it for food
> that after starving fill it with blood and pus . . .
> You the master of peace . . . and peace on the Lord.[54]

This may be an allusion to 'Glory to God in the heavens, peace on earth, and good will to men' from the New Testament. A paraphrase of the Lord's Prayer appears in the poem "Alā Ṣalīb Khaḍir al-Tarzī' [on the cross of Khaḍir al-Tarzī] by Mājid Abū-Ghūsh:

> On earth
> intifāḍa
> and in the hands of people
> stones
> Our father who art in jail
> peace
> Our father who art in the grave
> peace![55]

There is no mention of fundamentalist religious streams and no emphasis placed on Islamic religious motifs. Only once is reference made to the rallying call 'Allāh is great', and then only through use of the verb that refers to it – *kabbara* – rather than utterance of the slogan itself.

The motif of the stone appears often in poems or stories as a symbol of the intifāḍa: simple, strong, supported by the masses, clinging to the land, the struggle of the weak against the strong. Poets and writers praise it endlessly. A clear example of the feelings of rapture and euphoria that gripped the Arab world at the start of the intifāḍa can be found in the poem 'Simfoniyyat al-Arḍ' by Su'ād al-Ṣabāḥ, in which she writes:

> Spread carpets and roses for the children of the intifāḍa
> and engulf them with flowers
> Israel is a glass house
> and it has been shattered.[56]

Indeed, al-Ṣabāḥ perceives the stone-throwing to be a revolution that will shake up the entire Arab world: 'We [the Arab states] did not liberate one inch of Palestinian land . . . but these hands with a mission have liberated us.'[57]

In the first year of the intifāḍa, the stone appears almost exclusively in poems, except for one story by the Israeli-Palestinian writer Muṣṭafā Murrār.[58] From early in the second year of the intifāḍa, more detailed and realistic descriptions of the stone-throwing appear, and these are tied in with children or youth.[59] The stone is perceived to be as powerful as the occupation, which it challenges. In the poem 'Taqaddum' [progress], Samīḥ Faraj states, 'The stone spoke out against the chain-link [of the armoured vehicles].'[60] In the story 'Ḥijāra 'alā Jabīn al-Waṭan', published in March 1990, 'Awda has his protagonist say that the stone raised by his grandson lifted him out of the cave of his loss, dispersion and fear: 'The stone is the prophet of the future . . . it is the harbinger of the happiness to come.'[61]

In other stories stone-throwing is conceived as a children's game, as in the story where it is presented as a new sport – 'stone ball' – in which the children are eager to confront the soldiers.[62] Stone-throwing is also a game in which children amuse themselves, imitating what they see on television.[63] Linking the stone to children does not diminish from its status or importance.

The throwing of a stone by a youth is perceived as an expression of determined opposition, and under no circumstances is there doubt about its efficacy, despite the futility and clear imbalance in the face of the army's weapons. This can be found in 'al-Niṣf al-Ākhar' [the other half] by the Gazan 'Umar Ḥammash, whose hero is anaesthetized and undergoing an operation after being hit by army bullets in a clash in which he threw stones at soldiers. The feelings and voices that he absorbs during the operation evoke a dream in which he is throwing stones at the imaginary teeth of a cave threatening to devour him, which he shoots with live bullets, rubber bullets and tear gas. Even though his body is riddled with bullets, he continues to throw stones without pause, and he manages to smash the teeth of the cave. Although this is only a dream with the imaginary and impossible nature of dreams, and the hero actually loses part of his body, amputated in the operation, the story does not express loss, failure or futility, but rather unwavering determination. One wonders what the 'other half' – the amputated part – of his body is that the hero demands be returned to him: Is it part of the homeland? If so, is the reference to the West Bank or to the areas of Palestine that were lost in 1948?[64]

Toward the end of the second year of the intifāḍa, assertions of belief in the victory of the Palestinian struggle multiply, together with reference to a future Palestinian state. There is no analysis of the character or problems of the future state, and minimal discussion of its borders. It would exist beside the state of Israel and include the West Bank – Jerusalem, Bethel,

Qalandiyya, Ramallah, Nablus and Bir-Zeit – and the Gaza Strip, which would be connected to the West Bank by an air corridor.[65]

The PLO appears in the writing only once: in the poem 'Ghayr al-Ḥaqq mā bi-Ṣiḥḥ', the folk Palestinian poet Rājiḥ al-Salfītī calls upon Rabin and Shamir to negotiate with the Palestinian people represented by the PLO.[66] Apparently, the absence of the PLO is evidence of Israeli censorship. Indeed, an article about Palestinian poetry in the territories by Dr Muḥammad Shiḥāda notes that the occupation authorities forbade the folk poets from writing poems about Palestine and the PLO.[67] One very short story that appeared in *al-Kātib* criticizes leaders who delude the Palestinian people with promises. Because the wording is general and cautious, it is not perfectly clear who the subject of this criticism is among the leadership – the PLO or elements within it.[68]

There are references to territories or settlements within Israel (the Green Line border), sometimes for purposes of noting the territorial contiguity of Palestine: In her poem 'Simfoniyyat al-Arḍ', the Kuwaiti Su'ād al-Ṣabāḥ – the only writer in this category who is not Palestinian – maintains opposition to the state of Israel whether in the territories or in Israel proper. On the theme of stone-throwing, she writes: 'This magnificent symphony of land / continues / continues like fate striking / once in Bethlehem / once in Gaza/once in Nazareth.'[69] Mūsā Ḥāfiẓ from the Jenin refugee camp sets in poetry the farmers' pride in their wheat-growing 'from Rosh HaNikrah to Gaza',[70] while Yūsuf Shiḥāda from the West Bank cites Damascus, Hebron, the Galilee, the Carmel and Haifa in his poems.[71]

There is no call for returning territories to Palestinian sovereignty, on the pretext of censorship, but also apparently due to the unspoken distinction that has developed over the years among Palestinians in the territories between the broad sense of 'occupied Palestine' that includes the state of Israel (even rejecting the 1948 UN partition borders), and the narrow sense of Palestine – the West Bank and the Gaza Strip. Nevertheless, the claim of ownership over Palestine in its entirety is relinquished only implicitly.

Conspicuous in the stories and poems is the lack of attention to the problems of Israeli Arabs. There is no mention of contact with them, not even fictitious encounters with a Palestinian from the territories who comes to work in Israel, nor is there support or interest expressed in their national, cultural, social or economic issues (such as Land Day).

The obsessive preoccupation of the literature, particularly the poetry, with the struggle against the Israeli occupation is not viewed by the writers as 'mobilization' on behalf of the national cause. Although reservations are occasionally expressed about the quality of some of the writing, the writers believe that their success as artists rests upon their ability to give voice to the collective conscience and build the moral infrastructure: literature must serve the intifāḍa. As written by the Association of Palestinian Writers in Jerusalem in the introduction to a story that appeared in October 1989, 'Every literary work is an instrument of intifāḍa/resistance.'[72]

A good illustration of this can be found in 'Simfoniyyat al-Arḍ', in which Su'ād al-Ṣabāḥ perceives the intifāḍa as the greatest and truest poem:

Resign, you great poets
our poems have no masters or serfs
our poetry has one ruler called stone
this glorious symphony of land
continues . . . continues
like the rhythm of bells
And the melody of the song
that carries to us the lightning and the rain
has burned the paper of all the writers.[73]

Against this background, it is strange that there is no broad theoretical exploration of the role of the poet in the intifāḍa, other than the piece by Dr Ilhām Abū-Ghazāla of Bir-Zeit University about the woman in intifāḍa poetry, in which excerpts are quoted of poems from the territories.[74]

It is also worth noting that the arrest of writers and poets was not given prominence in the journal, but only random mention.[75] One reason for this is the mass nature of the arrests in the territories, which does not leave much room for being impressed by the arrest of a few individuals. Also, the arrest of these writers was perceived to be related to their political work, not their role as spiritual or opinion leaders, or due to the content of their writing. Confrontation with the Israeli occupation is not viewed as taking place in the cultural realm.

Almost every month, however, short stories or poems are published that were written by those interred in the Anṣār-3 detention camp ('Ketziot') or the Nafḥa, Ashkelon and Junayd prisons. Sometimes the date of this work is also given. The time gap between the writing of the work and its publication ranges from several weeks to several months, up to a year. A poem that appeared in November 1990 was reprinted from the first issue of a literary publication issued by the prisoners of Nafḥa prison in May 1990. These pieces are generally, though not always, related to the experience of imprisonment, the feelings of the prisoners, or what takes place in detention. Some poems recall *shahīd*s who were killed in detention.[76] Mention of the place where these poems and stories were written seems to be intended to indicate the close affinity between art and reality, and the role of art in the national struggle as literature of resistance. This literature is discussed in studies that appear in the journal. The term 'poetry of resistance' refers to Palestinian poetry that opposes all oppression, regardless of where it takes place, without geographical distinctions.

Testimony about the influence of Arab resistance literature written in Israel on the literature of the territories (also called 'resistance literature') can be found in a study carried out by Dr Muḥammad Shiḥāda about Palestinian poetry in the territories in the years 1967-88, in which he says:

> The occupation of the West Bank and the Gaza Strip gave Palestinian writers and intellectuals an opportunity to become closely acquainted with the [Israeli-] Palestinian literature of the resistance. Familiarity with the writing of Emile Ḥabībī, Maḥmūd Darwīsh, Samīḥ al-Qāsim, Tawfīq Zayyād, Sālim Jubrān, Nā'if Sālim, Ḥannā Ibrāhīm, and others served as a point of departure and basis for the writers of the occupied country, and also an example of humanist, national, and progressive literature, as well as a vivid picture of what Palestinian literature should be, as they served as a school not just for the writers of the occupied country, but also for the writers after the defeat of June 1967.[77]

He then brings the words of the poet Khalīl Tūmā, 'a representative figure of the poetry of resistance in the West Bank and the Gaza Strip' on 'the impact of resistance poetry from the Galilee on local poetry in the West Bank and the Gaza Strip',[78] and also personal testimonies of poets about the influence of 'Palestinian resistance poetry' from the Galilee on their own literary development. For example: 'The poems of al-Qāsim, Zayyād, and Darwīsh won my heart'; 'I was influenced by the poets of resistance, especially Tawfīq Zayyād, Maḥmūd Darwīsh, Sālim Jubrān, and Samīḥ al-Qāsim'; and:

> The spread of Palestinian resistance poetry, as embodied in the poetry collections of Maḥmūd Darwīsh, Samīḥ al-Qāsim, and Tawfīq Zayyād, raised the level of poetry in the West Bank and the Gaza Strip. And then lo and behold, our poets and writers passed beyond the longing, the tears, and the anticipation, renounced the yearning for childhood and orange groves, burned down the tent, rebelled against reality in an effort to change it, and began to take part in shaping their future and the lustrous future of their nation.[79]

Despite these testimonies to the influence of Israeli-Arab literature on the literature of the territories, no articles appeared in *al-Kātib* during the period under review that were exclusively devoted to prominent figures in Palestinian literature in Israel, although they were occasionally cited in articles, literary criticism, and in the column 'Aṣdā' Adabiyya'.[80]

We have seen in this chapter that the corpus of prose and poetry produced during the period of the intifāḍa has channelled Palestinian literature – especially that written in the territories – into new avenues. Almost all the writing that appeared during this period was focused on the events of the intifāḍa. The flood of writing in the first year of the intifāḍa diminished in the second and became a thin trickle in the third. The Gulf War reduced the level of interest in intifāḍa literature, just as it relegated the intifāḍa to the sidelines. The writing of the intifāḍa – fundamentally symbolic and mobilized for the cause – forms the backbone of modern Palestinian literature, as it would for any community with clear political goals and in the process of self-definition. This is true for other writing that addresses the intifāḍa, whether in Hebrew or various modern Arabic literatures. It is also quite evident that poetry is the preferred genre in the first year of the intifāḍa. This is also true of Hebrew literature that dealt with the intifāḍa. Poetry takes up considerable space in *al-Kātib* and not a single issue appears without it, unlike prose where only short stories appear, and not in every issue, though in most. Plays do not appear in the journal, although from time to time there have been articles about theatre and, infrequently, about art or the plastic arts, most of which were related to the intifāḍa. One piece appeared about Palestinian films and an occasional article about folklore.

Most of the stories that appeared in *al-Kātib* during this period were written in a realistic style, and fewer in a symbolic style. The characters are generally stereotyped, physical descriptions are rarely provided, and there is no in-depth exploration of character, which is superficial and undeveloped. Palestinian literature written during the intifāḍa is almost entirely mobilized for the national cause. From an artistic point of view, the better writing (in my opinion) is that in which nationalism is not a central axis (such as the stories of al-Qawāsmih).

Translated items figure prominently in the journal. Much of this is poetry and its authors are from Europe or Latin America. Most are written in a socialist or revolutionary communist tone, universal in character, and not related to the Palestinian problem or the intifāḍa.

During the period of the intifāḍa, Palestinian society is portrayed in its literature as patriotic and unified, free of internal divisions. It is depicted as espousing national and personal values, struggling, respectful of those who carry the burden of the intifāḍa and glorifying its fallen. Cracks in the solidarity appear in the writing only in the third year, and then primarily among the wealthy.

Notwithstanding the positive image of Palestinian society, the Arab states, especially Egypt, Jordan and the oil states, come in for acerbic criticism. This is directed at Arab leaders who pursue materialism and become enamoured with the West. In one case there is even criticism, if only implicit, of the PLO. The United States and Israel are depicted in a particularly negative light. Israelis are without exception portrayed as negative, with only differences of degree among them. Surprisingly, there is almost no reference to Israeli settlers in the territories, although other Palestinian writers both in the territories (such as Jamāl Bannūra) and in Israel (such as Riyāḍ Baydas) make significant reference to settlers, none of it complimentary. Only toward the end of the third year is there some restraint in portraying the Israeli soldier, and occasionally even acknowledgement that, with some Israelis, dialogue is possible.

One of the striking phenomena of the writing in *al-Kātib* – and indeed not just there – during the period under review, is the great importance attached to children, youth and women. It is crystal clear that the rising status of these three groups comes at the expense of the status of the Palestinian man. Whether or not social change as described actually reflects reality or merely the wishes of the writers is a question worth pursuing in sociological or anthropological research.

The motif of stone appears often as a symbol and slogan of the intifāḍa that embody its many characteristics: simple, strong, popular, of the earth, and suggesting the struggle of the weak against the strong. In the first year of the intifāḍa, the stone was cited only in poems, except for one story. From the beginning of the second year, more realistic descriptions appear of stone-throwing by children or youths. Stone-throwing is also perceived as a game of children confronting soldiers. The stone is grasped as a weapon against occupation, a weapon used almost exclusively by children and youths, and only in isolated instances by adults.

By the second half of the period under review, expressions increase of belief in the victory of the Palestinian struggle and a future Palestinian state. In the few items which refer to the borders of such a state, the reference is to a Palestinian state beside the state of Israel. There is no call to return the territories of Palestine within the Green Line, whether because of censorship or because of the unspoken distinction that has gradually formed in the consciousness of Palestinians in the territories between the West Bank plus Gaza Strip and the area within Israel. Nonetheless, claims of ownership over the entire land of Palestine are not explicitly renounced.

Finally, it should be emphasized that the conclusions presented here are based on articles that appeared in *al-Kātib*. Thus, three qualifying remarks are in order. First, writing appears in *al-Kātib* at the discretion of its editor, and naturally reflects his ideology. Second, the works that appeared in *al-Kātib* in the first three years of the intifāḍa do not reflect all Palestinian writing in the territories during the period under review, and certainly are not representative of the Palestinian work written in the various diasporas as well as the many works in Arabic and Hebrew written about the intifāḍa. And third, the conclusions I have drawn above based on the literary texts in *al-Kātib* in the period under review are my conclusions based on the entire corpus of Palestinian writing in the first three years of the intifāḍa, with two significant reservations. The first is that the links among the three branches of Palestinian literature have strengthened since the intifāḍa, in contrast with the findings of this study, where Israeli Arabs and their problems are not mentioned in *al-Kātib*. The second reservation is related to the image of the Israeli and possible cooperation between the two nations. The image of the Israeli in the totality of Palestinian writing in the territories that appeared during the first three years of the intifāḍa is not exclusively negative and demonized, unlike the work under review in this study. We have only to cite writers such as Jamāl Bannūra, al-Mutawakkil Ṭāha, or Maḥmūd al-Yūsuf who do not present the Israeli in an exclusively negative light, likewise their approach about possible dialogue between the two nations. They express this viewpoint not only in their writing, but in Israeli–Palestinian encounters in which they and other writers participate.

NOTES

1. Jamāl Bannūra, *Ayyām lā Tunsā*, Jerusalem, Ittiḥād al-Kuttāb al-Filasṭīniyyīn, 1988. As'ad al-As'ad, *Layl al-Banafsaj*, Jerusalem, Ittiḥād al-Kuttāb al-Filasṭīniyyīn, 1989.
2. 'Abd al-Sattār Qāsim, *Ayyām fī Mu'taqal al-Naqab*, Jerusalem, Lajnat al-Difā' 'an al-Thaqāfa al-Waṭaniyya al-Filasṭīniyya, 1989.
3. For the sake of brevity, I note here that all articles that appeared in *al-Kātib* were in Arabic. When the time of writing or publication appears significant, I note this in the body of the chapter (when the date is known), although the date of writing is known for only a few articles.
4. The format of the journal changed as of issue no. 129 (January 1991): the page size was increased, while the number of pages decreased to 64, and dropped further to 40 pages in issue no. 130 (February–March 1991). Perhaps the smaller scope was due to difficulties resulting from the Gulf War (in issue no. 130, the editor cites the extended curfew to explain the delay in publication date).
5. *al-Kātib*, 110 (June 1989), pp. 65–76.
6. *al-Kātib*, 119 (March 1990), pp. 45–60; *al-Kātib*, 120 (April 1990), pp. 65–76; and *al-Kātib*, 121 (May 1990), pp. 52–68.
7. *al-Kātib*, 122 (June 1990), pp. 58–70.
8. *al-Kātib*, 126 (October 1990), pp. 59–66.

9. 'Ḥayāt Unthā', *al-Kātib*, 106 (February 1989), pp. 73–6; 'al-Ḥayawān al-Habla', *al-Kātib*, 124 (August 1990), pp. 82–6.
10. 'Yā Ḥalālī yā Mālī', *al-Kātib*, 112 (August 1989), p. 90; 'Mawāwīl li'Uyūniki yā Balad', *al-Kātib*, 115 (November 1989), pp. 82–3.
11. 'Alī al-Jarīrī, 'Lan U'ātiyahum siwā ismī', *al-Kātib*, 113 (September 1989), pp. 80–1; Zakī al-'Īla, 'Ḥīṭān min Damā', *al-Kātib*, 119 (March 1990), pp. 95–8; Taysīr 'Abd al-'Azīz, 'Taḍāmun', *al-Kātib*, 125 (September 1990), pp. 90–1; Qāsim Manṣūr, 'al-Aṭfāl Yarfuḍūna al-Ḥalwā', *al-Kātib*, 125 (September 1990), pp. 84–5; Ibrāhīm al-'Alam, 'Fī Intiẓār Rizq', *al-Kātib*, 123 (July 1990), pp. 83–6.
12. Ibrāhīm al-'Alam, 'Jasad al-Shahīd', *al-Kātib*, 119 (March 1990), pp. 92–4; Ṣubḥī Ḥamdān, 'al-Ṭifl wa'l-Dūrī', *al-Kātib*, 126 (October 1990), pp. 86–90.
13. See, for example, the poems of Aḥmad Fū'ād Najm, 'Ghunwat Salām', *al-Kātib*, 107 (March 1989), pp. 85–7, or the nostalgic poetry of Sulāfa Ḥijjāwī, 'al-Judhūr', *al-Kātib*, 113 (September 1989), p. 89, which is perhaps more personal in nature.
14. Edith Thomas, 'al-Brūfisūr wa'l-Maḥār', *al-Kātib*, 114 (October 1989), pp. 65–8.
15. *al-Kātib*, 128 (December 1990), p. 87.
16. See 'Yawm' by Sāmī al-Kīlānī, *al-Kātib*, 100 (August 1988), pp. 87–9.
17. Such as the story 'Limādhā Ibtasama al-Shāṭir Ḥasan?' by Ibrāhīm Jawhar, *al-Kātib*, 105 (January 1989), pp. 86–8.
18. al-'Alam, 'Jasad al-Shahīd', *al-Kātib*, 119 (March 1990), pp. 92–4; Taysīr 'Abd al-'Azīz, 'Karam', *al-Kātib*, 122 (June 1990), p. 81; Manṣūr, 'al-Aṭfāl Yarfuḍūna al-Ḥalwā', *al-Kātib*, 125 (September 1990), pp. 84–5; Ya'qūb al-Aṭrash, 'Muhimma 'Ājila', *al-Kātib*, 125 (September 1990), pp. 86–9; Ibrāhīm al-'Alam, 'al-Dhi'b', *al-Kātib*, 128 (December 1990), pp. 80–2; al-'Alam, 'Fī Intiẓār Rizq', *al-Kātib*, 123 (July 1990), pp. 83–6.
19. *al-Kātib*, 114 (October 1989), pp. 69–70.
20. Fāṭimā Khalīl Ḥamad, 'al-Nīsān Yatanashshaq al-Azhār', *al-Kātib*, 115 (November 1989), pp. 78–80.
21. *al-Kātib*, 119 (March 1990), p. 94.
22. See, for example, 'Mahr' by Zakī al-'Īla, *al-Kātib*, 109 (May 1989), pp. 80–3.
23. Maḥmūd Shuqayr, 'Liqā'', *al-Kātib*, 112 (August 1989), pp. 79–80; 'Umar Abū-'Iqāb, 'Riḥla ilā al-Madīna', *al-Kātib*, 120 (April 1990), pp. 87–9.
24. *al-Kātib*, 125 (September 1990), pp. 90–1.
25. Ibid., p. 95.
26. Jamīl al-Salḥūt, 'Kūz al-Mā'', *al-Kātib*, 109 (May 1989), p. 85; Aḥmad Gharīb, 'Laylā', *al-Kātib*, 124 (August 1990), pp. 87–8.
27. Maḥmūd Shuqayr, 'Wadīda', *al-Kātib*, 112 (August 1989), p. 77; Sāmī al-Kīlānī, 'Jam' al-Asrā Jam'', *al-Kātib*, 121 (May 1990), p. 81; Gharīb, 'Laylā', *al-Kātib*, 124 (August 1990), pp. 87–8; Nawāl al-As'ad, 'Abū-Muḥammad', *al-Kātib*, 106 (February 1989), pp. 77–9; al-'Alam, 'Jasad al-Shahīd', *al-Kātib*, 119 (March 1990), pp. 92–4; Samīr al-Rantīsī, 'al-Dā'ira', *al-Kātib*, 121 (May 1990), pp. 87–8; al-'Alam, 'Fī Intiẓār Rizq', *al-Kātib*, 123 (July 1990), pp. 83–6.
28. In the story 'Waẓīfa' by Ashraf Ghīṭān, *al-Kātib*, 93 (January 1988), pp. 78–9: the Jordanian security service prevents a Palestinian from getting a job; in the story 'Abū-Muḥammad' by al-As'ad, *al-Kātib*, 106 (February 1989), pp. 77–9: the Arab states take no interest in the Palestinians and the United States, Israel and King Hussein are held responsible for their situation; in the poem 'Ajā al-Shaqiyy 'Alā Sha'bī Yughālibuhu',

by 'Alī al-Jarīrī, *al-Kātib*, 108 (April 1989), p. 92; the story 'Dhālika al-Miṣrī' by Iyād Ḥalas, *al-Kātib*, 127 (November 1990), pp. 86–7.

29. *al-Kātib*, 95 (March 1988), p. 91.
30. *al-Kātib*, 111 (July 1989), pp. 83–4. See also the poem 'Mādhā Taqūl Shahrazād lī wa-Mādhā aqūl li-Shahrazād' by Ra'd Mushtat, *al-Kātib*, 98 (June 1988), p. 90, in which disgust is expressed for a Bahrainian princess in London who gives a speech on the trivial subject of coffee.
31. In the poem 'Madīnat al-Layālī al-Bayḍā'' by 'Umar Maḥāmīd from Umm al-Faḥm, *al-Kātib*, 114 (October 1989), p. 83, and in the story 'Zahrāt Barriyya' by Taysīr 'Abd al-'Azīz, *al-Kātib*, 117 (January 1990), p. 83, it is the Soviets who express their sympathy; in the story 'Nihāyat al-Maṭāf' by Ya'qūb al-Aṭrash, *al-Kātib*, 117 (January 1990), pp. 80–2 – the Swedes; and in the story 'Kitāba 'alā al-Shams' by al-Aṭrash, *al-Kātib*, 123 (July 1990), pp. 80–2 – the Greeks.
32. See the critical writing of Dr Ilhām Abū-Ghazāla, *al-Kātib*, 116 (December 1989), pp. 54–62; and of Dr Ibrāhīm al-'Alam, *al-Kātib*, 117 (January 1990), pp. 61–3.
33. On the figure of Ḥanẓala, see Guy Bechor, *Leksikon Ashaf*, Tel-Aviv, Ministry of Defence Publications, 1991, p. 140. Nājī al-'Alī himself was murdered in 1987, and was considered a martyr by the Palestinians and a symbol of the intifāḍa, especially since it is not clear who killed him. For more about al-'Alī, see ibid., pp. 260–1.
34. *al-Kātib*, 113 (September 1989), pp. 67–72.
35. Maḥmūd Shuqayr, 'Amūna', *al-Kātib*, 109 (May 1989), p. 79; Jamīl al-Salḥūt, *al-Kātib*, 109 (May 1989), p. 74; al-Aṭrash, 'Nihāyat al-Maṭāf', *al-Kātib*, 117 (January 1990), pp. 80–2.
36. *al-Kātib*, 125 (September 1990), pp. 84–5.
37. *al-Kātib*, 119 (March 1990), March 1990, p. 101.
38. In the story 'Ḥīna Takāmala al-Binā'' by Ibrāhīm al-'Alam, *al-Kātib*, 113 (September 1989), pp. 73–5.
39. As in the stories by al-'Alam, 'Fī Intiẓār Rizq', *al-Kātib*, 123 (July 1990), pp. 83–6; and Qāsim Manṣūr, 'Aqmār Tishrīn', *al-Kātib*, 128 (December 1990), pp. 83–4.
40. Shuqayr, 'Wadīda', *al-Kātib*, 112 (August 1989), p. 77.
41. *al-Kātib*, 106 (February 1989), pp. 77–9.
42. Ibid., pp. 73–6.
43. Muḥammad Rajab, 'Ṭuqūs 'Ādiyya Jiddan', *al-Kātib*, 108 (April 1989), pp. 90–1; Maḥmūd Shuqayr, 'Zujāj', *al-Kātib*, 109 (May 1989), p. 76.
44. al-'Īla, 'Mahr', *al-Kātib*, 109 (May 1989), pp. 80–3.
45. al-'Alam, 'Fī Intiẓār Rizq', *al-Kātib*, 123 (July 1990), pp. 83–6.
46. *al-Kātib*, 119 (March 1990), p. 76.
47. *al-Kātib*, 118 (February 1990), p. 90.
48. *al-Kātib*, 124 (August 1990), p. 92.
49. Ibid., p. 93.
50. *al-Kātib*, 119 (March 1990), p. 101.
51. *al-Kātib*, 118 (February 1990), p. 87.
52. See, for example, Mājid Abū-Ghūsh, "Alā Ṣalīb Khaḍir al-Tarzī', *al-Kātib*, 103 (November 1988), p. 91; 'Abd al-'Azīz, 'Zahrāt Barriyya', *al-Kātib*, 117 (January 1990), p. 83.
53. *al-Kātib*, 95 (March 1988), p. 92.
54. *al-Kātib*, 111 (July 1989), pp. 83–4.

55. *al-Kātib*, 103 (November 1988), p. 91.
56. *al-Kātib*, 95 (March 1988), p. 91.
57. Ibid., p. 92.
58. 'Jidār al-Qabr', *al-Kātib*, 98 (June 1988), pp. 78–81.
59. As in the story 'Limādhā Ibtasama al-Shāṭir Ḥasan?' by Jawhar, *al-Kātib*, 105 (January 1989), pp. 85–8; and also the poem 'Qaṣīda Muhdāt ilā Khulūd 'Adnān Dāghir' by Fayṣal al-Zu'bī, *al-Kātib*, 114 (October 1989), pp. 75–6, where the Israeli soldier is searching for stones and poems in the schoolbag of the girl.
60. *al-Kātib*, 109 (May 1989), p. 91.
61. *al-Kātib*, 119 (March 1990), p. 101.
62. 'Umar Abū-'Iqāb, 'Riḥla Naḥwa al-Mustaqbal', *al-Kātib*, 122 (June 1990), pp. 77–9.
63. Manṣūr, 'al-Aṭfal Yarfuḍūna al-Halwā', *al-Kātib*, 125 (September 1990), pp. 84–5.
64. *al-Kātib*, 126 (October 1990), pp. 84–5.
65. al-Salfītī, 'Naḥnu min Ḥaqqinā Dawla wa-Huwiyyā', *al-Kātib*, 109 (May 1989), pp. 87–8; Abū-'Iqāb, 'Riḥla Naḥwa al-Mustaqbal', *al-Kātib*, 122 (June 1990), pp. 77–9; al-Jarīrī, 'Ajā al-Shaqiyy 'Alā Sha'bī Yughālibuhu', *al-Kātib*, 108 (April 1989), p. 92.
66. *al-Kātib*, 109 (May 1989), p. 88.
67. *al-Kātib*, 120 (April 1990), p. 67.
68. 'Abd al-'Azīz, 'al-'Ālam yastayqiẓ mubakkiran', *al-Kātib*, 122 (June 1990), pp. 81–2.
69. *al-Kātib*, 95 (March 1988), p. 91.
70. 'Hizzī Ghurbālaki', *al-Kātib*, 121 (May 1990), p. 89.
71. 'Ṣabāḥ al-Khayr Maryam al-Filasṭīniyya', *al-Kātib*, 106 (February 1989), pp. 80–3: Damascus, Hebron, the Galilee, the Carmel, Haifa; 'Ẓilāl min Qaṣīda li-Kharīf al-Jalīl', *al-Kātib*, 96 (April 1988), pp. 94–5: the Galilee.
72. *al-Kātib*, 119 (March 1990), p. 76.
73. *al-Kātib*, 95 (March 1988), p. 91.
74. *al-Kātib*, 110 (June 1989), pp. 65–76.
75. In an item in 'Aṣdā' Adabiyya' (*al-Kātib*, 113 [September 1989], p. 92), it was reported that Sihām Daūd of the Israeli delegation in the Berlin Festival condemned the oppression of the Palestinian people in the territories, their expulsions and the arrests of authors and poets. In an article about a collection of poetry by Sāmī al-Kīlānī (*al-Kātib*, 114 [October 1989], p. 45), it was noted that at the time of publication, the poet had been arrested for the second time. In an article about Palestinian poetry in the territories, the author writes that 'the occupation authorities arrested several writers of *zajal* [popular poem in strophic form] and folk poets, and demanded that they [should] not write poems about Palestine and the PLO' (*al-Kātib*, 120 [April 1990], p. 67). He also writes, in reference to folk poetry: 'The well-known Palestinian folk poet Rājiḥ al-Salfītī suffered from the arbitrary behaviour of Jordanian and Israeli authorities alike: the Israeli authorities arrested him in 1974 and they continue to arrest him periodically. In 1976, al-Salfītī was elected to the Salfit town council' (ibid., p. 68). In the same volume, an article by 'Alī al-Jarīrī written in the Anṣār detention camp in September 1990 offers a critique the stories of al-Kīlānī: 'Sāmī al-Kīlānī is a Palestinian poet and author . . . and a member of the Executive Committee of the Association of Palestinian Writers in the West Bank and Gaza Strip. The occupation authorities arrested him several times for political activity. The most recent time was a second administrative detention in April 1989 in the desert detention camp in the Negev, where I had the honor of meeting him among a group of artists, writers, and poets' (ibid., p. 77).

76. 'Abd al-Nāṣir Ṣāliḥ, 'Hal Ghādara al-Shuhadā'', *al-Kātib*, 102 (October 1988), pp. 91–2; al-Mutawakkil Ṭāha, 'al-Khurūj min Anṣār–3', *al-Kātib*, 106 (February 1989), pp. 85–7.
77. *al-Kātib*, 119 (March 1990), p. 50.
78. Ibid., p. 54.
79. Ibid., p. 58.
80. The figures cited are Muṣṭafā Murrār ('the known author'), Muḥammad 'Alī Ṭāha ('secretary of the Association of Palestinian Writers'), Samīḥ al-Qāsim, Anton Shammās, Shakīb Jahshān (an item in 'Aṣdā' Adabiyya' speaks of a poetry collection of the Israeli poet Shakīb Jaḥshān, in the preface of which the Israeli poet Sālim Jubrān wrote that this is the poem that predicted the intifāḍa before it erupted [no. 112, August 1989, p. 93]), and Eliās Anīs Khūrī of Acre. In a critique in the June 1988 volume, reprinted from *al-Nidā'* on 4 October 1989, the 'poets of resistance' are cited, led by Maḥmūd Darwīsh, Samīḥ al-Qāsim and Tawfīq Zayyād. Also published in the January 1988 issue was an interview with Emile Ḥabībī about his style of language.

5

Danger, High Voltage

The Image of the Jew/Israeli in Palestinian Intifāḍa Literature (1987–90)

In this chapter we shall examine the image of the Jew and/or the Israeli in Palestinian literature, primarily during the period of the intifāḍa. We have already touched on this sensitive and difficult subject in previous chapters, especially in relation to Jerusalem; here, an attempt will be made to grapple with it in the writing of Arabs, both Palestinian and not, during one of the most difficult periods in the long history of confrontation between Jews and Arabs, Israelis and Palestinians: as the conqueror and the conquered.

Inevitably with two political–national communities in violent contention for more than a century, feelings run deep and negative images of the rival find their way into writing as well. In modern Hebrew literature, the image of the Arab bears an 'ugly face', ranging from one who threatens the Jewish–Zionist presence in Israel to a romantic and exotic persona; in either event, the Arab is both a stranger and a neighbour.[1] Likewise, until the late 1960s, the image of the Jew and/or Israeli served many major Palestinian writers, such as Emile Ḥabībī, Ghassān Kanafānī and Ḥannā Ibrāhīm,[2] as a key motif, and not always a negative one. Literary interest in the Jew waned in the 1970s and 1980s among young Palestinian writers such as Ibrāhīm Naṣrallāh, Muḥammad Naffā', Muḥammad 'Alī Ṭāha and Nājī Ẓāhir. Exceptions were Israeli Palestinians such as Emile Ḥabībī, Riyāḍ Baydas and Salmān Nāṭūr, who in the 1980s and especially since the intifāḍa have dealt extensively with the image of the Jew and/or Israeli. Thus, we find that the intifāḍa – like the war of 1967 – rekindled and fanned the flames of conflict and alienation among the Arabs, igniting an avid new interest of Palestinian writers in the Jew.

A MAJOR NEGATION AND A MINOR AFFIRMATION

In the period of the intifāḍa, treatment of the Jew and/or the Israeli underwent a significant transformation in Palestinian literature. Since then, more space has been devoted to portraying Jews among all three groups of Palestinian writers and the image is, by and large, a negative one. The Israelis that Palestinians encounter most frequently are soldiers, followed by policemen, secret servicemen and Jewish settlers in the occupied territories. There is little reference to Jews within the previous 'Green Line' border of Israel, whether Israeli employers or left-wing activists. In the intifāḍa writing of Palestinians, little distinction is drawn between types of Israelis or Jews, whether reflecting the pluralism of ideologies or their attitudes to Palestinians. The negative image of Israelis appears in two main areas: the inhuman behaviour of soldiers and the soldiers' coarse attitudes toward Palestinians and the values they hold dear. This dehumanization of the Israeli soldier is derived first and foremost from his daily humiliation of Palestinians, as one who treats young and old with equal contempt. The Israeli soldier also comes under attack for taking advantage of his position to sully the honour of Palestinian women and to abuse them sexually.[3] Here we find the use of demonization in driving a wedge between the peoples, fomenting the primordial wrath of a society sensitive to matters of the honour of its women. Israeli soldiers are portrayed as behaving with brutality that borders on savagery. In general during the period of the intifāḍa – as well as before – Israeli society is characterized as militaristic, disciplined, but lacking ethical values and sexually corrupt, in contrast with Palestinian society that clings to its traditional values and its land.[4]

A striking example of this is the famous poem by the Palestinian Maḥmūd Darwīsh, "Ābirūn fī Kalām 'Ābir' [those passing in passing words].[5] In this poem, which appeared early in the intifāḍa, Darwīsh depicts Israeli and Palestinian societies. There is perhaps no Palestinian writer more interesting who writes about Israeli society than Darwīsh, who was born in Israel and lived there for a good part of his life. Darwīsh's views about Israelis and Palestinians are not just the voice of an individual, but reflect the collective view of the other, of those who comprise a major portion in the equation of the two political and cultural communities locked in struggle with each other. Without entering a superfluous debate of 'what the poet meant', let us briefly examine the characteristics of Israelis and Jews as presented there. The title itself – 'those passing in passing words' – already attests to the poet's viewpoint. These words underscore the impermanence of Israeli society, an entity that will pass with time because it is foreign and exists by virtue of power and technology, while the Arabs form part of the natural terrain of Palestinian land. Emphasis is placed on transience in time and space. The words 'those passing' not only open the poem, but introduce each of the four stanzas, serving as a leitmotif. Thus the poet depicts Israeli society as one in constant transition, one that does not excel at staying in one place. The verb 'leave' recurs no fewer than eight times in Darwīsh's poem. And there is a clear distinction between them, the Israelis, and us, the Palestinians:

> From you the sword – and from us our blood
> from you steel and fire – and from us our flesh
> from you another tank – and from us a stone
> from you a hand grenade – and from us the rain.[6]

Darwīsh captures well the sense of the Palestinian collective in his recurring refrain of the temporary sojourn of Israelis on Palestinian soil. And counterpoised to the transience and impermanence that characterize Jewish-Israeli society – the lot of all foreign conquerors of Palestine – is the steadfastness of the Palestinians, their clinging to the land. It is Palestinian land, according to Darwīsh, and thus he concludes that the Israelis will never be bound to this land or to the Palestinians, not in their lives nor in their deaths:

> Live wherever you like, but not among us
> the time has come to leave
> and die wherever you like, but don't die among us
> . . . and get out of our land.[7]

Darwīsh notes both the link of the Palestinians to their land and also the absence of Jewish ties not only to the region but to nature at all. He thus intensifies the image of the Jew wandering from place to place, one who took control of land not his by force of arms. This description is diametrically opposed to the Palestinians who are not power driven, but are at one with their land; hence it is no wonder that in addition to their past and present, they also have a future.

Sometimes comparisons are drawn between the behaviour of Israeli and Nazi soldiers.[8] One of the most striking examples of this appears in the poem 'Risāla ilā Jundī Isrā'īlī' [letter to an Israeli soldier] by al-Mutawakkil Ṭāha, chair of the Association of Palestinian Writers in the Territories:

Years ago you bent under the whips of Dachau
your father died in Warsaw
you wept for your sister broiled in the purgatory of Auschwitz
have you forgotten?
how is it that you have made me an Auschwitz in the desert
and how banished the husbands
and burned the sons
have you forgotten?? or does it just seem to you that the world
always proceeds backwards?![9]

Yet there are Palestinian writers whose attitude to Jews in the context of the Holocaust is totally different. They treat Jews as those who suffered from the Nazis and have now reached a safe haven, demanding that the Jews understand the plight of the Palestinians and accept their right to their own state.[10]

From the opposing camp, use made by Israeli Jews of the Holocaust and Nazism in the context of the intifāḍa and in comparison with it is particularly harsh. The frequency that this subject comes up, again and again, can testify to its centrality in the collective consciousness of Israeli society. Yossi, a soldier serving in Gaza, defines it well: 'Damn it, we're Jews who went through the Holocaust, and now we're starting – excuse me for saying this – but we're starting to re-enact it! . . . I mean it, just so.'[11] The positive side of Israel is also presented, though in smaller doses at the beginning of the intifāḍa. By the third year, however, references increase to Israelis not as a monolithic bloc, but as a multifarious society. Perhaps this stems from the Palestinian desire to maximize the political fruits of their struggle through the intifāḍa. Another possible reason is the declaration by the PLO in November 1988 of the establishment of a Palestinian state. Evidence of greater moderation can be found in both political and literary writing by Palestinians. As of the third year, even Israeli soldiers are no longer depicted as just monsters, but as human beings who do their work according to the rules, with little emotional involvement.[12] Jamāl Bannūra, a prominent Palestinian writer from the West Bank, depicts the human side of an Israeli in 'al-Junūd Yabkūna Ayḍan' [soldiers also cry], the story of a soldier who does not lose his humanity while dealing with a demonstration of Palestinian youth:

'Are you crying?!!'
He hid his tears and said, 'I can't watch a child being hit.'
'How can you have sympathy for these people?'
He nodded his head, looked the other soldier in the eye and said, 'I just thought of my own children. I wish I could see them right now!'[13]

In the context of Palestinian differentiation of various kinds of Israelis, some Palestinian writers have engaged in dialogue with Israeli-Jewish writers, searching out the human face of the conflict. For example, the poet Maḥmūd al-Yūsuf directly addresses an Israeli writer. His poem is called 'Ilā Dalya Rafikovitz' [to Dalia Ravikovitch] and, in a footnote, he explains that she is a progressive Hebrew poet. He writes:

> Perhaps you'll write about a labourer whose lover was killed and
> they laughed
> about a labourer who was burned alive, Dalia, and they laughed
> perhaps you'll write about us, and about me, oh Dalia
> about the child who was hanged in Jabaliya or Jenin and about the
> cross and the bullets . . . .[14]

This poet was not aware that – during that same period – a macabre poem appeared by Dalia Ravikovitch that bore the title 'HaSipur 'al Ha'Aravi SheMet BeSrayfa' [the story of the Arab who died by burning]. An excerpt:

> He caught fire at once
> this is no metaphor,
> it peeled his clothes,
> grabbed his flesh
> the nerves of his skin went first
> the hair became devoured by flame.[15]

The encounter between Hebrew literature written in Israel and Palestinian intifāḍa literature written primarily in the territories has great significance. In the first months of the intifāḍa, a large body of Hebrew writing appeared, especially poetry (Avidan, Amichai, Ravikovitch), written in a blunt and straightforward style. The second wave in the second year of the intifāḍa saw fewer works about the uprising, and most of these were prose. Examples are *Shahīd* [martyr] by Avi Valentin, *Agadot HaIntifāḍa* [tales of the intifāḍa] by Dror Green, and *Ta'atu'on* [illusion] by Yitzhak Ben-Ner.[16] These works are not among the finest Hebrew stories from the late 1980s. They appeal strongly to emotion and contain a spontaneous emotional response to the traumatic events, which they equate with the atrocities of the Holocaust.

In the third wave of Hebrew writing related to the intifāḍa in the early 1990s, attention to the uprising waned and became a backdrop to the collective and personal consciousness of the writers. This is evident in the novels *Mar Mani* [Mr Mani] by Abraham B. Yehoshua and *Otiyot*

HaShemesh Otiyot HaYare-aḥ [letters of the sun letters of the moon] by Itamar Levi, or in the book of poetry by Zvi Atzmon, *Me'urav Yerushalmi* [Jerusalem mixed grill].[17]

A small number of Palestinian writers can be found who acknowledge the right of Israel to a state of its own, but who also demand that Israelis acknowledge a reciprocal right for Palestinians. These writers propose establishment of a Palestinian state side-by-side with Israel in the hopes that recognition of these mutual rights will promote negotiations between Israel and the PLO on the establishment of a Palestinian state bordering the state of Israel.

Rājiḥ al-Salfītī, a Palestinian from the West Bank, directly addresses the Israeli collective in two poems. In the first, 'Naḥnu min Ḥaqqinā Dawla wa-Huwiyya' [we have a right to a state and an identity], the poet acknowledges Israelis as having suffered injustice from the Nazis and now reached still waters, noting that this should now apply to Palestinians. He proposes a Palestinian state alongside Israel. In the second poem, 'Ghayr al-Ḥaqq mā bi-Ṣiḥḥ' [it would only be the right thing], al-Salfītī calls upon Israelis to recognize the rights of the Palestinians, and invites both Rabin and Shamir (Minister of Defence and Prime Minister at the time, respectively) to negotiate with the PLO about a state alongside Israel: 'Come let us live eternally as neighbours, in friendship and mutual respect/with two states for you and for us, this calls for no explanation.'[18]

Parallels are drawn between the tragedy of the Palestinians, especially during the intifāḍa, and the tragedies of Israel on both the personal and the collective levels. A particularly moving example of this is 'Mawsim al-Uqḥuwān' [season of the camomile] by the Palestinian poet Samīr al-Rantīsī. This poem was written on the first anniversary of the incident of the settlers' outing near the Palestinian village of Beita, in which two villagers and a girl from one of the Jewish settlements were killed, followed by the demolition of several homes in the village as punishment. The poet mentions the names of those who featured in this tragic event – Romem Aldoubi, the guard who fired toward the villagers when they approached the settlers on the outing; Mūsā al-Bītāwī, the Palestinian villager who was killed by one of the bullets; his sister Munīra al-Bītāwī, who threw a stone as revenge on Aldoubi, who was shot and injured; and then the bullet fired by Aldoubi's gun that killed Tirza Porat, a girl on the outing. Rantīsī has the Palestinian victim, Mūsā al-Bītāwī, speak to the Israeli victim, Tirza Porat, in a tone that suggests a parallel between the two tragedies – the Palestinian and the Israeli – and presents the dead not as glorified heroes, but as victims of a cruel fate:

How many more ordinary mornings
will fill us with horror
and transform our day to another sky?
who chose us
to be the victim and the symbol
to be the beginning of the beginnings
the moment of historical trial
we, the two dreamers
the routine, the ordinary
who chose us
Tirza Porat
to be the heart of the conflict
and the crossroads of time
. . . I have never wanted to be
the headline of the conflict – of any conflict
I didn't even want to be a moment of explosion
the greatest of my dreams was Amīn and Munīra al-Bītāwī
who no longer has
a ceiling or a wall
. . . come back, ask
who is it who left the pickaxe
and made do with what time handed him
made do with collecting garbage
on the streets of Beit Shean
for a paltry wage
O Tirza of the bad luck!
why didn't you find someone besides me to be a symbol?
why didn't they find someone besides you to be a victim?
Tirza Porat
why could they only find Beita in the spring.[19]

Israelis in positive contexts appear infrequently, and not in the fiction. For example, there are photos of Israelis who oppose the continued occupation of the territories; a report in the 'Aṣdā' Adabiyya' column in *al-Kātib* about the raising of the Palestinian issue in the Berlin festival, citing by name the participation of Israeli poets, several of whom condemned Israel's policies in the territories; a statement that Israeli (Jewish) artists have shown positive attitudes toward the Palestinian theatre; and the translation of an op-ed piece that had appeared in the Hebrew newspaper *Ha-aretz* asserting that the intifāḍa cannot be defeated and that the only solution is through political negotiation.[20]

THE RELIGIOUS CONFRONTATION BETWEEN ISLAM AND JUDAISM

Until now, we have examined the image of the Jew from political, military and human points of view. There is another significant aspect, especially during the period of the intifāḍa: the religious facet, which generally appears in the context of places holy to Islam and Christianity, especially Jerusalem, as examined in Chapter 6. Let it be said at the outset: non-Palestinian Arab writers who write about Jews and/or Israelis in the context of the struggle between Islam and Judaism do so in much harsher and more extreme terms than their Palestinian counterparts, who have a more secular ideology. Examples of this appear in the works of the Egyptian poet of Sudanese origin, Muḥammad al-Faitūrī, the Egyptian poet Sa'd Di'bis, the Syrian poet Farīd 'Aqīl, and the Kuwaiti poet Su'ād al-Ṣabāḥ.[21]

In her poem 'Simfoniyyat al-Arḍ', for example, Su'ād al-Ṣabāḥ presents the Arab–Israeli conflict as a religious conflict:

> Here our children . . .
> are rising up against the heritage of 'Ād and
> Thamūd [ancient peoples destroyed for their sins and heresy,
> according to the Koran]
> Here our children
> are killing Hebrew time
> throwing the Ten Commandments into the fire
> and refuting Jewish myths.[22]

The religious dimension of the Israeli–Palestinian conflict is emphasized not just by Arab writers who brandish their religiosity, such as the Egyptian poet Sa'd Di'bis, but even by Arab writers who declare themselves secular with socialist or communist leanings that are ostensibly in conflict with religion. In this part of the world, the political struggle between the Palestinian and the Israeli communities has on more than one occasion turned into a struggle between Islam and Judaism. Israeli soldiers are described as not just politically but primarily *religiously* aggressive. This is expressed most fiercely regarding Jerusalem.

In addition to its enormous political significance, the religious significance of Jerusalem finds clear voice in Palestinian literature during the intifāḍa, as noted in the next chapter. Strong evidence for this can be found in the immediate and forceful reactions of some Palestinian poets to the violent incident on the Temple Mount in October 1990 in which

17 Palestinians were killed and some 200 wounded. This tragic event penetrated the Palestinian collective consciousness as one of the pinnacles of national Palestinian martyrdom, together with traumatic historical events such as Dīr Yāsīn, Kafr Qibya, Kafr Qāsim, and the more recent slaughter at the Cave of the Patriarchs in Hebron. Muslim fear of 'conquest' of the Temple Mount by the Jews after the war of 1967 had already been stoked at the beginning of the century by Ḥājj Amīn al-Ḥusaynī. Confrontations, incidents and massacres that took place in Jerusalem since 1967 reinforced this feeling among Palestinians. It is sufficient to recall Michael Dennis Rohan, who set fire to the al-Aqṣā Mosque in August 1969; or Alan Harry Goodman, the American Jew who, in April 1982, entered the Temple Mount plaza disguised as an Israeli soldier and opened fire, killing two and wounding 68; or the attempt to blow up the mosques on the Temple Mount by members of the Lifta underground in January 1984.[23] Powerful reactions to these incidents appear in some works by the Israeli–Palestinian poet Maḥmūd Dusūqī, whose venomous tone against Jews and Zionists in religious issues merges with his passionate political stance on behalf of the Palestinian 'right of return'.[24]

In contemporary Arab writing, Jews and/or Israelis are often compared to the Crusaders, i.e., a foreign body that invaded the Middle East. The foreignness of Israel is perceived as Western, hence the terms of disparagement used against Israel, such as 'a Western wedge in the Middle East' and the like. The difficult straits during the intifāḍa led some Palestinian writers – as well as other Arab writers – to seek refuge in the glorious Muslim past.[25] This should not be surprising since, from the late 1970s, the process of growing Islamic fundamentalism has been linked to a return to more illustrious periods in Islamic history. Thus, there is an appeal to Arab and/or Muslim myths such as the twelfth-century victories of Ṣalāḥ al-Dīn al-Ayyūbī over the Crusaders and restoration of the glory of Islam.[26] Clearly the Zionist 'invasion' of Palestine, led by Europeans from a culture foreign to the region, was perceived by the indigenous Arabs as yet another fleeting version of the Crusaders. Evidence for this appears among many Palestinian writers, such as Maḥmūd Dasūqī in his Koranic poem 'Ṭayr Abābīl' [flocks of *abābīl*], the very title of which alludes to its strong connection with the Koran.[27] An excerpt:

> The Byzantines returned to al-Shām [Damascus] and all are asleep
> and the nation lives in futile imaginings
> and continues to hum without stop . . .
> salaam to Jerusalem . . .

salaam to Jerusalem . . .
and Jerusalem calls . . . the walls of Jerusalem call . . .
do you hear O hero of Islam
the Arabs are asleep
the Arabs are asleep . . .[28]

Later in the poem, al-Dasūqī underscores the transience of the Crusaders. Like other Palestinian-Arab writers, he emphasizes Muslim–Christian solidarity, which seems to contradict the enmity felt toward the Byzantines and the Christian Crusaders. This is a nationalist position, of course, that mediates the Christian–Muslim friction. Indeed, in discussions over the future of Jerusalem, Muslim religious leaders often stress that Christians are also free subjects in a Muslim country [*Ahl al-Dhimma*] of Islam.

At times the religious, nationalist and personal elements come together. For example, the Palestinian writer Ibrāhīm al-'Alam describes in his story 'al-Dhi'b' how a young girl who is raped by her Israeli employer recalls the ninth-century 'Abbāsīd Caliph al-Mu'taṣim, who took revenge on the Byzantines for the rape of a Muslim woman, and the words of 'Urwa Ibn al-Ward, a renowned and beneficent leader from the days of the *Jāhiliyya*, the pre-Islamic period, who speaks of the need to use force to regain what is lost to thieves. Thus her private justice merges with the general justice for her people.[29]

During the intifāḍa, as before, Palestinians viewed Jewish control over Palestine, and over Jerusalem in particular, as an occupation in every sense. They evince no willingness to compromise with the foreign conqueror, and almost none recognize the parallel claim of Jews to Jerusalem. Instances are rare in which the rights of Jews to Jerusalem are acknowledged, and these generally refer to rights regarding the Western Wall or some perfunctory sites in Jewish west Jerusalem. Expressions of religious reconciliation toward the Jews are the exception to the rule, such as the poems of the Israeli-Palestinian Edmūn Shiḥāda, a Christian who integrates religious Christian, Islamic and Jewish symbols into his poem 'Madīnat al-Salām wa'l Ālām' [city of peace and pains], which he concludes with a wish for peace:

And when we cross the ancient roads
in the joy of the white doves
in the song of the morning and the loss
and in the blueness of the dome of the sky
the incense holders will become intoxicated

and spread their incense fragrance
and from the flower gardens
the perfume smell of our Jerusalem will rise
and peace will be born.[30]

CONNECTIONS AND RELATIONS BETWEEN ISRAELIS AND PALESTINIANS

One of the common themes in Palestinian literature during the intifāḍa period, as well as before, is Jewish hatred and loathing for Arabs, or, in this case, for Palestinians. The subject of forced transfer of Arabs out of Israel occupies much attention and reflects ancient fears of Palestinian society, especially Israeli Arabs. Some Palestinian writers claim that the hatred of Arabs was not confined to the late Rabbi Meir Kahane and his flock, but is deeply rooted in broad segments of Israeli-Jewish society. One local writer who addresses this extensively is Riyāḍ Baydas from Shfaram, a small town in the Galilee. In 'al-Bu'ra' [the focus], one of his more outspoken stories, the author brings together three Jews and an Arab on a bus ride. The three Jews betray considerable ignorance about everything having to do with Palestinian-Arab society and are united in their hatred of the Arab – the 'Arabush' as they call him – not distinguishing between Israeli-Arabs and Arabs from the territories. Even Amos, who is more moderate than the others (Yossi and Nili), calls for transfer of the Arabs. Baydas has deliberately chosen a relatively moderate figure, a Holocaust survivor whose son had gone to jail rather than do army service in the occupied territories, in order to malign all Jews. Sarcasm is one of the techniques Baydas uses, as in this series of rhetorical questions asked by Amos: '. . . Have we attacked you? Have we stolen anything from you? Have we kicked you out? Have we taken over your property? Have we killed your sons? What have we done to you? For God's sake, tell me . . . .'[31]

In the fabric of relations between Palestinians and Israelis and/or Jews, contemporary Palestinian literature takes a complex view of the Jewish woman in Israeli society. In contrast with the Jewish or Israeli male in modern Palestinian literature, who often symbolizes the Jewish collective in Israel and therefore sometimes remains nameless, the attitude toward the Jewish woman in modern Palestinian literature is both personal and collective. Two categories of Jewish women come into contact with Palestinians: prostitutes or women in a personal, human relationship with a Palestinian.

With regard to prostitutes, Palestinian writers who wrote about these women during the intifāḍa were following in the footsteps of pre-intifāḍa Arab writers, Palestinians in particular, who depicted romantic ties between Jewish women and Arab men.[32] Arab writers may have approached this from the viewpoint of the collective honour of the woman [*'Irḍ*], which would explain the sparse attention they gave in the first half of the century to 'immoral' Muslim women or prostitutes. These writers preferred to describe 'immoral' Christian or Jewish women. It was not until the 1960s that major Muslim-Arab writers began to write about Muslim prostitutes.[33]

With regard to the second category – personal human relationships – Palestinian writers have described these between Palestinian men and Jewish women, relegating the political conflict to the background. One notable example is the story 'Bākiran, fī Had'at al-Ṣabāḥ' [early in the calm of the morning] by Riyāḍ Baydas. Here we witness a relationship between the narrator, Riyāḍ, who, together with his Arab girlfriend, rents a room from Rachel, the Jew. The story of Rachel, a Jewish immigrant from Iraq, captivates the narrator and undermines his relationship with his Arab girlfriend. Rachel, who does not know Hebrew well, nor is fluent in Arabic, is described as one who likes Arabs and is torn between both cultures, Jewish and Arab.[34]

As noted in this chapter, a situation of two political communities locked in violent struggle for over a century inevitably fosters the creation of a constellation of negative images, but also covert admiration of the rival, which is not manifested in *belles-lettres*, but expressed between the lines in political writing and in the privacy of one's home. The Palestinian–Israeli struggle, soaked in blood, with years of hostility and animosity, has fostered negative stereotypes of the Jew in Arab and particularly Palestinian literature, as well as negative clichés of the Arab and the Palestinian in contemporary Hebrew writing.

One can state with considerable certainty that at the beginning of the nationalist struggle between these two political entities, the Jew/Israeli was a key motif, but that literary preoccupation with the Jew decreased over the years, especially since 1967 in Palestinian-Israeli literature, as a result of the disintegration of borders and the renewal of ties among the three groupings of the Palestinian people.

The intifāḍa reversed this trend, just as it altered many areas of politics and literature. Since then, the level of interest in the Jewish Israeli has increased and again claims a significant place in Palestinian writing, as it does in the work of other Arab writers. The renewed interest in the

Jew/Israeli in literature of the intifāḍa period was a product of increased friction between the civilian Palestinian population and the Israeli ruling power and its representatives, especially the soldiers. It was inevitable that an encounter of this type would bring about greater absorption with the Jew, and not to the good.

NOTES

1. Risa Domb, *The Arab in Hebrew Prose, 1911–1948*, London, Vallentine Mitchell, 1982. Gila Ramras-Rauch, *The Arab in Israeli Literature*, Bloomington and Indianapolis, Indiana University Press, London, I.B. Tauris, 1989. Adir Cohen, *Panim Mekhu'arot BaMarah: Hishtakfut HaSikhsukh HaYehudi-'Aravi BeSifrut HaYeladim Ha'Ivrit*, Tel-Aviv, Reshafim, 1985. Ehud Ben-Ezer, *BeMoledet HaGa'agu'im HaMenugadim: Ha'Aravi BaSifrut Ha'Ivrit*, Tel-Aviv, Zmora-Bitan, 1992. Dan Oriyan, 'MeOyev LeMe'Ahev: Demut Ha'Aravi BaTe-atron HaYisraeli', *Bamah*, 122 (1990), pp. 5–21. Ghānim Maz'al, *al-Shakhṣiyya al-'Arabīyya fi al-Adab al-'Ibri al-Ḥadīth*, Acre, Dār al-Aswār, 1985.
2. Sasson Somekh, 'Batim Gevohim, Karim: Demut HaShakhen HaYehudi BeYetziratam Shel Sofrim 'Aravim MeḤaifa VehaGalil', *Mifgash*, 4–5 (winter 1986), pp. 21–5 (Hebrew). Maḥmūd 'Abbāsī, 'Demut HaYehudi BaSifrut Ha'Aravit BeYisrael', *Migvan*, 27 (June 1978), pp. 55–61. Muḥammad Jalāl Idrīs, *al-Shakhṣiyya al Yahūdiyya, Dirāsa Adabiyya Muqārana*, Cairo, 'Ayn li'l-Dirāsāt wa'l-Buḥūth al-Insāniyya al-Ijtimā'iyya, 1993. 'Ādil al-Usṭā, *al-Yahūd fi al-Adab al-Filasṭīnī bayna 1913–1987*, Jerusalem, Ittiḥād al-Kuttāb al-Filasṭīniyyīn fī al-Ḍaffa wa-Qiṭā' Ghazza, 1992. Evidence of the need to know the 'other' – the Jew and/or the Israeli – can be found in the space devoted to this subject in the first issue of two Palestinian periodicals published in 1995: *al-Ghirbāl*, Ramallah, 1995, pp. 5–15; and *Mashārif*, edited by Emile Ḥabībī, Haifa, 1995, pp. 13–50. In *Mashārif* it was continued in issue no. 2 (September 1995), pp. 13–46 and issue no. 4 (November 1995), pp. 15–28. See also Maḥmūd Ghanāyim, *al-Madār al-Ṣa'b, Riḥlat al-Qiṣṣa al-Filasṭīniyya fi Isrā'īl*, Kafr Qar', Dār al-Hudā, 1995, pp. 297–328.
3. Some examples: In Maḥmūd Shuqayr's story 'al-Umm', *al-Kātib*, 109 (May 1989), pp. 76–7, soldiers rip off the clothing of teenage girls. In Ibrāhīm al-'Alam's 'Fī Intiẓār Rizq', *al-Kātib*, 123 (July 1990), pp. 83–6, a young Israeli tries to rape a Palestinian girl who works in his parents' home. In 'Laylā' by Aḥmad Gharīb, *al-Kātib*, 124 (August 1990), pp. 87–8, Israeli secret servicemen drug a young woman, film her naked, and then attempt to extort information from her about an intifāḍa activist. In a story by Ibrāhīm al-'Alam, 'al-Dhi'b', *al-Kātib*, 128 (December 1990), pp. 80–2, an Israeli rapes a young Palestinian woman who works for him.
4. See 'Yawm Ghā'im' by Ḥalīma Jawhar, *al-Kātib*, 108 (April 1989), pp. 88–9 for a comparison of soldiers with snakes; in the poem 'Ajā al-Shaqiyy 'Alā Sha'bī Yughālibuhu', by 'Alī al-Jarīrī, *al-Kātib*, 108 (April 1989), p. 92: 'The city of Jerusalem is awake on the loins of night/and pursues the wolves in their lair'; in the poem 'Māta Ṣamtan' by 'Abd al-Qādir al-'Izza, *al-Kātib*, 111 (July 1989), p. 84: 'a fat monster whose name is Border Patrol'; in the story 'Liqā'' by Maḥmūd Shuqayr, *al-Kātib*, 112 (August 1989), pp. 79–80: pigs; in the story 'Ḥīṭān min Dam' by Zakī al-'Īla, *al-Kātib*, 119

(March 1990), pp. 95–8: a black bird with curved talons sniffing for blood and lapping it up intoxicatedly; in the story 'Jasad al-Shahīd' by al-'Alam, *al-Kātib*, 119 (March 1990), one of the young people says to the soldiers: 'they hide like cockroaches, but attack like wolves' (p. 92). Another youth requests of his friend, 'If I am killed, hide my body from them so they won't touch me, lest their impurity cling to me' (p. 93); in the story 'Riḥla ilā al-Madīna' by 'Umar Abū-'Iqāb, *al-Kātib*, 120 (April 1990), pp. 87–9: monsters, hangmen; in the story 'al-Zujāj al-Maksūr' by Ilhām Abū-Ghazāla, *al-Kātib*, 121 (May 1990), p. 85, the wave of immigration to Israel from the former Soviet Union is described as a swarm of locusts; in the story 'al-Dā'ira', by Samīr al-Rantīsī, *al-Kātib*, 121 (May 1990), pp. 87–8: the settler is called 'dog' by the youths; in the poem '30 Ayyār' by Mājid Abū-Ghūsh, *al-Kātib*, 123 (July 1990), p. 93: 'fangs of the conquerors'; in the story 'al-Dhi'b', by al-'Alam (ibid), the Jew is described as a predatory hawk and a wolf.

5. Maḥmūd Darwīsh, *'Ābirūn fī Kalām 'Ābir, Maqālāt Mukhtāra*, Casablanca, Dār Tūbqāl li'l-Nashr, 1991, pp. 41–3. For Israeli reactions to this poem and that of Darwīsh himself, see pp. 45–55. The Hebrew reader can find translations and responses to the poem in: Ido Disanchik, 'Shratzim VeḤarakim Me'ofefim', *Ma'ariv* (25 March 1988), p. 7; and Tom Segev, 'Kavanat HaMeshorer – Hemshekh', *Ha-aretz* (25 March 1988). For a deep and thorough analysis of this poem, see Angelika Neuwirth, 'Kulturelle Sprachbarrienen Zwischen Nachbarn', *Orient*, 3 (1988), pp. 440–66.
6. Darwīsh, *'Ābirūn*, p. 41.
7. Ibid., p. 43.
8. Jabr Jazmāwī, 'al-Saṭr al-Awwal min Kitāb al-Ḥubb', *al-Kātib*, 111 (July 1989), pp. 81–2; Ḥannā Abū-Ḥannā, 'Ṣabāḥ Yawm 'Ādī', *Qaṣā'id min Ḥadīqat al-Ṣubār*, Acre, Maṭba'at Abū-Raḥmūn, 1988, pp. 99–100.
9. Ami Elad [-Bouskila], 'Gam BeVatei HaKeleh Kotvim Sifrut', *Yediot Aḥaronot* (25 October 1991), p. 22.
10. Rājiḥ al-Salfītī, 'Naḥnu min Ḥaqqinā Dawla wa-Huwiyya', *al-Kātib*, 109 (May 1989), pp. 87–8.
11. Rolly Rosen and Ilana Hammerman, *Meshorerim Lo Yikhtevu Shirim*, Tel-Aviv, 'Am 'Oved, Proza Aḥeret, 1990, p. 33.
12. al-Rantīsī, 'al-Dā'ira', *al-Kātib*, 121 (May 1990), pp. 87–8. Nabīl 'Awda, 'Ḥijāra 'alā Jabīn al-Waṭan', *al-Kātib*, 119 (March 1990), pp. 99–102.
13. Jamāl Bannūra, *Ḥamām fī Sāḥat al-Dār*, Jerusalem, Ittiḥād al-Kuttāb al-Filasṭīniyyīn, 1990, pp. 63–4.
14. Elad [-Bouskila], *Gam Bevaki HaKeleh Kotvim Sifrnut; Yediot Aḥaronot*, p. 22.
15. Dalia Ravikovitch, 'Stones', *Ha-aretz* (19 April 1989). The translation into Arabic by Sihām Dāūd bore the same title. See Muḥammad 'Alī al-Yūsufī (ed.), *Abjadiyyat al-Ḥijāra*, Nicosia, Mu'assasat Bīsān li'l-Ṣiḥāfa wa'l-Nashr wa'l Tawzī', 1988, pp. 198–9.
16. Avi Valentin, *Shahīd*, Tel-Aviv, 'Am 'Oved, 1989; Dror Green, *Agadot HaIntifāḍa*, Jerusalem, Eikhut, 1989; Yitzhak Ben-Ner, *Ta'atu'on*, Jerusalem, Keter, Tsad HaTefer, 1990.
17. Avraham B. Yehoshua, *Mar Mani*, Tel-Aviv, HaKibbutz Hameuḥad, Hasifriya HaḤadasha, 1990; Zvi Atzmon, *Me'urav Yerushalmi*, Tel-Aviv, Sifriyat HaPo'alim, 1990; Itamar Levi, *Otiyot HaShemesh Otiyot HaYare-aḥ*, Jerusalem, Keter, Tsad HaTefer, 1991.
18. Rājiḥ al-Salfītī, 'Ghayr al-Ḥaqq mā bi-Ṣiḥḥ', *al-Kātib*, 109 (May 1989), p. 88.

19. Samīr al-Rantīsī, 'Mawsim al-Uqḥuwān', *al-Kātib*, 109 (May 1989), pp. 89–90.
20. In the inside back cover of *al-Kātib*, 114 (August 1989), there is a photograph in which, according to the caption, Israeli soldiers are prevented by 'peace movement activists' from reaching the Tekoa settlement, where they were asked to come. In *al-Kātib*, 123 (July 1990), p. 86, there is a photograph of a demonstration of 'Yesh Gvul' [there is a border] in which the demonstrators redraw the 'green line'. Also see *al-Kātib*, 115 (September 1989), pp. 92–3; an article about Palestinian theatre in *al-Kātib*, 117 (January 1990), p. 76; and *al-Kātib*, 122 (June 1990), p. 82.
21. *Abjadiyyat al-Ḥijāra*, pp. 113–14; Sa'd Di'bis, *Qaṣā'id li'l Islām wa'l-Quds*, Cairo, al-Markaz al-Islāmī li'l-Ṭibā'a, 1989, pp. 23–8; Su'ād al-Ṣabāḥ, 'Simfoniyyat al-Arḍ', *al-Kātib*, 95 (March 1989), pp. 91–2; Farīd 'Aqīl, *Filasṭīn al-Ḥijāra*, Damascus, Maṭba'at al-Kātib al-'Arabī, n.d., pp. 12, 44–6.
22. al-Ṣabāḥ, 'Simfoniyyat al-Arḍ', *al-Kātib*, 95 (March 1989), pp. 91–2.
23. Meron Benvenisti, *Conflicts and Contradiction*, New York, Villard Books, 1986. Ziad Abu-Amr, *Islamic Fundamentalism in the West Bank and Gaza*, Bloomington, Indiana University Press, 1994.
24. Maḥmūd Dusūqī, *Ṭayr Abābīl*, Taybe, Maṭba'at 'Umar Jibālī, 1988, pp. 18–19, 24–8.
25. 'Aṭāllāh Jabr, 'al-Farāsha', *Wahaj al-Fajar*, Nazareth, Rābiṭat al-Kuttāb wa'l–Udabā' al-Filasṭīniyyin fī Isrā'il, 1989, pp. 103–7. 'Aqīl, *Filasṭīn al-Ḥijāra*, pp. 12, 44–6. Di'bis, *Qaṣā'id li'l Islām*, p. 5.
26. Emmanuel Sivan, *Mytosim Politiyim 'Arviyim*, Tel-Aviv, 'Am 'Oved, 1988, pp. 85–120.
27. The title of the poem 'Ṭayr Abābīl' alludes to the Elephant surah in the Koran (*The Elephant*, 105), in which God punishes the 'elephant people' (the Yemenite army under their commander Abrahā) for planning to assault Mecca and destroy the shrine of the Ka'bah. God sent flocks of birds against them, who pelted them with burning clay-stones. In Islam this story is viewed as a metaphor for God's protection of the Arabs.
28. Dasūqī, 'Ṭayr Abābīl', pp. 18–19.
29. Ibrāhīm al-'Alam, 'al-Dhi'b', pp. 80–2.
30. *Kull al-'Arab* (9 July 1993), p. 22.
31. Riyāḍ Baydas, *Takhṭīṭāt Awwaliyya*, Casablanca, Dār Tūbqāl li'l-Nashr, 1988, p. 15. For a discussion of Riyāḍ Baydas and his work, see Ami Elad [-Bouskila], 'Bein 'Olamot Mesoragim: Riyāḍ Baydas VehaSipur Ha'Aravi HaKatzar BeYisrael', *HaMizraḥ HeḤadash*, 35 (1993), pp. 65–87.
32. Maḥmūd 'Abbāsī, 'Hitpatḥut HaRoman VehaSipur HaKatzar BaSifrut Ha'Aravit BaShanim 1948–1976', PhD thesis, Jerusalem, Hebrew University, 1983, p. 165. Shmuel Moreh, 'Demuto Shel HaYisraeli BaSifrut Ha'Aravit Me-az Kom HaMedinah', in *Sikhsukh 'Arav-Yisrael BeRe-i HaSifrut Ha'Aravit*, ed. Yehoshafat Harkabi, Yehoshua Porath and Shmuel Moreh, Jerusalem, Van Leer Institute, 1975, p. 48. Riyāḍ Baydas, 'Hadhayān', *al-Jadīd*, 11–12 (November–December 1989), pp. 80–1.
33. Striking examples of this can be found in work by the Egyptian writer Najīb Maḥfūẓ, for example, the figure of Nūr in his novel *al-Liṣṣ wa'l-Kilāb*, Cairo, Maktabat Miṣr, 1961.
34. *al-Jadīd* (January 1990), pp. 25–9.

6

The Holiness of a City
Jerusalem in the Literature of the Intifāḍa (1987–90)

In the previous two chapters, we examined Palestinian and non-Palestinian literature that appeared in the first three years of the intifāḍa, until the outbreak of the Gulf War. In Chapter 4, the periodical *al-Kātib* served as our prime source of information about what transpired during that period, especially in the three branches of Palestinian literature. We noted how, during the intifāḍa, new symbols were created and old ones revived in constructing the Palestinian ethos.

In this chapter, we trace the image of Jerusalem as it emerges from the Arabic literature of the intifāḍa years. Jerusalem was central to both Arab and Palestinian works, not just in the period preceding the intifāḍa, but from the end of the nineteenth century. The research of Dr 'Abdallāh 'Awaḍ al-Khabbāṣ has identified thousands of works of poetry, prose and plays published during the years 1900–84 in which Jerusalem was central.[1]

The works written under the shadow of the intifāḍa clearly communicate a sense of shock, pride and shame: shock aroused by the desperate situation of the Palestinians, which led to their revolt against the Israeli oppressor; pride from the participation in the war of stones by children, women and old people, and shame at the inadequacy of the Arab world, which did nothing to change the condition of the Palestinians, except utter slogans and empty phrases. The intifāḍa's impact on non-Palestinian Arab writers can be seen in a number of poems in the anthology *Abjadiyyat al-Ḥijāra* [alphabet of stone] (1988), edited by Muḥammad 'Alī al-Yūsufī[2] and in the collection by the well-known Syrian poet, Nizār Qabbānī (1923–98), *Thulāthiyyāt Aṭfāl al-Ḥijāra*, [trilogy of stone babies] (1988).[3]

THE RELIGIOUS–POLITICAL MEANING OF JERUSALEM

Jerusalem, or, in Arabic, *al-Quds* [the holy], has been a centre of religious and political significance since the beginning of Islam, as is clear from the specific literary genre known as *Faḍā'il al-Quds*, that is, 'Praises of Jerusalem'. This unique literary genre saw a revival after the conquest of Jerusalem by the Crusaders in 1099. Before this event Jerusalem was praised as were the other Islamic holy cities.

However, since the twelfth century the *'ulamā'* [the Islamic scholars] have repeatedly called for jihād and the liberation of Jerusalem from Christian occupation. Parallel to this, the literary genre 'Praises of Jerusalem' became very important in a growing literature that emphasized the holiness of Jerusalem in Islam. Thus, this special literary genre became famous in Arabic literature and religion.[4] Jerusalem's religious significance remained great despite Muḥammad's changing of the direction of prayer (the *qibla*) from Jerusalem to Mecca after he despaired of persuading the Medina Jews to join him. Today Jerusalem is still called *Ūlā al-Qiblatayn*, 'the first of the two directions of prayer'.[5] The Umayyad caliphs (661–750), as well as later rulers such as the Mameluks and Ottomans, renovated and constructed places sacred to Islam in Jerusalem, thus adding a political dimension to the historical and religious significance of the city.

Many towns are mentioned in the literature of the intifāḍa – Jaffa and Haifa are associated with the historical and political past, representing part of the collective Palestinian experience and Nablus, Jenin and Gaza are towns that play a distinct role in the heroic struggle of the intifāḍa period. Indeed a special place is reserved for Gaza since it was the first town to rise up against Israel. However, Jerusalem occupies the place of honour in the literature, particularly in poetry. As time passed, the priority accorded to Gaza has changed in favour of the West Bank and Jerusalem.

Jerusalem is reflected in the intifāḍa literature written in Israel and abroad as a religious, political, national and historical ethos. The Egyptian poet of Sudanese origin Muḥammad al-Faitūrī (1930–) writes in his 'Shāhid 'Iyān' [eye-witness], written shortly after the beginning of the intifāḍa:

> You are not a child. Thus you were born in the Jewish time
> And sank down in dream before it
> Naked except for Jerusalem, and the olive tree of al-Aqṣā
> And the bell of the Holy Sepulchre.[6]

Not only does a political ideology emerge here, but also a religious stance. The use of the term 'the Jewish time' and not, for instance, 'the Israeli period', carries a religious rather than a national meaning. The religious sensibility expressed in this poem derives from the Islamic outlook on life. According to Islam, Jews and Christians are inferior to Muslims although they are accorded the name *ahl al-kitāb*, 'people of the book'. Living in Muslim countries, they enjoyed the protection of the Muslim citizens in return for paying the capital tax. Deep religious pain was felt by Muslims after June 1967 when the Jews became the new rulers not only of new parts of the Holy Land but also of the holy city. The message of the poem is that the Jew has taken everything from the Palestinian except Jerusalem and its religious symbols – the mosque of al-Aqṣā and the Church of the Holy Sepulchre.

In general in intifāḍa literature, whether Palestinian or otherwise, the religious element is mainly Islamic, though Christian symbols are occasionally introduced. Perhaps this reflects the fact that Palestinian-Muslim notables guarded the Christian holy places during the period of Muslim rule over Jerusalem. An anonymous Palestinian poet writing in the Anṣār-3 (Ketziot) detention camp in the Negev, also refers to the two religions in a poem called 'al-Quds': 'Her mosques weep and her churches lament.'[7]

Similarly, another Palestinian poet, Abū al-Fādī, writes in his 'Nahr al-Ḥajar' [river of stone] printed in the same collection: 'Our flags flutter over the churches and the mosques.'[8]

The West Bank poet Muḥammad Ḥunayḥan writes in 'li'l-Lajna al-Ātiya' [to the next conference]:

> Peace to you, my country
> Peace to you from every mosque
> From the Holy Sepulchre and from the Church of the Nativity.[9]

The poet al-Mutawakkil Ṭāha (chairman of the Writers' Association of the West Bank and the Gaza Strip), in a poem called 'God be with you', uses the Christian reference *Masīḥu al-Intifāḍa* [messiah of the intifāḍa].[10] Another Palestinian poet, 'Izz al-dīn al-Manāṣra (1946–) also uses Christian symbols, for example, 'Mary the African' or 'Mary of the Intifāḍa'.[11]

It might seem that such Christian references are evidence of interfaith cooperation. According to Islam, Jesus [*'Īsā* in Arabic] is one of the prophets though not the son of God. Politically, since the inception of the Arab national movement, both Muslims and the Christians have fought for independence. The Palestinian struggle is not exceptional in this regard, since there has long been a tradition of cooperation between Christians and Muslims except for the fundamental Islamic groups. However, a careful reading of works written during the intifāḍa, particularly those concerned with Jerusalem, shows that the examples cited above are in fact the exceptions in a heavily Islam-oriented literature.

The religious stance evident in the poem by Muḥammad al-Faitūrī emerges both before and during the intifāḍa period in many poems about Jerusalem composed by Palestinian and other Arab writers. This stance is associated with the ineluctable bond between the city and its glorious Arab, especially Islamic, past. Thus the word *qibla*, the direction of Muslim prayer, appears in various contexts where Jerusalem is described, and the religious sentiment linked to the events and legends drawn from Islamic tradition is exalted. A particularly conspicuous example of the Jerusalem of Islamic traditions is the motif of Muḥammad's nocturnal journey [*al-Isrā'*] to the outermost mosque – al-Aqṣā – on his legendary human-faced horse al-Burāq, and his ascent to heaven [*al-mi'rāj*]. This famous story only gradually became firmly associated with Jerusalem, other traditions assigning it to Mecca. The definite identification with Jerusalem probably dates to the time of 'Abd al-Malik.[12] Palestinian and non–Palestinian poets use this famous legend in various ways, especially in the context of the occupation of Jerusalem. For instance, 'Alī al-Jarīrī, who lives in Ramallah on the West Bank, writes in a poem called 'Ajā al-Shaqiyy 'Alā Sha'bī Yughālibuhu' [the mischievous one turned to attack my people]:

> And the city of Jerusalem . . .
> Is the first direction of prayer and none is worthier
> That in her the horses should be reined, O Arabs.[13]

In this poem and others, Palestinian and non-Palestinian alike, Jerusalem emerges as the embodiment of a unique religious ethos.

In intifāḍa literature no contradiction is expressed by either the Palestinian or the non-Palestinian poets between Islam and their ideological belief, though most of them are secular and politically 'left wing'. The word 'secular' must be used with caution because of the dominant role that Islamic history and tradition play in the life of a Muslim. Being Muslim (like being Jewish) transcends religion and entails a history, a tradition and cultural assumptions. One can be 'secular' in religious observance, but one cannot step outside one's history, community, or culture. These poets, therefore, do not hesitate to use Islamic religious symbols. (It is interesting to note that the same phenomenon holds true for Israeli writers, and for the same reason: the holiness of Jerusalem, its ethos, symbols and central historical importance for both religions, provide a vocabulary that resonates for the reader.) The writer of the above poem, a secular Palestinian, links the sacred past of Jerusalem with the future of the Palestinian people, and sees it as the capital of the future Palestinian state. The interrelation between faith and politics expressed in this poem, as in many others, is not surprising, for the two have been closely connected in the history and tradition of Islam from its beginning.[14]

Tawfīq Fayyāḍ (1939–), another secular Muslim, is an Israeli-Arab author and playwright who was expelled from Israel in 1974 and now lives in Tunis. In his writings he emphasizes the sanctity of Jerusalem and includes a religious dimension when dealing with the struggle for Palestine and Jerusalem. In the story 'al-Ṣabiyy Salāma' [the boy Salāma],[15] Fayyāḍ portrays the religious conflict between Islam and Judaism. Among the characters in the story are two Israeli soldiers, Ezer and Natan, who are serving in the Gaza Strip. Ezer tells Natan of his promise to his girlfriend Ruthie that, after Gaza is wiped off the face of the earth, he will take her to Egypt to see Aswan, the pyramids and the Nile. He will stand at the top of a pyramid and blow the shofar to the Lord of Hosts, the God of Israel, and will put out Pharaoh's eyes. As for the Holy City, 'I promised her that when Jerusalem gives up its soul, I will stand on the golden dome of the mosque and blow the shofar on Friday night, and smash the crescent on the dome.' Natan smiles at this, and asks 'And the silver dome of al-Aqṣā?' Ezer glowers angrily and only answers 'I shall set candlesticks there.'[16]

This rather ridiculous dialogue nonetheless conveys the writer's sense of the political and especially the religious, aggressiveness of Israelis and Jews. Because he lived in Israel, Fayyāḍ is able to use ancient Jewish religious symbols such as the shofar and candlesticks to indicate the connection between past and present in the Jewish tradition. The soldier not only flaunts his contempt and scorn for the Arabs and the symbols of the Egyptian past that have been under attack in Egypt since the Sadat regime (especially by Islamic thinkers opposing Pharaonic ideas). His violent words correlate politics, faith and fanatical nationalism with the God of Israel and with such messianic premonitions as the blowing of the shofar. The final expression of his attitude to the holiest places of Islam in Jerusalem is his determination to shatter the silver crescent and put candlesticks in its place. It is their perception of Jewish views that prompts the Palestinian poets to conclude that there is a need to strengthen Muslim religious symbols in Jerusalem.

The Egyptian poet Sa'd Di'bis takes the religious character of the struggle for Jerusalem during the intifāḍa to new heights. The title of his collection, *Qaṣā'id li'l-Islām wa'l-Quds* [odes to Islam and to Jerusalem],[17] indicates the tone of the work. Di'bis sees the struggle for control over Jerusalem not only as a national and political conflict between the Arabs and Israel, but primarily as a religious conflict between Muslims and Christians, on the one hand, and Jews, on the other. The book of odes contains two striking religious elements. One is the author's clear belief that Islam is the solution to all Muslim sufferings – such as seeing Jerusalem under Jewish rule. As Di'bis himself states, he is a religious poet, in contrast to the secular Palestinian and non-Palestinian poets cited so far. His perception of Islam as a solution to the problems of Muslims everywhere reflects the doctrine of new Islam radical movements such as the Muslim Brotherhood. This pan-Islamic outlook underlies his linkage of the Afghan guerrilla fighters, the *Mujāhidīn*, with the Muslim combatants in Lebanon and Palestine, including Jerusalem.

The second element in the writing of Di'bis is a sharp anti-Jewish attitude in which he seems to take pride. He traces this back to early Islam, when the Jews were accused of falsifying the Bible, paraphrasing this notion in modern terms. An example of this can be seen in his poem 'Innahum Yasrikūna al-Quds min *Mu'jam al-Buldān*' [they are stealing Jerusalem from the *Mu'jam al-Buldān*].[18] Here he harshly berates the Jews without actually naming them, claiming that they falsified dictionaries and stole the holy city of Jerusalem from the Muslims by misrepresenting the *Mu'jam al-Buldān* (the important geographical lexicon by Yāqūt, 1178–1229). The poet uses many derogatory epithets about those responsible for these deeds, calling them 'forgers', 'thieves', 'cattle', 'hangmen' and 'servants of Satan'. It is not surprising that he issues energetic calls for a jihād to rescue Jerusalem from the yoke of occupation.

In fact, extremist expressions of opposition to Israel and the Jews, and of ardent support for the intifāḍa, appear chiefly in works by non-Palestinians. There are several possible reasons for this: Arab and Islamic solidarity with the Palestinians, the need of the Arab world to pay lip-service to the Palestinians, and the confidence in the early stages of the intifāḍa that the uprising would succeed in paving the way for an independent Palestinian state. The non-Palestinians wanted to share in both the most difficult and the most joyous moments of the struggle. And perhaps the distance from the intifāḍa and the effect of media reporting, especially television, about what is happening to their fellow Arabs, played a role. The extreme religious and political views that Di'bis adopts are also expressed by Muḥammad al-Faitūrī in 'Shahīd 'Iyān', and by the Kuwaiti

Su'ād al-Ṣabāḥ (1942–) in her political poem 'Simfoniyyat al-Arḍ', referred to in Chapter 4, which was published shortly after the outbreak of the intifāḍa.[19]

THE HISTORICAL MYTH OF JERUSALEM

The religious aspect of Jerusalem as a central motif in intifāḍa literature is often accompanied by political and historical references to the glorious Islamic past. One can say that the worse the present situation – in spite of the hope that the intifāḍa will bring about radical change – the more use is made of the history of the famous commanders of the faithful who contributed to the construction and independence of Jerusalem. The period of Islamic glory began in the seventh century and was accompanied by a superior feeling of religious conquest, especially regarding the Jews who were not the military or political threat that the Christians were. The fact that the issue today concerns the position of one of the holiest places in Islam increases Muslim bitterness and prompts them even more to look to their glorious past. The historical, political and religious link between the present and the past was first forged in the *Jāhiliyya* (pre-Islamic period) with the heroic figure of 'Antara Ibn Shaddād (525–615), who was one of the great poets of his time. The link really took root, however, with the coming of Islam and the prophet Muḥammad. Writers use leading political, religious and military personalities associated with Jerusalem, for example, 'Umar Ibn al-Khaṭṭāb, the second Caliph (reigned 634–644), to whom Hārūn Hāshim Rashīd (1927–), a Palestinian now living in Tunis, dedicates a poem,[20] or the Umayyad Caliph, 'Umar Ibn 'Abd al-'Azīz (717–720), under whose leadership and that of the other Umayyad rulers Jerusalem underwent much renovation and construction, enjoying important political and religious status. Ibn 'Abd al-'Azīz, also known as 'Umar II, was celebrated for his fervent religious faith. References to him occur in a poem by Muḥammad Ḥunayḥan, 'Burāq al-Quds fī al-'Ulā' [Burāq, Jerusalem on the heights], written in September 1988, in the first year of the intifāḍa.[21] Other commanders also appear in the literature, for example, Khālid Ibn al-Walīd (d. 642), who won many victories over the Persians and Byzantines, and 'Amrū Ibn al-'Āṣ (574–664), who conquered Egypt. All these figure appear in Rashīd's poem to 'Umar Ibn al-Khaṭṭāb.

The most celebrated Muslim figure, who appears repeatedly in intifāḍa literature, as well as in pre-intifāḍa literature and the visual arts, particularly on Jerusalem, is the Ayubbid commander, Ṣalāḥ al-Dīn (1138–93).

Ṣalāḥ al-Dīn, one of the greatest Muslim generals (he was not an Arab), is a national symbol and an example to be emulated in times of crisis. Apart from his achievements in overcoming the Fatimids in Egypt and his conquest of Syria and parts of Iraq that had fallen into rebel hands, his supreme glory is his rout of the Crusaders at Hittin (1187) and his subsequent capture of Jerusalem. Moreover, he cleared Jerusalem of Christian symbols, removed the cross from the Dome of the Rock and cleaned the Temple Mount with rose water.

The parallel with the intifāḍa is clear: Jerusalem is occupied by a foreign power and must be cleansed by the Muslims. Since the establishment of the state of Israel, Jewish domination of Israel and Palestine has been compared in the Muslim-Arab world to the rule of the Crusaders, with Israel seen as a foreign body in the region. Accordingly, it is not surprising that the figure of Ṣalāḥ al-Dīn is used in various ways in comparison of the Muslim–Christian conflict in the Middle Ages with the modern antagonism between Israel and the Palestinians. Ṣalāḥ al-Dīn is perceived as a religious, military and political figure, who responded to the difficult situation of the Palestinians in Jerusalem and elsewhere. Moreover, he is the redeemer of the Muslim Palestinians. The yearning for him is expressed, for instance, in the story 'al-Farāsha' [the butterfly] by the Israeli-Arab writer 'Aṭāllāh Jabr,[22] in a collection of poems by the Syrian Farīd 'Aqīl, *Filasṭīn al-Ḥijāra* [Palestine of stones], and by Sa'd Di'bis in the introduction to his *Qaṣā'id li'l-Islām wa'l-Quds*, which he dedicates to the Palestinian child who restored the heroism of Ṣalāḥ al-Dīn to the Arabs.[23]

A much-admired modern figure is that of Abū-Jihād, who, until his assassination in Tunis in 1988, was second-in-command to PLO leader Yasser Arafat. Hārūn Hāshim Rashīd, in a poem called 'Lan Naqbal al-'Azā'' [No, we will not be comforted],[24] written in May 1988, 40 days after Abū-Jihād's death, says that his pure soul is in Jerusalem, on the dome of al-Aqṣā, calling to the brave at heart. Here a connection is made between the Palestinian poet living in Tunis, where Abū-Jihād was killed, and a central figure in the Palestinian liberation movement and the intifāḍa. This figure is raised to the level of a military, political and national myth, who continues to act after death as a symbol and model for Palestinians fighting in Jerusalem for independence.

Another interesting aspect of intifāḍa literature is the use made of the name 'al-Quds' and its variants. A frequent expression or combination is *Quds al-Aqdās*, the holy of holies. This usage occurs in the poem by Sa'd Di'bis 'Waṭan al-Muslim' [land of the Muslim], and in one of the earliest poems of the intifāḍa by the Bethlehem poet Jamīl Mukaḥḥal, 'al-Quds fī al-Bāl' [Jerusalem in my mind].[25] Other versions are *al-ḥajar al-muqaddas* [the sanctified stone], or *al-ghaḍab al muqaddas* [the holy rage], as in the poem 'Ḥijārat al-Ghaḍab al-Muqaddas' [stones of holy rage] by 'Ādil a-Ra'īfī.[26]

JERUSALEM AS A SYMBOL OF THE BELOVED

Apart from its importance as a political and religious centre, Jerusalem is also portrayed as a symbol of love, both personal and collective. In one of the most striking poems written about Jerusalem in the intifāḍa period, 'al-Quds', the Ramallah poet Mājid Abū-Ghūsh[27] speaks of the bond of blood between himself and the city. He portrays himself as a lover, and his beloved as having both a spiritual, heavenly character as well as an earthly one. Their relationship is described in human terms, the jealous poet spending his nights under her window to prevent her from meeting anyone else:

> My beloved
> Hiding place of my insignificant dreams
> I spent the night below your window
> And how many lovers wait for redemption
> At your door!
> Will you admit anyone but myself
> To your miḥrāb?
> I am sure that you will not
> Will you place your hand
> In any other man's hand?
> I am sure that you will not
> Will you listen to anything but my song and my 'ūd playing?
> I am sure that you will not.[28]

Notwithstanding the personal aspect of the poem, its religious and political levels are manifest. Here, the *miḥrāb*, the niche in the wall of every mosque indicating the *qibla*, is also a sexual symbol, linked with the poet's choice of Jerusalem his beloved as the capital of the future state of Palestine. Not only is the interweaving of faith and politics that has been part of Islam from the first, expressed in the intifāḍa literature, but even the most passionate personal love poem can carry a religious and political message. This poem concludes on an optimistic note: 'Wa'Inna al-shams la tushriqu illā li tulqiya al-salām' [the sun only shines to bless us with peace].[29]

In this chapter we have seen that Jerusalem as a symbol and a religious, political and national ethos can also be treated as a beloved, based on its historical importance as a holy place of Islam. All this has long existed in Arabic literature, but the intifāḍa has quickened and heightened the perception of Jerusalem as being at the forefront of the uprising. Palestinian and other authors praise and glorify the city, continuing the Islamic tradition of 'Praises of Jerusalem', and bestow upon it a modern political and religious status.

This kind of writing is found more in poetry, as the traditional Arabic genre, than in prose. Other genres are Western, not Arab, in origin. Thus, poetry is dominant and has more influence on Arabic readers. Intifāḍa poetry is written in classical rather than colloquial Arabic, unlike the popular poems composed to be read before audiences in public places or recorded on cassette. Both written and oral poetry are fine examples of rhetoric and both are forms of propaganda, the former composed for the intellectual, the latter for the ordinary citizen.

Intifāḍa literature in general, and particularly that about Jerusalem, plays a role in constructing a history for Palestine as a state with Jerusalem as its capital. This literature is also used for revolutionary purposes, the primary aim being to bring about the establishment of a Palestinian state. Intifāḍa literature, especially that dealing with Jerusalem, has its roots in pre-Islamic history and, more importantly, in later Islamic times as well.

Despite these trends, Jerusalem does not appear in literature as often as might be expected. It is not the only city mentioned in intifāḍa literature, although of course it is the most important. It has historical, religious, political and personal status, in contrast to places like Jaffa, Haifa, Acre, Jenin and Nablus, which have all but the religious status. The repeated references to Jerusalem are particularly interesting since, as has been said, most Palestinian writers are secular (with the aforementioned reservations about use of this term). However, the intifāḍa literature that deals with Jerusalem presents a unified stance concerning Palestine as a whole, in contrast to other intifāḍa writing which distinguishes between Palestine within the Green Line (i.e., within the state of Israel) and Palestine outside it. Thus as regards Jerusalem, there is no separation between the three groups of Palestinians: authors in Israel, such as Jamāl Q'awār; diaspora authors, such as Hārūn Hāshim Rashīd; and most of all authors in the West Bank and the Gaza Strip – all write about Jerusalem under the intifāḍa.

Jerusalem as a central, national–religious symbol for the Palestinians is a unifying symbol which emphasizes its importance for the entire people.

Despite the common reverence all groups of authors hold for Jerusalem, the non-Palestinian writers go to much greater political and religious extremes than their Palestinian colleagues. If Jews or Israelis make an appearance in intifāḍa literature, the picture that emerges is uncomplimentary, that of soldiers and rulers dealing roughly with the Palestinian population and holding on to the Holy City by force.

The special situation of Jerusalem under Israeli rule encourages writers to look to better times and return to past eras: the distant pre-Islamic past, especially the Golden Age of Islam. As has been said, the most important figure authors turn to is Ṣalāḥ al-Dīn, as the supreme political and religious model, and as a symbol of the liberation of Jerusalem. At the same time the great commander is known to have signed a treaty with the Crusader enemy.

NOTES

1. 'Abdallāh 'Awaḍ al-Khabbāṣ, 'al-Quds fī al-Adab al-'Arabī al-Ḥadīth, in *al-Quds Miftāḥ al-Salām*, 2nd edn., Tunis, Maktab al-Shu'ūn al-Fikriyya wa'l–Dirāsāt, 1993, pp. 44–5. Fārūq Mawāsī, *al-Quds fī al-Shi'r al-Filasṭīnī al-Ḥadīth*, Nazareth, Manshūrāt Mawāqif (3), 1996.
2. Muḥammad 'Alī al-Yūsufī, *Abjadiyyat al-Ḥijāra*, Nicosia, 'Mu'assasat Bisān li'l-Ṣiḥāfa wa'l-Nashr wa'l Tawz'ī, Thaqāfat al-Intifāḍa, 1988.
3. Nizār Qabbānī, *Thulāthiyyāt Aṭfāl al-Ḥijāra*, 2nd edn., Beirut; Manshūrāt Nizār Qabbānī, 1990.
4. For more details see: G. von Grunebaum, 'The Sacred Character of Islamic Cities', Cairo; Mélanges Ṭāha Ḥusayn, 1942, pp. 25–37; Shlomo Dov Goitein, 'The Sanctity of Jerusalem and the Palestinians in Early Islam' in *Studies in Islamic History and Institutions*, Leiden; E.J. Brill, 1966, pp. 135–48; Heribert Busse, 'The Sanctity of Jerusalem in Islam', *Judaism*, XVII (1968), pp. 441–68; Emmanuel Sivan, 'The Beginning of *Faḍā'il al-Quds* Literature', *Israel Oriental Studies*, I (1971), pp. 263–71; Franz Rosenthal, *A History of Muslim Historiography*, 2nd edn., Leiden, E.J. Brill, 1968; Abū Bakr Muḥammad b. Aḥmad, in Isaac Hasson (ed.), *Faḍā'il al-Bayt al-Muqaddas*, Jerusalem, Hebrew University of Jerusalem, 1979; Isaac Hasson, 'Muslim Literature in Praise of Jerusalem: *Faḍā'il al-Bayt al-Maqdis*', *The Jerusalem Cathedra*, I (1981), pp. 168–84.
5. On this term, see *The Encyclopedia of Islam*, 2nd edn., Leiden, E.J. Brill, 1986, vol. V, pp. 82–8.
6. *Abjadiyyat al-Ḥijāra*, pp. 113–14. A poem by the same writer with the same title but different in content is included in the collection *Ibdā'āt al-Ḥajar*, Jerusalem, Ittiḥād al-Udabā' wa'l-Kuttāb al-Filasṭīniyyīn, 1989, Vol. II, pp. 127–9.
7. *Ibdā'āt al-Ḥajar*, Jerusalem, Ittiḥād al-Udabā' wa'l-Kuttāb al-Filasṭīniyyīn, 1988, vol. I, p. 17.

8. Ibid., p. 95.
9. *Ibdā'āt al-Ḥajar*, vol. II, p. 74.
10. Ibid., vol. I, p. 19.
11. al-Yūsufī, *Abjadiyyat al-Ḥijāra*, p. 123.
12. *The Encyclopedia of Islam*, 2nd edn, Leiden, E.J. Brill, vol. I, 1986, pp. 76–7.
13. *al-Kātib*, 108 (April 1989), p. 92.
14. Ibid.
15. *al-Kātib*, 110 (June 1989), p. 77–8.
16. Ibid., p. 77.
17. Sa'd Di'bis, *Qaṣā'id li'l-Islām wa'l-Quds*, Cairo, al-Markaz al-Islāmī li'l-Ṭibā'a, 1989.
18. Ibid., pp. 23–8.
19. *al-Kātib*, 95 (March 1988), pp. 91–2.
20. Hārūn Hāshim Rashīd, *Thawrat al-Ḥijāra*, Tunis, Dār al-'Ahd al-Jadīd li'l–Nashr, 1988, pp. 70–81.
21. *Ibdā'āt al-Ḥajar*, vol. I, pp. 36–43.
22. Rashīd, *Thawrat al-Ḥijāra*, pp. 70–81.
23. *Wahaj al-Intifāḍa*, Nazareth, Rābiṭat al-Kuttāb wa'l-Udabā' al-Filasṭīniyyin fī Isrā'īl, 1989, pp. 103–7; Farīd 'Aqīl, *Filasṭīn al-Ḥijāra*, Damascus, Maṭba'at al-Kātib al-'Arabī, n.d., pp. 12, 44–6; Di'bis, *Qaṣā'id li'l-Islām wa'l-Quds*, p. 5.
24. Rashīd, *Thawrat al-Ḥijāra*, pp. 82–93.
25. Di'bis, *Qaṣā'id li'l-Islām wa'l-Quds*, pp. 17–22; *al-Kātib*, 94 (February 1988), p. 94.
26. *Ibdā'āt al-Ḥajar*, vol. II, pp. 152–3.
27. *al-Kātib*, 125 (September 1990), pp. 93–4.
28. Ibid.
29. Ibid., p. 94.

Epilogue

In peace as in war, there is an inalienable bond between literature and the society that it reflects. The roots of modern Palestinian literature, like most modern Arabic literatures, reach back into the late nineteenth century. The struggle waged between Palestinian and Israeli societies have left their imprint on the literature of each. In the course of this study, four key dates have been defined as watersheds, three of which (1948, 1967, 1987) relate to wars between Israel and the Arabs, including the Palestinians, and a fourth relates to peace: the Declaration of Principles between Israel and the PLO (1993) and the peace agreement between Israel and Jordan (1994).

The present study was written between 1990 and 1996, the peace agreements still too fresh to allow perspective on the changes they wrought in Palestinian and Israeli societies. Just as the wars and the Palestinian uprising that began in 1987 were reflected in modern Palestinian literature, the changes in Palestinian society as a result of the peace agreements will undoubtedly find expression in Palestinian literature. It is still too early to expect the writing to reflect these fundamental changes, which will be manifest at a later stage. I would like to raise here three fundamental issues that are key to the complexity of Palestinian literature.

The first is the landscape of modern Palestinian literature, i.e., the kind of relationship that will develop between Israel and Palestinian society and/or the Palestinian political entity established by the peace agreements, and how it will be expressed in Palestinian literature. These relationships extend beyond the three branches of the Palestinian community, and concern the fabric of relations among Palestinian society, modern Arabic literatures and, to a lesser extent, world literature.

The second issue is the state of the various genres in modern Palestinian literature. This, too, is difficult to assess, since among the four common literary forms (novel, short story, poetry and plays), poetry has been the most outstanding, acknowledged for its quality and quantity. Modern Palestinian poetry unquestionably overshadows the other literary genres. This was true for modern Arabic literature in general until the late 1950s and early 1960s, when the short story began to win the prominence previously accorded to the poem. This does not mean that Arabic poetry has declined over the past 35 years; modern Arabic poetry still holds a warm place in the hearts of Arab readers. Since Arabic poetry, unlike other literary genres, was not an import from the West, it continues to bask in the glory of the magnificent classical Arabic poetry – that written during the *jāhiliyya* and then under Islam.

Regarding other Palestinian literary genres, plays are sparse and few would praise the existing works in this genre, unlike the short story and novella. The Palestinian short story has come a long way from the early short stories of the 1940s and 1950s the outstanding short stories of Ghassān Kanafānī and Samīra 'Azzām in the 1960s, and the more advanced stories in the past two decades, especially those of Emile Ḥabībī, Zakī Darwīsh, Yaḥyā Yakhluf, Liyāna Badr and Riyāḍ Baydas.

The novel is also not an outstanding genre in modern Palestinian literature. Rather than offer a comprehensive explanation for this phenomenon, two assumptions should perhaps be mentioned. The first relates to the fact that writing a good novel requires an expanse of time and a tradition of novel-writing, neither of which exists for most Palestinian writers. This is not to overlook the achievements of Emile Ḥabībī, Ghassān Kanafānī, Jabrā Ibrāhīm Jabrā and Ibrāhīm Naṣrallāh. Interestingly, recent years – especially since the 1960s – have spawned modern Arab novelists who are excellent by any criteria, to wit, Najīb Maḥfūẓ, Fatḥī Ghānim, 'Abd al-Ḥakīm Qāsim, Ibrāhīm 'Abd al-Majīd, al-Ṭayyib Ṣāliḥ, 'Abd al-Raḥman Munīf and Muḥammad Barrāda; and the list could go on. But while the modern Arabic novel has flourished in recent decades, this is not true for the novel of Palestinian literature. The second assumption is that in order to write a novel, some preconditions must be met, first and foremost, the existence of an independent nation. Just as we have noted that the 1960s were a decade of dramatic changes in the world of the Arabic short story, note also the transformation of various Arabic literatures in the 1940s and 1950s in the years when independence was achieved by most Arab states. One cannot overlook the link between the attainment of independence for these states and the development of their literature, especially the narrative genres, the novel in particular. These genres, which evolved in Western countries with a tradition of political independence of some sort, could develop and take root during the period of the struggle for independence. In contrast, during the late 1940s, Palestinian society underwent a dramatic crisis in its confrontation with the Jewish community: loss of its land in Mandatory Palestine leading to establishment of the state of Israel and hostile confrontation with a community in competition for the land called Palestine. Thus, in the 1940s and 1950s the Palestinian community underwent a process that was the direct opposite of that undergone by other Arab communities. At a time when other Arab communities were consolidating for the achievement of political independence, the Palestinian community was being split and separated. This process had additional repercussions: the Palestinian urban population shrank dramatically, while large portions of Palestinian society, especially inside Israel, became rural. And in a primarily rural population the processes of urbanization, industrialization, acquisition of education and the like are slow, and this was reflected in the literature itself. Thus we find that Palestinian literature, particularly the narrative genres, was not at its best in the 1950s. Some harbingers of change were evident with the revival of parts of the Palestinian community, especially inside Israel, as processes of modernization swept across Palestinian – and Jewish – society in Israel. These included urbanization, increased education and the establishment of publishing houses, newspapers and periodicals. All these together with a growing closeness to Jewish society that had adopted Western modernization patterns had a profound impact on the Palestinian-Arab community in Israel. As a result of accelerated Israelization and, on the other hand, difficulties with the other Palestinian communities, many changes took place, including the Palestinization of the Israeli Arabs and their brethren in the territories and in the various Palestinian diasporas. The gradual emergence of the Palestinian nation into a nationalist political community from the mid 1960s eventually led to its recognition of the need to establish a Palestinian entity. Thus, consolidation of all three branches of Palestinian society contributed to the flourishing of Palestinian literature in quantity and quality. To date, however, the Palestinian community has not yet won independence, either political or otherwise. This fact has significant impact on the pace of development of genres, particularly the novel.

Another reason for the delayed development of the novel, in comparison with other genres of modern Palestinian literature, such as poetry, seems to be related to the character of Palestinian society. This is a small nation whose living conditions differ from those of other Arab communities. It is a closed community, all of whose branches live abroad or under the rule of other Arab states or Israel, and even the birth pains of autonomy in parts of the West Bank and Gaza Strip have not placed these areas under their complete control. In such a closed society it is not easy to be creative in a lengthy and complex genre about the surrounding society, especially in a novel with direct or implied criticism of one's own community. Thus, political, social, cultural and religious conditions influence not just the theme but also the choice of genre. Perhaps this also explains the small number of female Palestinian writers, of whom the most prominent are Fadwā Ṭūqān, Samīra 'Azzām, Saḥar Khalīfa (1941–), Zulaykha Abū-Rīsha (1942–), Liyāna Badr (1952–), Sihām Dāūd (1952–) and Nidā Khūrī (1959–). This may also be one reason for the small number of Palestinian novels that exist today. Evidence in support of this hypothesis is publication of the novel *Arabeskot* in Hebrew: at the time he was writing, Anton Shammās could not write a novel critical of Arab society in Arabic. Shammās could criticize Israeli-Jewish society as much as he liked in either Hebrew or Arabic; there is a significant difference, however, between criticizing one's own culture and society in its own language, and criticizing that community in the language of the majority that is not that of the community, even if they are fluent in Hebrew. I believe that the only Palestinian writer who dared this in Arabic in Israel was Emile Ḥabībī. (I do not wish to address the question here of whether the works of Ḥabībī are novels *per se*, but in this context the reference is to his more lengthy literary works, which are of high quality and reflect a virtuoso use of Arabic.) Ḥabībī, in captivating style, has criticized and satirized Jewish society and its concerns over security. Of particular interest are his most recent works in which he lampoons not just Jewish society but also Arab society, Arab states and members of his own community – the Palestinians – in their own language and culture.

Finally we may say that contemporary Palestinian poetry holds a special place, its major poets having stature not just among Palestinians but in modern Arabic poetry at large and by international standards. This is especially true of the last 35 years, thanks to poets such as Maḥmūd Darwīsh, Jabrā Ibrāhīm Jabrā and others, testifying to the importance of this genre in modern Arabic and in Palestinian literature in particular. In poetry, the three Palestinian branches are on a par with each other, and this is also true of the few novels and plays in modern Palestinian literature. It is should also be noted that Palestinian writers living in Israel who had been branded as traitors by Arab states and by many Palestinian colleagues, and who were later crowned with laurel wreaths – only partially justified – and inappropriately referred to as writers of 'the literature of resistance' were those at the forefront of modern Palestinian literature in poetry as well as in prose. And yet some major prose writers such as Jabrā Ibrāhīm Jabrā, Ghassān Kanafānī and Emile Ḥabībī are evidence to the contrary . . . or the exceptions that prove the rule.

The role and status of Palestinian literature in time of war is clear. The question is, what will be the role of Palestinian writing in an era of peace, after the Palestinians have attained independence in a state or in an autonomous region, or some other variation. This is a fascinating question: only time will tell.

Bibliography

IN ARABIC

'Abd al-Ghaniyy, Muṣṭafā, *Naqd al-Dhāt fī al-Riwāya al-Filasṭīniyya*, Cairo, Sīnā li'l-Nashr, 1994.

'Abd al-Hādī, Fayḥā', *Ghassān Kanafānī, al-Riwāya wa'l-Qiṣṣa al-Qaṣīra*, Jerusalem, al-Jam'iyya al-Filasṭīniyya al-Akademiyya li'l-Shu'ūn al-Dawliyya, 1990.

Abū-'Amsha, 'Ādil (ed.), *Shi'r al-Intifāḍa*, Jerusalem, Ittiḥād al-Kuttāb al-Filasṭīniyyin fī al-Ḍaffa wa'l-Qiṭā', 1991.

Abū-'Awf, 'Abd al-Raḥmān, *al-Baḥth 'an Ṭarīq Jadīd li'l-Qiṣṣa al-Qaṣīra al-Miṣriyya, Dirāsa Naqdiyya*, Cairo, al-Hay'a al-Miṣriyya al-'Āmma li'l-Ta'līf wa'l-Nashr, 1971.

Abū Bakr, Walīd, *Aḥzān fī Rabi' al-Burtuqāl, Dirāsa fī Fann Samīra 'Azzām al-Qaṣaṣī*, 2nd edn., Acre, 1987 (1st edn, 1985).

Abū-Ḥannā, Ḥannā, *Qaṣā'id min Ḥadīqat al-Ṣubār*, Acre, Maṭba'at Abū Raḥmūn, 1988. 'al-Adab al-Filasṭīnī fī al-Arḍ al-Muḥtalla', *Adab wa-Naqd*, 65 (January 1990), pp. 11–102.

Aḥmad, Yūsuf Nāṣir, al-*Qaṣas al-Filasṭīnī al-Maktūb li'l-Aṭfāl 1975–1984*, Dā'irat al-Thaqāfa Munaẓẓamat al-Taḥrīr al-Filasṭīniyya, 1989 (place of publication unknown).

'Alayyān, Muḥammad Shiḥāda, *al-Jānib al-Ijtimā'ī fī al-Shi'r al-Filasṭīnī al-Ḥadīth*, Amman, Dār al-Fikr li'l-Nashr wa'l-Tawzī', 1987.

'Aqīl, Farīd, *Filasṭīn al-Ḥijāra*, Damascus, Maṭba'at al-Kātib al-'Arabī, n.d.

'Arāidī, Na'īm, *Qaṣā'id Karmiliyya fī al-'Ishq al-Baḥrī*, Shfaram, Dār al-Mashriq li'l-Tarjama wa'l-Ṭibā'a wa'l-Nashr, 1984.

'Arāidī, Na'īm, *Masīrat al-Ibdā', Dirāsāt Naqdiyya Taḥlīliyya fī al-Adab al-Filasṭīnī al-Mu'āṣir*, Haifa, Maktabat kul Shay', 1988.

'Arāidī, Na'īm, *Maḥaṭṭāt 'alā Ṭarīq al-Ibdā', Dirāsāt Naqdiyya fī al-Adab al-Filasṭīnī al-Mu'āṣir*, Haifa, Maktabat kull Shay', 1992.

al-As'ad, As'ad, *Layl al-Banafsaj*, Jerusalem, Ittiḥād al-Kuttāb al-Filasṭīniyyīn, 1989.

'Āshūr, Raḍwā, *al-Ṭarīq ilā al-Khayma al-Ukhrā, Dirāsa fī A'māl Ghassān Kanafānī*, Beirut, Dār al-Ādāb, 1977.
'Aṭiyya, Aḥmad Muḥammad, *al-Riwāya al-Siyāsiyya, Dirāsa Naqdiyya fī al-Riwāya al-Siyāsiyya al-'Arabīyya*, Cairo, Maktabat Madbūlī n.d. (1981).
'Aṭiyya, Aḥmad Muḥammad, *Ḥarb Uktūbir fī al-Adab al-'Arabī al-Ḥadīth*, Cairo, Dār al-Ma'ārif, Iqra' 480, 1982.
'Aṭiyya, Aḥmad Muḥammad, *Aṣwāt Jadīda fī al-Riwāya al-'Arabīyya*, Cairo, al-Hay'a al-Miṣriyya al-'Āmma li'l-Kitāb, 1987.
Avidan, David, *Idhā'a min Qamar Iṣṭinā'ī* (trans. Anton Shammās), Tel-Aviv, David Avidan the Thirtieth Century, 1982.
al-'Awfī, Najīb, *Muqārabat al-Wāqi' fī al-Qiṣṣa al-Qaṣīra al-Maghribiyya, min al-Ta'sīs ilā al-Tajnīs*, Beirut, Casablanca, al-Markaz al-Thaqāfī al-'Arabī, 1987.
al-'Awdāt, Ḥusayn, *al-Sīnimā wa'l-Qaḍiyya al-Filasṭīniyya*, Cairo, al-Ahālī li'l-Ṭibā'a wa'l-Nashr wa'l-Tawzī', 1987.
al-'Aẓm, Ṣādiq Jalāl, *al-Naqd al-Dhātī ba'd al-Hazīma*, Acre, Dār al-Jalīl li'l-Ṭibā'a wa'l-Nashr, 1969.
'Azzām, Muḥammad, *Ittijāhāt al-Qiṣṣa al-Mu'āṣira fī al-Maghrib, Dirāsa*, Damascus, Manshūrāt Ittiḥād al-Kuttāb al-'Arab, 1978.
'Azzām, Samīra, *al-Ẓill al-Kabīr*, Beirut, Dār al-'Awda, 1982.
Badr, 'Abd al-Muḥsin Ṭāha, *Ḥawla al-Adīb wa'l-Wāqi'*, 2nd edn, Cairo, Dār al-Ma'ārif, 1981.
Badr, Liyāna, *Shurfa 'alā al-Fākihānī*, 2nd edn, Jerusalem, Manshūrāt al-Waḥda, 1985.
Bala'āwī, Ḥakam, *al-Ḥājja Rashīda, Qiṣṣaṣ Filasṭīniyya*, Beirut and Nicosia, Dār al-Kalima li'l-Nashr, 1986.
Ba'labakkī, Laylā, *Anā Aḥyā*, Beirut, Dār Majallat Shi'r, 1958.
Bannūra, Jamāl, *Dirāsāt 'Arabīyya*, Acre, Dār al-Aswār, 1987.
Bannūra, Jamāl, *Ayyām lā Tunsā*, Jerusalem, Ittiḥād al-Kuttāb al-Filasṭīniyyīn, 1988.
Bannūra, Jamāl, *Ḥamām fī Sāḥat al-Dār, Majmū'at Qiṣṣaṣ*, Jerusalem, Ittiḥād al-Kuttāb al-Filasṭīniyyīn, 1990.
Barākis, Ghāzī Fū'ād, *Jubrān Khalīl Jubrān fī Dirāsa Taḥlīliyya Tarkībiyya l'Adabihi wa Rasmihi wa Shakhṣihi*, Beirut, Dār al-Kitāb al-Lubnānī, 1981.
Baydas, Riyāḍ, *al-Jū' wa'l-Jabal*, Jerusalem, Dār Ṣalāḥ al-Dīn, 1980.
Baydas, Riyāḍ, *al-Maslak, Majmū'at Qiṣaṣ Qaṣīra*, Jerusalem, Intermīdiyā, 1985.
Baydas, Riyāḍ, *al-Rīḥ, Majmū'at Qiṣaṣ*, Nicosia, Dār al-Ṣumūd al-'Arabī, 1987.
Baydas, Riyāḍ, *Takhṭīṭāt Awwaliyya*, Casablanca, Dār Tūbqāl li'l-Nashr, 1988.

Baydas, Riyāḍ, *Ṣawt Khāfit, Qiṣṣaṣ Qaṣīra*, Nicosia, Maṭbū'āt Faraḥ, 1990.

Baydas, Riyāḍ, *al-Hāmishī, Riwāya*, Jerusalem, Manshūrāt Ghassān Kanafānī, 1992.

Baydas, Riyāḍ, *al-Ṣafīr, Qiṣṣaṣ Qaṣīra*, Jerusalem, Intermīdiyā, 1992.

Baydas, Riyāḍ, *Filfil Ḥārr*, Beirut, Dār Ab'ād, 1992.

Baydas, Riyāḍ, *Bāṭ Būṭ*, Nazareth, Maktabat Samīr al-Ṣafadī, 1993.

Baydas, Riyāḍ, *Shubbāk Fān Gūkh al-Aṣfar*, Tarshīḥā, Manshūrāt Ikhwān Mikhwal, 1994.

Bayḍī, Aḥmad, *Ma'a Ghassān Kanafānī, bayna al-Manfā wa'l-Huwiyya wa'l-Ibdā'*, Casablanca, Dār al-Rashād al-Ḥadītha, 1986.

al-Bi'r al-Mashūra wa Qiṣas Ukhrā, Tel-Aviv, Dār al-Nashr al-'Arabī, 1969.

Bsīsū, 'Abd al-Raḥmān, *Istilhām al-Yanbū', al-Ma'thūrāt al-Sha'abiyya wa-Athāruhā fī al-Binā' al-Fannī li'l-Riwāya al-Filasṭīniyya*, Beirut, Mu'assasat Sanābil li'l-Nashr wa'l-Tawzī', 1983.

Būlus, Ḥabīb (ed.), *al-Qiṣṣa al-'Arabīyya al-Filasṭīniyya al-Maḥaliyya al-Qaṣīra, Anṭolojiyā*, Nazareth and Shfaram, al-Maṭba'a a-Sha'biyya, Dār al-Mashriq, 1987.

Dāghir, Sharbal, 'Arābesk Filasṭīniyya,' *al-Nāqid*, 2 (August 1988), pp. 74–5.

Darwīsh, Maḥmūd, *'Ābirūn fī Kalām 'Ābir, Maqālāt Mukhtāra*, Casablanca, Dār Tūbqāl li'l-Nashr, 1991.

Darwīsh, Maḥmūd, *Ḥiṣār liMadā'iḥ al-Baḥr*, Amman, al-Dār al-'Arabīyya li'l-Nashr wa'l-Tawzī', 1986.

Darwīsh, Maḥmūd, *Dhākira li'l-Nisyān*, 2nd edn, Jatt, Manshūrāt al-Yasār, 1987.

Darwīsh, Maḥmūd, *Dīwān Maḥmūd Darwīsh*, 12th edn, Beirut, Dār al-'Awda, 1987.

Darwīsh, Maḥmūd, *Arā Mā Urīd, Shi'r*, 2nd ed., Casablanca, Dār Tūbqāl li'l-Nashr, 1990.

Darwīsh, Maḥmūd, *Aḥada 'Ashara Kawkaban*, 2nd edn, Casablanca, 1993 (1st edn 1992).

Darwīsh, Maḥmūd, *Limādha Tarakta al-Ḥiṣān Waḥīdan*, London, Riyāḍ a-Rayyis li'l-Kitāb wa'l-Nashr, 1995.

Darwīsh, Maḥmūd and Samīḥ al-Qāsim, *al-Rasā'il*, Haifa, Dār Arābesk, 1989.

Darwīsh, Zakī, *Shitā' al-Ghurba' wa-Qiṣaṣ Ukhrā*, Jerusalem, Majallat al-Sharq, 1970.

Darwīsh, Zakī, *Aḥmad, Maḥmūd wa'l-Aakharūn*, 2nd edn, Nicosia, Mu'assasat Bīsān Press li'l-Ṣiḥāfa wa'l-Nashr, 1989.

Dasūqī, Maḥmūd, *Ṭayr Abābīl, Shi'r*, Taybe, Maṭba'at 'Umar Jibālī, 1988.

Dāūd, Sihām, *HāKadhā Ughannī, Shi'r*, Jerusalem, Manshūrāt Ṣalāḥ al-Dīn, 1979.

Di'bis, Sa'd, *Qaṣā'id li'l-Islām wa'l-Quds*, Cairo, al-Markaz al-Islāmī li'l-Ṭibā'a, 1989.

Elad-Bouskila, Ami, 'Infitaḥ wa Inghilāq al-Mujtama' al-Isrā'īlī fī al-Sharq al-Awsaṭ fī Zaman al-Salām', *Mashārif*, 10 (August 1997), pp. 35–43.

Elad-Bouskila, Ami (ed.) *Aḍwā' Dāniya, Mukhtārāt min al-Qiṣṣa al-'Arabīyya al-Ḥadītha*, Jerusalem, Akademon, 1991.

Fā'ūr, Yāsīn Aḥmad, *al-Thawra fī Shi'r Maḥmūd Darwīsh*, Sūsa/Tunis, Dār al-Ma'ārif li'l-Ṭibā'a wa'l-Nashr, 1989.

Fā'ūr, Yāsīn Aḥmad, *al-Sukhriyya fī Adab Emile Ḥabībī*, Sūsa/Tunis, Dār al-Ma'ārif li'l-Ṭibā'a wa'l-Nashr, 1993.

Ghanāyim, Maḥmūd, *Fī Mabnā al-Naṣṣ, Dirāsa fī Riwāyat Emile Ḥabībī al-Waqā'i' al-Gharība fī Ikhtifā' Sa'īd Abī al-Naḥs al-Mutashā'il*, Jatt, Manshūrāt al-Yasār, 1987.

Ghanāyim, Maḥmūd, *Tayyār al-wa'ii, fī al-Riwāya al-'Arabīyya al-Ḥadītha*, Beirut and Cairo, Dār al-Jīl, Dār al-Hudā, 1992.

Ghanāyim, Maḥmūd, *al-Madār al-Ṣa'b, Riḥlat al-Qiṣṣa al-Filasṭīniyya fī al-Isrā'īl*, Kafr Qar', Dār al-Hudā, 1995.

Ghānim, Fatḥī, *al-Jabal*, Cairo, Dār al-Hilāl, 1965 (1st edn, 1959).

al-Ghazzāwī, 'Izzat, *Naḥwa Ru'yā Naqdiyya Ḥadītha*, Jerusalem, Ittiḥād al-Kuttāb al-Filasṭīniyyin, 1989.

Haniyya, Akram, *Ṭuqūs li Yawm Ākhar*, Nicosia, Mu'assasat Bīsān Press li'l-Ṣiḥāfa wa'l-Nashr wa'l-Tawzī', 1986.

Ḥabībī, Emile, *Sudāsiyyat al-Ayyām al-Sitta wa-Qiṣaṣ Ukhrā*, Haifa, Maktabat al-Ittiḥād al-Ta'āwuniyya, n.d. (1st edn, 1969).

Ḥabībī, Emile, *al-Waqā'i' al-Gharība fī Ikhtifā' Sa'īd Abī al-Naḥs al-Mutashā'il*, 3rd edn, Jerusalem, Manshūrāt Ṣalāḥ al-Dīn, 1977 (1st edn, 1974).

Ḥabībī, Emile, *Ikhṭayya*, Nicosia, Mu'assasat Bīsān Press, 1985.

Ḥabībī, Emile, *Khurrāfiyyat Sarāyā bint al-Ghūl*, Haifa, Dār Arābesk, 1991.

Ḥabībī, Emile, 'Wa Ammā al-Ummahāt faYamkuthna fī al-Arḍ', *Mukhtārāt al-Qiṣṣa al-Qaṣīra fī 18 Baladan 'Arabiyyan*, Cairo, Markaz al-Ahrām li'l–Tarjama wa'l-Nashr, 1993, pp. 239–51.

al-Ḥakīm, Tawfīq, *Yawmiyyāt Nā'ib fī al-Aryāf*, Cairo, al-Dār al-Namūdhajiyya, n.d. (1st edn, 1937).

Ḥammash, 'Umar, *Azhār ilā Maqbarat al-Mukhayyam, Majmū'at Qaṣaṣiyya*, Jerusalem, Ittiḥād al-Kuttāb al-Filasṭīniyyīn, 1990.

al-Ḥusayn, Quṣayy, *al-Mawt wa'l Ḥayāt fī Shi'r al-Muqūwama*, Beirut, Dār al-Rā'id al-'Arabī, n.d.

Ḥusayn, Rāshid, *Ḥayyim Naḥmān Biyālīk, Nukhba min Shi'rihi wa-Nathrihi*, Jerusalem, Hebrew University, 1966.

Ḥusayn, Ṭāha, *al-Ayyām*, vol. 1, Cairo, Dār al-Ma'ārif, 1974 (1st edn, 1929).

al-Ḥusaynī, Isḥāq Mūsā, *Mudhakkirāt Dajāja*, 4th edn, Beirut, al-Ittiḥād al-'Āmm li'l-Kuttāb wa'l-Suḥufiyyīn al-Filasṭīniyyīn, 1981.

Ibdā'āt al-Ḥajar, *al-Kitāb al-Awwal*, Jerusalem, Ittiḥād al-Udabā' wa'l-Kuttāb al-Filasṭīniyyin, 1988.

Ibdā'āt al-Ḥajar, al-Kitāb al-Thānī, Jerusalem, Ittiḥād al-Udabā' wa'l-Kuttāb al-Filasṭīniyyin, 1988.

al-'Īd, Yumnā, *Taqniyyāt al-Sard al-Riwā'ī fi Ḍaw' al-Manhaj al-Bunyawī*, Beirut, Dār al-Fārābī, 1990.

Idrīs, Muḥammad Jalāl, al-Shakhṣiyya al-Yahūdiyya, Dirāsa Adabiyya Muqārana, Cairo, 'Ayn li'l-Dirāsāt wa'l-Buḥūth al-Insāniyya al-Ijtimā'iyya, 1993.

Idrīs, Suhayl, al-Ḥayy al-Lātīnī, 6th edn, Beirut, Dār al-Ādāb, 1973 (1st edn 1953).

Jabrā, Ibrāhīm Jabrā, *al-Majmū'a al-Shi'riyya al-Kāmila*, London, Riyāḍ al-Rayyis li'l-Kitāb wa'l-Nashr, 1990.

'Kalima fī al-Bidāya, Qiṣas Qaṣīra 'Arabiyya bi'l-'Ibriyya, Taḥiyya li'l-Mutarjimīn wa-li Dār al-Nashr', *al-Ittiḥād* (21 July 1989), p. 4.

Kanafānī, Ghassān, *Rijāl fī al-Shams*, 2nd edn, Beirut, Mu'assasat al-Abḥāth al-'Arabīyya, 1980 (1st edn, 1963).

Kanafānī, Ghassān, *al-Adab al-Filasṭīnī al-Muqāwim taḥt al-Iḥtilāl, 1948–1968*, 2nd edn, Beirut, Mu'assasat al-Abḥāth al-'Arabīyya, 1981 (1st edn, 1968).

Kanafānī, Ghassān, *Adab al-Muqāwama fī Filasṭīn al-Muḥtalla, 1948–1966*, 2nd edn, Beirut, Mu'assasat al-Abḥāth al-'Arabīyya, 1982 (1st edn, 1966).

Kanafānī, Ghassān, *Fī al-Adab al-Ṣahyūnī*, 2nd edn, Beirut, Mu'assasat al-Abḥāth al-'Arabīyya, 1982 (1st edn, 1966).

Kanafānī, Ghassān, *Mā Tabaqqā Lakum*, 3rd edn, Beirut, Mu'assasat al-Abḥāth al-'Arabīyya, 1983 (1st edn, 1966).

Kanafānī, Ghassān, *Arḍ al-Burtuqāl al-Ḥazīn*, 3rd edn, Beirut, Mu'assasat al-Abḥāth al-'Arabīyya, 1983 (1st edn, 1962).

Kanafānī, Ghassān, *'Ā'id ilā Ḥayfā*, 4th edn, Beirut, Mu'assasat al-Abḥāth al-'Arabīyya, 1987 (1st edn, 1969).

al-Khabbāṣ, 'Abdallāh 'Awaḍ, 'al-Quds fī al-Adab al-'Arabī al-Ḥadīth', in *al-Quds Miftāḥ al-Salām*, 2nd edn, Tunis, Maktab al-Shu'ūn al-Fikriyya wa'l–Dirāsāt, 1993, pp. 44–5.

Khaddāsh, Zayyād, 'Ṣūrat al-Yahūdī fī al-Naṣṣ al-Ibdā'i al-Maḥallī', *al-Ghirbāl*, 1 (February 1995), pp. 6–15.

Khalīfa, Khālid (ed.), *Filasṭīniyyūn 1948–1988*, Shfaram, Dār al-Mashriq li'l-Tarjama wa'l-Ṭibā'a wa'l-Nashr, 1988.

Khalīfa, Saḥar, *al-Ṣubbār*, Beirut, Dār al-Ādāb, n.d, (1st edn, 1976).

Khalīfa, Saḥar, *'Abbād al-Shams*, 3rd edn, Damascus, Dār al-Jalīl, 1984.

Khalīl, Khālida Sheikh, *al-Ramz fī Adab Ghassān Kanafānī al-Qaṣaṣī*, Nicosia, Sharq Press, 1989.
Khūrī, Eliās, *al-Dhākira al-Mafqūda, Dirāsāt Naqdiyya*, Beirut, Mu'assasat al-Abḥāth al-'Arabiyya, 1982.
Khūrī, Salīm, *al-Widā' al-Akhīr*, Tel-Aviv, Maṭba'at Dūkmā, 1961.
Lu'lu', 'Abd al-Wāḥid, 'Ṣūrat Jabrā fī Shabābihi, Shi'r bi'l Inklīziyya', *al-Nāqid*, 10 (April 1989), pp. 26–31.
Maḥfūẓ, Najīb, *al-Liṣṣ wa'l-Kilāb*, Cairo, Maktabat Miṣr, 1977 (1st edn, 1961).
Maḥmūd, Ḥusnī, *Emile Ḥabībī wa'l-Qiṣṣa al-Qaṣīra*, Zarqa, al-Wikāla al-'Arabīyya li'l-Tawzī' wa'l-Nashr, n.d.
Makkī, al-Ṭāhir Aḥmad, *al-Shi'r al-'Arabī al-Mu'āṣir, Rawā'iuhu wa-Madkhal li-Qirā'atihi*, 3rd edn, Cairo, Dār al-Ma'ārif, 1986 (1st edn, 1980).
Manṣūr, 'Aṭāllāh, *Wabaqiyat Samīra*, Tel-Aviv, Dār al-Nashr al-'Arabī, 1962.
Manṣūr, 'Aṭāllāh, "Arab Yaktubūn bil-'Ibriyya: al-Wuṣūl ilā al-Jār', *Bulletin of the Israeli Academic Centre in Cairo*, 16 (1992), pp. 63–6.
Maqāli': Qaṣā'id min Waḥy al-Intifāḍa, Jerusalem, Ittiḥād al-Kuttāb al-Filasṭīniyyīn fī al-Ḍaffa al-Gharbīyya wa-Qiṭā' Ghazza, 1988.
al-Maqāliḥ, 'Abd al-'Azīz, *Talāqī al-Aṭrāf, Qirā'a Ūlā fī Namādhij min al-Adab al-Maghribī al-Kabīr, al-Maghrib, al-Jazā'ir, Tūnis*, Beirut, Dār al-Tanwīr, 1987.
Maṣārwa, Riyāḍ, *al-Ṭifl al-Ḍā'i', Masraḥiyya*, Nazareth, 1982 (publisher unknown).
El-Masīrī, 'Abd al-Wahhāb, 'Naẓra 'alā al-Shi'r al-Filasṭīnī', *Fikr*, 17 (October 1985), pp. 173–89.
Mawāsī, Fārūq, *Mā Qabla al-ba'd, Shi'r*, Bāqa al-Gharbiyya, 1990 (publisher unknown).
Mawāsī, Fārūq, *Qubla ba'd al-Firāq, Shi'r*, Bāqa al-Gharbiyya, Maṭba'at Bāqa al-Gharbiyya, 1990.
Mawāsī, Fārūq, *al-Quds fī al-Shi'r al-Filasṭīnī al-Ḥadīth*, Nazareth, Manshūrāt Mawāqif (3), 1996.
Maz'al, Ghānim, *al-Shakhṣiyya al-'Arabīyya fī al-Adab al-'Ibrī al-Ḥadīth*, Acre, Dār al-Aswār, 1985.
Moreh, Shmuel, *al-Kutub al-'Arabīyya allatī Ṣadarat fī Isrā'īl (1948–1977)*, Haifa, Bet HaGefen, 1977.
Moreh, Shmuel, *al-Qiṣṣa al-Qaṣīra 'inda Yahūd al-'Irāq 1924–1978*, Jerusalem, Magnes Press, 1981.
Moreh, Shmuel and Maḥmūd 'Abbāsī, *Tarājim wa-Āthār fī al-Adab al-'Arabī fī Isrā'īl 1948–1986*, 3rd edn, Shfaram, Dār al-Mashriq li'l-Tarjama wa'l-Ṭibā'a wa'l-Nashr, 1987.
Munīf, 'Abd al-Raḥman, *al-Nihāyāt*, 3rd edn, Beirut, Dār al-Ādāb, 1982.

Murrār, Muṣṭafā, *al-Khayma al-Mathqūba waQiṣaṣ Ukhrā*, Tel-Aviv, Dār al-Nashr al-'Arabī, 1970.

Nabahānī, Subḥī, *Fī al-Adab al-Filasṭīnī, al-Bu'd al-Insānī fī Riwāyat al-Nakba*, Cairo, Dār al-Fikr li'l-Dirāsāt wa'l-Nashr wa'l-Tawzī', 1990.

Naffā', Muḥammad, 'Mudhakkirāt Lāji'', *al-Jadīd*, 1 (January 1965), pp. 37–40.

al-Naqqāsh, Rajā', *Udabā' Mu'āṣirūn*, Cairo, Maktabat al-Anglo al-Miṣriyya, 1968.

al-Naqqāsh, Rajā', *Maḥmūd Darwīsh, Shā'ir al-Arḍ al-Muḥtalla*, 2nd edn, Cairo, Dār al-Hilāl, 1971 (1st edn, 1969).

al-Nassāj, Sayyid Ḥāmid, *Bānūrāmā al-Riwāya al-'Arabiyya al-Ḥadītha*, Cairo, Dār al-Ma'ārif, 1980.

al-Nassāj, Sayyid Ḥāmid, *al-Adab al-'Arabī fī al-Maghrib al-Aqṣā*, Cairo, al-Hay'a al-Miṣriyya al-'Āmma li'l-Kitāb, 1985.

Nāṭūr, Salmān (ed.), *'Āda li'l-Riḥ, Majmū'a min al-Qiṣas al-'Ibriyya*, Tel-Aviv, Mifras, n.d.

Nāṭūr, Salmān, *Yamshūna 'alā al-Rīḥ*, Nazareth, Markaz Yāfā li'l-Abḥāth, 1991.

al-Nā'ūrī, 'Isā, *Adab al-Mahjar*, 3rd edn, Cairo, Dār al-Ma'ārif, 1977.

Nazzāl, Nāhida, *Fī Intiẓār al-Ḥulm*, Jerusalem, Ittiḥād al-Kuttāb al-Filasṭīniyyīn fī al-Arḍ al-Muḥtalla, 1989.

Qabbānī, Nizār, *Hawāmish 'alā Daftar al-Naksa, Qaṣīda Ṭawīla*, 3rd edn, Beirut, Nizār Qabbānī, 1968.

Qabbānī, Nizār, *Thulāthiyyat Aṭfāl al-Ḥijāra*, 2nd edn, Beirut, Manshūrāt Nizār Qabbānī, 1990 (1st edn 1988).

al-Qāḍī, Muḥammad, *al-Arḍ fī Shi'r al-Muqāwama al-Filasṭīniyya*, Libya-Tunis, al-Dār al-'Arabīyya li'l-Kitāb, 1982.

al-Qa'īd, Muḥammad Yūsuf, *Yaḥduth fī Miṣr al-Ān*, 2nd edn, Beirut, Dār Ibn Rushd, 1979.

Qāsim, 'Abd al-Sattār, *Ayyām fī Mu'taqal al-Naqab*, Jerusalem, Lajnat al-Difā' 'an al-Thaqāfa al-Waṭaniyya al-Filasṭīniyya, 1989.

al-Qāsim, Afnān, *al-'Ajūz*, Baghdad, Wizārat al-I'lām wa'Ittiḥād al-Kuttāb wa'l-Ṣuḥufiyyīn al-Filasṭīniyyīn, 1974.

al-Qāsim, Afnān, *Mas'alat al-Shi'r wa'l-Malḥama al-Darwīshiyya fī Madīḥ al-Ẓill al-'Ālī, Dirāsa Sūsyū-Bunyawiyya*, Beirut, 'Ālam al-Kutub, 1987.

al-Qāsim, Afnān, *Umm al-Jamī'*, Beirut, 'Ālam al-Kutub, 1989.

al-Qāsim, Afnān, *Kutub wa'Asfār*, Cairo, al-Hay'a al-Miṣriyya al-'Āmma li'l-Kitāb, 1990.

al-Qāsim, Afnān, *Mūsā wa Juliet*, Casablanca, Dār Qurtuba li'l-Ṭibā'a wa'l-Nashr, 1991.

Qāsim, Muḥammad Khalīl, *al-Shamandūra*, Cairo, Dār al-Kitāb li'l-Ṭibā'a wa'l-Nashr, 1968.

al-Qāsim, Nabīh, *Dirāsāt fī al-Qiṣṣa al-Maḥalliyya*, Acre, Dār al-Aswār, 1979.

al-Qāsim, Nabīh, *Iḍā'a 'alā al-Shi'r al-Filasṭīnī al-Maḥallī*, Shfaram, Dār al-Mashriq li'l-Tarjama wa'l-Ṭibā'a wa'l-Nashr, 1987.

al-Qāsim, Nabīh, *al-Qiṣṣa al-Filasṭīniyya fī Muwājahat Ḥazīrān, Dirāsa Naqdiyya*, Shfaram, Dār al-Mashriq li'l-Tarjama wa'l-Ṭibā'a wa'l-Nashr, 1989.

al-Qāsim, Nabīh, *Ḥarakatunā al-Shi'riyya ilā Ayna?*, Kufr Qara', Dār al-Hudā, 1991.

al-Qāsim, Nabīh, *Dirāsāt fī al-Adab al-Filasṭīnī al-Maḥallī*, Acre, Dār al-Aswār, n.d.

al-Qāsim, Samīḥ (ed.), *Matāli' min Antolojiyya al-Sh'ir al-Filasṭīnī fī Alf 'Ām*, Haifa, Dār Arābesk, 1990.

al-Qāsim, Samīḥ, *al-Qaṣā'id*, Kafr Qara', Dār al-Hudā, 1991.

al-Qāsim, Samīḥ and Nazīh Khayr (ed. and trans.), *al-Dhākira al-Zarqā'*, Tel-Aviv, Mifras 1991.

al-Qawwāl, Anṭwān, *Jubrān Khalīl Jubrān*, Beirut, Dār Amwāj li'l-Ṭibā'a wa'l-Nashr, 1993.

27 Qiṣṣa Qaṣīra min al-Qaṣaṣ al-Filasṭīnī fī al-Manāṭiq al-Muḥtalla, Manshūrāt Āfāq, 1977 (place of publication unknown).

Rakībī, 'Abdallāh Khalīfa, *al-Qiṣṣa al-Qaṣīra fī al-Adab al-Jazā'irī al-Mu'āṣir*, Cairo, Dār al-Kitāb al-'Arabī li'l-Ṭibā'a wa'l-Nashr, 1969.

Rakībī, 'Abdallāh Khalīfa, *Filasṭīn fī al-Adab al-Jazā'irī al-Ḥadīth*, Damascus, Ṣabrā li'l-Ṭibā'a wa'l-Nashr, 1986.

Rashīd, Hārūn Hāshim, *Thawrat al-Ḥijāra*, Tunis, Dār al-'Ahd al-Jadīd li'l-Nashr, 1988.

Rashīd, Hārūn Hāshim, *al-Shi'r al-Muqātil fī al-Arḍ al-Muḥtalla*, Sidon-Beirut, al-Maktaba al-'Aṣriyya, n.d.

al-Rifā'ī, Jamāl Aḥmad, *Athar al-Thaqāfa al-'Ibriyya fī al-Shi'r al-Filasṭīnī al-Mu'āṣir: Dirāsa fī Shi'r Maḥmūd Darwīsh*, Cairo, Dār al-Thaqāfa al-Jadīda, 1994.

al-Sa'āfīn, Ibrāhīm, *Nash'at al-Riwāya wa'l-Masraḥiyya fī Filasṭīn ḥattā 'Ām 1948*, Amman, Dār al-Fikr li'l-Nashr wa'l-Tawzī', 1990.

al-Ṣabāḥ, Su'ād, 'Simfoniyyat al-Arḍ', *al-Kātib*, 95 (March 1988), pp. 91–2.

al-Sa'd, Jawdat, *al-Adab al-Ṣahyūnī al-Ḥadīth bayn al-Irth wa'l-Wāqi'*, Beirut, al-Mu'assasa al-'Arabiyya li'l-Dirāsāt wa'l-Nashr, 1981.

Ṣā'igh, Tawfīq, *Iḍā'a Jadīda 'alā Jubrān*, Beirut, al-Dār al-Sharqiyya li'l-Ṭibā'a wa'l-Nashr, 1966.

al-Salāwī, Muḥammad Adīb, *al-Shi'r al-Maghribī, Muqāraba Ta'rīkhiyya 1830–1960*, Casablanca, Ifrīqiyā al-Sharq, 1986.

Ṣāliḥ, Fakhrī, *al-Qiṣṣa al-Filasṭīniyya al-Qaṣīra fī al-Arāḍī al-Muḥtalla*, Beirut, Dār al-'Awda, 1982.

Ṣāliḥ, Fakhrī, *Fī al-Riwāya al-Filasṭīniyya*, Beirut, Mu'assasat Dār al-Kitāb al-Ḥadīth, 1985.

Ṣāliḥ, al-Ṭayyib, *Mawsim al-Hijra ilā al-Shamāl*, 2nd edn, Beirut, Dār al-'Awda, 1969 (1st edn, 1967).

Ṣāliḥ, al-Ṭayyib, *Dawmat wad Ḥāmid, Sab' Qiṣaṣ*, 3rd edn, Beirut, Dār al-'Awda, 1970 (1st edn 1967).

Ṣāliḥ, al-Ṭayyib, *'Urs al-Zayn*, 3rd edn, Beirut, Dār al-'Awda, 1977 (1st edn 1967).

al-Sawāfīrī, Kāmil, *al-Adab al-'Arabī al-Mu'āṣir fī Filasṭīn min Sanat 1860–1960*, Cairo, Dār al-Ma'ārif, 1979.

al-Sawāfīrī, Kāmil, *al-Shi'r al-'Arabī al-Ḥadīth fī Ma'sāt Filasṭīn min Sanat 1900 ilā Sanat 1960*, 2nd edn, Cairo, Maṭābi' Sijill al-'Arab, 1985 (1st edn, 1964).

Shāhīn, Aḥmad 'Umar and Warda al-Ṭawīl, *Tashābuk al-Judhūr, Dirāsa Wamukhtārāt 'an al-Shā'ir al-Isrā'īlī Yahūdā Amiḥāi*, Cairo, Dār Shuhdī li'l-Nashr, 1988.

Sha'ir, Fatḥī, *'Aṣāfīr al-Ḥijāra*, Cairo, Maktabat Madbūlī, 1991.

al-Shāmī, Rashād 'Abdallāh, *'Ajz al-Naṣr, al-Adab al-Isrā'īlī wa-Ḥarb 1967*, Cairo, Dār al-Fikr li'l-Dirāsāt wa'l-Nashr wa'l-Tawzī', 1990.

Shahrabāni, Na'īm, *al-Nizā' al-'Arabī al-Isrā'īlī, Biblīyūghrāfiyā Mashrūḥa liKutub waNashrāt 'Arabīyya*, 2nd edn, Jerusalem, Ma'had Trūman li'l-Dirāsāt al-Silmiyya, 1988.

Shammās, Anton, *Asīr Yaqẓatī wa Nawmī*, Jerusalem, Maṭba'at al-Sharq, 1974.

Shammās, Anton (ed.), *Ṣayd al-Ghazāla*, Shfaram, Dār al-Mashriq, 1984.

al-Sharqāwī, 'Abd al-Raḥmān, *al-Arḍ*, Cairo, 3rd edn, Dār al-Kitāb li'l-Ṭibā'a wa'l-Nashr, 1968 (1st edn, 1954).

Shiḥāda, Edmūn, *al-Ṭarīq ilā Bīr Zeit*, 2nd edn, Nicosia, Mu'assasat Bīsān li'l-Ṣiḥāfa wa'l-Nashr, 1989.

Shukrī, Ghālī, *Burj Bābil, al-Naqd wa'l-Ḥadātha al-Sharīda*, London, Riyāḍ a-Rayyis li'l-Kitāb wa'l-Nashr, 1989.

Ṣidqī, Najātī, *al-Akhawāt al-Ḥazīnāt, Qiṣaṣ*, 2nd edn, Beirut, al-Ittiḥād al-'Āmm li'l-Kuttāb wa'l-Ṣuḥufiyyīn al-Filasṭīniyyīn, 1981.

Somek, Ronni, *Yāsmīn, Qaṣā'id* (trans. Samīḥ al-Qāsim), Haifa, Maṭba'at al-Karma, 1995.

Suwaidān, Sāmī, *Abḥāth fī al-Naṣṣ al-Riwā'ī al-'Arabī*, Beirut, Mu'assasat al-Abḥāth al-'Arabīyya, 1986.

Ṭāha, Muḥammad 'Alī, *Salāman wa-Taḥiyya*, Acre, Dār al-Jalīl, 1969.

Ṭāha, al-Mutawakkil and Ibrāhīm Jawhar (eds), *Ba'd Alf Yawm min al-Intifāḍa, al-Thaqāfa wa'l Intifāḍa*, Jerusalem, Ittiḥād al-Kuttāb al-Filasṭīniyyīn fī al-Ḍaffa al-Gharbīyya wa-Qiṭā' Ghazza, n.d.

al-Tamīmī, Farīd al-Qā'ūd, *al-Wurūd, Shi'r*, Zarqa, Maktabat al-Qā'ūd al-Shāmila, 1992.

Ṭūqān, Fadwā, *Riḥla Jabaliyya, Riḥla Ṣa'ba, Sīra Dhātiyya*, 2nd edn, Amman, Dār al-Shurūq li'l-Nashr wa'l-Tawzī', 1985.

al-Usṭā, 'Ādil, *al-Qiṣṣa al-Qaṣīra fī al-Ḍaffa al-Gharbīyya wa-Qiṭā' Ghazza 1967–1981* (place, date, and year of publication unknown).

al-Usṭā, 'Ādil, *al-Yahūd fī al-Adab al-Filasṭīnī bayna 1913–1987*, Jerusalem, Ittiḥād al-Kuttāb al-Filasṭīniyyīn fī al-Ḍaffa wa-Qiṭā' Ghazza, 1992.

'Uthmān, I'tidāl, *Iḍā'āt al-Naṣṣ*, Beirut, Dār al-Ḥadātha, 1988.

Wādī, Fārūq, *Thalāth 'Allāmāt fī al-Riwāya al-Filasṭīniyya*, 2nd edn, Acre, Dār al-Aswār, 1985 (1st edn, 1981).

Wahaj al-Fajr: Min Adabiyyāt al-Intifāḍa, Nazareth, Rābiṭat al-Kuttāb wa'l-Udabā' al-Filasṭīniyyīn fī Isrā'īl, 1989.

al-Waraqī, al-Sa'īd, *Ittijāhāt al-Riwāya al-'Arabiyya al-Mu'āṣira*, Cairo, al-Hay'a al-Miṣriyya al-'Āmma li'l-Kitāb, 1982.

Watad, Muḥammad, *Zaghārīd al-Intifāḍa*, 2nd edn, Nicosia, Mu'assasat Bīsān li'l-Ṣiḥāfa wa'l-Nashr, 1989.

Yāghī, 'Abd al-Raḥmān, *Shi'r al-Arḍ al-Muḥtalla fī al-Sittīnāt, Dirāsa fī al-Maḍāmīn*, 2nd edn, Kuwait, Sharikat Kāẓima li'l-Nashr wa'l-Tarjama wa'l-Tawzī', 1982.

Yāghī, 'Abd al-Raḥmān, *Fī al-Adab al-Filasṭīnī al-Ḥadīth qabla al-Nakba wa-Ba'dahā*, Kuwait, Sharikat Kāẓima li'l-Nashr wa'l-Tarjama wa'l-Tawzī', 1983.

Yāghī, Hāshim, *Ḥarakat al-Naqd al-Adabī al-Ḥadīth fī Filasṭīn*, Cairo, Ma'had al-Buḥūth wa'l Dirāsāt al-'Arabiyya, 1973.

Yāghī, Hāshim, *al-Qiṣṣa al-Qaṣīra fī Filasṭīn wa'l Urdunn 1850–1965*, 2nd edn, Beirut, al-Mu'assasat al-'Arabiyya li'l-Dirāsāt wa'l Nashr, 1981 (1st edn, 1966).

Yāghī, Hāshim, *al-Shi'r al-Ḥadīth bayna al-Naẓar wa'l Taṭbīq*, Beirut, al-Mu'assasa al-'Arabiyya li'l-Dirāsāt wa'l Nashr, 1981.

al-Yūsuf, Yūsuf Sāmī, *Ghassān Kanafānī: Ri'shat al-Ma'sāt, Dirāsa*, Amman, Dār Manārāt li'l-Nashr, 1985.

al-Yūsufī, Muḥammad 'Alī, *Abjadiyyat al-Ḥijāra*, Nicosia, Mu'assasat Bīsān li'l-Ṣiḥāfa wa'l-Nashr wa'l Tawzī', 1988.

Ẓāhir, Nājī, *Majnūn Hind, Qiṣṣaṣ wa-Ḥikāyāt*, Nazareth and Shfaram, Manshūrāt al-Thaqāfa al-Taqaddumiyya, Dār al-Mashriq, 1987.

IN HEBREW

'Abbāsī, Maḥmūd, 'Hitpatḥut HaRoman VehaSipur HaKatzar BaSifrut Ha'Aravit BaShanim 1948–1976', PhD thesis Jerusalem, The Hebrew University, 1983.

Amir, Aharon, 'Ge'ūla VeHitbolelut', *Be-Eretz Yisrael* (October 1986), p. 9.

'Amit, Dalia, 'Milim SheMenasot Laga'at', an interview with Anton Shammās, 1988.

'Arāidī, Na'īm, *Eikh Efshar Le-Ehov*, Tel-Aviv, Traklin-'Eked, 1972.

'Arāidī, Na'īm, *Ḥemla U-Faḥad*, Tel-Aviv, 'Eked, 1975.

'Arāidī, Na'īm, *HaNozlim HaMenagnim BeYitzirat Uri Tzvi Greenberg*, Tel-Aviv, 'Eked, 1980.

'Arāidī, Na'īm, *Ḥazarti El Hakfar: Shirim*, Tel-Aviv, 'Am 'Oved, 1986.

'Arāidī, Na'īm, *Ḥayalim Shel Mayim*, Tel Aviv, Sifrei Ma'ariv and Sifrei HaKibbutz HaMeuḥad, HaSidra HaPetuḥa, 1988.

'Arāidī, Na'īm, *Ulai Zo Ahava*, Tel-Aviv, Ma'ariv, 1989.

'Arāidī, Na'īm, 'Sifrut 'Ivrit, Ma Na'amt', *Moznayim*, 65:4 (January 1991), 42–3.

'Arāidī, Na'īm, *BeḤamisha Memadim*, Tel-Aviv, Sifriyat HaPo'alim, 1991.

'Arāidī, Na'īm, *Tevila Katlanit*, Tel-Aviv, Bitan, 1992.

Atzmon, Zvi, *Me'urav Yerushalmi*, Tel-Aviv, Sifriyat HaPo'alim, 1991.

'Azzī, Asad, *LeMargelot HaGoral HaMar*, Haifa, Renaissance, 1976.

'Azzī, Asad, *'Onat HaLeḥishot*, Haifa, Renaissance, 1978.

'Azzī, Asad and Fāḍil 'Alī, *Shirei Reḥov*, Daliyat al-Karmil, Milim, 1979.

Balaban, Avraham, ''HaGal HeḤadish' Neged 'HaGal HeḤadash'', *Yediot Aḥaronot* (5 June 1992), pp. 34–5.

Balaban, Avraham, *Gal Aḥer BaSifrut Ha'Ivrit: Siporet 'Ivrit Postmodernistit*, Jerusalem, Keter, 1995.

Ballas, Shimon, *HaSifrut Ha'Aravit BeTsel HaMilḥama*, Tel-Aviv, 'Am 'Oved, Ofakim, 1978.

Ballas, Shimon (ed. and trans.), *Sipurim Palestinyim*, Tel-Aviv, 'Eked, 1970.

Baydas, Riyāḍ, 'HaMoked' (trans. Ami Elad [-Bouskila]), *Ma'ariv* (27 September 1992), pp. 27, 30.

Bechor, Guy, *Leksikon Ashaf: Ishim, Irgunim Ve-Iru'im*, Tel-Aviv, Ministry of Defence Publications, 1991.

Ben, Menaḥem, 'HaShalom HaMe-ayem 'Aleinu', *Yerushalayim* (28 October 1994).

Ben-Ezer, Ehud (ed.), *BeMoledet HaGa'agu'im HaMenugadim: Ha'Aravi BaSifrut Ha'Ivrit*, Tel Aviv, Zmora-Bitan, 1992.

Ben-Ner, Yitzhak, *Ta'atu'on*, 6th edn, Jerusalem, Keter, Tsad HaTefer, 1990.

Benvenisti, Meron, *Maḥol HaḤaradot, Intifāḍa, Milḥemet HaMifratz, Tahalikh HaShalom*, Jerusalem, Keter, Te'udat Zehut, 1992.

Bishara, 'Azmi, ''Al She'elat HaMi'ut HaPalestini BeYisrael', *Te-oriya U-Vikoret*, 3 (winter 1993), pp. 7–20.

Blau, Joshua, *Dikduk Ha'Aravit-Yehudit Shel Yemei HaBeinayim*, 2nd edn, Jerusalem, Magnes, 1979–80.

Cohen, Adir, *Panim Mekhu'arot BaMarah: Hishtakfut HaSikhsukh HaYehudi-'Aravi BeSifrut HaYeladim Ha'Ivrit*, Tel-Aviv, Reshafim, 1985.

Cohen, Ephi, *Ahava BeTsel HaIntifāḍa*, Tirat Carmel, Ashdat, 1990.

Darwīsh, Maḥmūd, *Zekher LaShikheḥa* (trans. Salmān Maṣālḥa), Tel-Aviv and Jerusalem, Schocken, 1989.

Darwīsh, Maḥmūd and Samīḥ al-Qāsim, *Bein Shnei Ḥatsa-ei HaTapuz* (trans. Hannah 'Amit-Kochavi), Tel-Aviv, Mifras, 1991.

Dāūd, Sihām, *Ani Ohevet BeDyo Levana*, Tel-Aviv, Sifriyat HaPo'alim, 1981.

Drori, Rina, *Reshit HaMaga'im Shel HaSifrut HaYehudit 'Im HaSifrut Ha'Aravit BaMe-ah Ha'Asirit*, Tel-Aviv, HaKibbutz HaMeuḥad and Tel-Aviv University, 1988.

Elad [-Bouskila], Ami (ed.), *Me'ever LaOfek HaKarov: Sipurim 'Arviyim Bnei Yameinu*, Jerusalem, Bidāyāt, Keter, 1989.

Elad [-Bouskila], Ami, 'HaMar-a HaSeduka: LeVa'ayat Hitkabluta Shel HaSifrut Ha'Aravit BeYisrael', *Moznayim*, 64: 8 (April 1990), pp. 27–30.

Elad [-Bouskila], Ami, 'Gam BeVatei HaKeleh Kotvim Sifrut', *Yediot Aḥaronot* (25 October 1991), p. 22.

Elad [-Bouskila], Ami, 'Kedushata Shel 'Ir: Yerushalayim BeSifrut HaIntifāḍa', *HaMizraḥ HeḤadash*, 34 (1992), pp. 151–61.

Elad [-Bouskila], Ami, 'Riyāḍ Baydas VehaSifrut HaPalestinit', *Ma'ariv*, (17 September 1992), pp. 27, 30.

Elad [-Bouskila], Ami (ed.), *Sifrutam Shel Ha'Aravim BeYisrael, HaMizraḥ HeḤadash*, 35 (1993).

Elad [-Bouskila], Ami, 'Avanim 'Al Mitzḥa Shel HaMoledet: 'Al HaSifrut HaPalestinit BeTekufat HaIntifāḍa', *Alpaim*, 7 (1993), pp. 96–117.

Elad [-Bouskila], Ami, 'Bein 'Olamot Mesoragim: Riyāḍ Baydas VehaSipur Ha'Aravi HaKatzar BeYisrael', *HaMizraḥ HeḤadash*, 35 (1993), pp. 65–87.

Elad [-Bouskila], Ami, *Yerushalayim BeSifrutam Shel 'Arviyei Yisrael BeTekufat HaIntifāḍa 1987–93*, Jerusalem Institute, 1994.

Elad [-Bouskila], Ami, 'HaḤipus Aḥar Zehut: Shalosh Sugiyot BeSifrutam Shel 'Arviyei Yisrael', *Alpaim*, 11 (1995), pp. 173–84.

Elad-Bouskila, Ami, 'Petihut USegirut Shel HaḤevra HaYisraelit BaMizraḥ HaTikhon Be'Et HaShalom', *Moznayim*, 70: 3 (December 1995), pp. 3–7.

Elad-Bouskila, Ami, *Sifrut 'Aravit BeLevush 'Ivri*, Jerusalem, Ministry of Education, Culture and Sport, 1995.

Elad-Bouskila, Ami, 'Shivḥei Ha'Ir HaKedosha: HaMytos Shel Yerushalayim BaSifruyot Ha'Arviyot HaḤadashot', in *Mytos VeZikaron* (ed. David Ohana and Robert Wistrich), Tel-Aviv and Jerusalem, HaKibbutz HaMeuḥad and Van Leer Institute, 1996, pp. 181–99.

Ghanāyim, Maḥmūd, 'Megamot Ḥadashot VeShinuyim BaSiporet Ha'Aravit BeYisrael', *HaMizraḥ HeḤadash*, 35 (1993), pp. 27–45.

Ghānim, Fatḥī, *HaHar* (trans. Ami Elad [-Bouskila]), Jerusalem, Keter, Bidāyāt, 1988.

Green, Dror, *Agadot HaIntifāḍa*, Jerusalem, Eikhut, 1989.

Grossman, David, *Nokheḥim Nifkadim*, Tel-Aviv, HaKibbutz HaMeuḥad, HaSifriya HaḤadasha, 1992.

Ḥabībī, Emile, *Ha-Opsimist: HaKhronika HaMufla'ah Shel He'almut Sa'id Abū al-Naḥs al-Mutashā'il* (trans. Anton Shammās), Tel-Aviv, Mifras, 1984.

Ḥabībī, Emile, *Ikhṭayya* (trans. Anton Shammās), Tel-Aviv, 'Am 'Oved, Proza Aḥeret, 1988.

Ḥabībī, Emile, 'K'mo Petza'', *Politika*, 21 (1988), pp. 6–21.

Ḥabībī, Emile, *Saraya, Bat HaShed HaRa'* (trans. Anton Shammās), Tel-Aviv, HaSifriya HaḤadasha, HaKibbutz HaMeūḥad, 1993.

Hareven, Alouph (ed.), *Eḥad MeKol Shisha Yisraelim: Yaḥasei Gomlin Bein Hami'ut Ha'Aravi VehaRov HaYehudi BeYisrael*, Jerusalem, Van Leer Institute, 1981.

Harkabi, Yehoshafat, Yehoshua Porath and Shmuel Moreh (eds), *Sikhsukh 'Arav-Yisrael BeRe-i HaSifrut Ha'Aravit*, Jerusalem, Van Leer and Truman Institute, 1975.

Hasson, Isaac, 'Yerushalayim BeRe'iya HaMuslemit: HaKoran VeSifrut HaMasoret', in *Sefer Yerushalayim: HaTekufa HaMuslemit HaKedosha 638–1099* (ed. Joshua Prawer), pp. 283–313.

Hever, Hannan, 'Lehakot Ba'Akevo Shel Akhiles', *Alpaim*, 1 (June 1989), pp. 186–93.

Hever, Hannan, ''Ivrit Be'Ito Shel 'Aravi, Shisha Prakim 'Al *Arabeskot* Me-et Anton Shammās', *Te-oriya U-Vikoret*, 1 (Summer 1991), pp. 23–38.

Hever, Hannan, ''HaPlitot LaPlitim': Emile Ḥabībī VeKanon HaSifrut Ha'Ivrit', *HaMizraḥ HeḤadash*, 35 (1993), pp. 102–14.

Ḥusayn, Fū'ād, *Yom Shīshī*, Tel-Aviv, Sa'ar, 1990.

Jiryis, Ṣabrī, *Ha'Aravim BeYisrael*, Haifa, Hotza'at HaMeḤaber, 1966.

Kanazi, George, 'Bea'ayat HaZehut BaSifrut Shel 'Arviyei Yisrael', in *Eḥad MiKol Shisha Yisraelim: Yaḥasei Gomlin Bein HaMi'ut Ha'Aravi VehaRov BeYisrael* (ed. Alouph Hareven), Jerusalem, Van Leer Institute, 1981, pp. 149–69.

Kanafānī, Ghassān, *Gevarim BaShemesh* (trans. Daniella Brafman and Yanni Demianus), Tel-Aviv, Mifras, 1979.

Khalīfa, Saḥar, *HaTzabar* (trans. Salmān Masālḥa), Jerusalem, Galileo, 1978.
Khalīfa, Saḥar, *HaḤamanit* (trans. Rahel Halabé), Haifa, Mifras, 1987.
Khayr, Nazīh (ed.), *Mifgash Ve'Imut BaYetzira Ha'Aravit Veha'Ivrit*, Haifa, Dfus al-Karma, 1993.
Kister, Ya'akov Meir, 'He'ara 'Al Kadmutan Shel Masorot Shivḥei Yerushalayim', in *Sugiyot BeToldot Eretz Yisrael Taḥat Shilton Ha-Islam* (ed. Moshe Sharon), pp. 69–71.
Laor, Dan, 'HaFasuta-im: HaSipur Shelo Nigmar', *Ha-aretz* (30 May 1986), p. B6, B7.
Layish, Aharon (ed.), *Ha'Aravim BeYisrael: Retzifut u-Temurah*, Jerusalem, Magnes Press, 1981.
Layish, Aharon (ed.), *Ha'Aravim BeYisrael: Bein Teḥiya Datit LeHit'orerut Le-umit*, *HaMizraḥ HeḤadash* (42), 1989.
Levi, Itamar, *Otiyot HaShemesh, Otiyot HaYare-aḥ*, Jerusalem, Keter, Tsad HaTefer, 1991.
Mansour, Jacob (ed.), *Meḥkarim Be'Aravit Uve-Islam*, vol. 1, Ramat-Gan, Bar-Ilan University, 1973.
Manṣūr, 'Aṭāllāh, *Be-Or Ḥadash*, Tel-Aviv, Karni, 1966.
Mawāsī, Fārūq, *Ha'Etzvonim Shelo Hūvnū, Shirim* (trans. Roge Tavor), Kafr Qar', al-Shafaq, 1989.
Michael, B., 'Kosot Ru-aḥ, Pitzpon Ve-Anton', *Ha-aretz* (17 January 1986), p. 9.
Mikhael, Sami, 'Shylok BeKartago', *Yedi'ot Aḥaronot* (28 October 1994), p. 28.
Mikhael, Sami, *Viktorya*, Tel-Aviv, 'Am 'Oved, HaSifrya La'Am, 1994.
Mikhael, Sami, 'Historiya Katlanit', *Yedi'ot Aharonot* (18 August 1995), p. 24.
Moreh, Shmuel, 'HaSifrut BaSafa Ha'Aravit BeMedinat Yisrael', *HaMizraḥ HeḤadash*, 9 (1958), pp. 26–39.
Moreh, Shmuel, 'Demuto Shel HaYisraeli BaSifrut Ha'Aravit Me-az Kom HaMedina', in *Sikhsukh 'Arav-Yisrael BeRe-i HaSifrut Ha'Aravit* (ed. Yehoshafat Harkabi, Yehoshua Porath and Shmuel Moreh), Jerusalem, Van Leer, 1975.
Naqqāsh, Samīr, 'Ma Atem Rotzim MiMeni? Ani Shomer 'Al HaOtonomiya Sheli!', *Mifgash*, 7 (spring 1986), p. 34.
Nāṭūr, Salmān, *Holkhim 'Al HaRu-aḥ*, Beit Berl, HaMerkaz LeḤeker HaḤevra Ha'Aravit BeYisrael, 1992.
Oz, Amos (interview), 'Mumḥeh LeRomantika', *Ha-aretz* (13 July 1990).
Peled, Mattityahu, 'Hashpa'at HaKoreh BeGirsa-ot Holkhim 'Al HaRu-aḥ Me-et Salmān Nāṭūr', *HaMizraḥ HeḤadash*, 35 (1993), pp. 115–28.
Prawer, Joshua (ed.), *Sefer Yerushalayim: HaTekufa HaMuslemit HaKeduma 638–1099*, Jerusalem, Ben-Zvi Institute, 1987.
Prawer, Joshua and Haggai Ben-Shammai (eds), *Sefer Yerushalayim:*

HaTekufa HaTzalbanit Veha-Ayubit 1099–1250, Jerusalem, Ben-Zvi Institute, 1991.

al-Qa'īd, Yūsuf, *Zeh Koreh BeMitzrayim Akhshav* (trans. Zeev Klein), Jerusalem, Keter, Bidāyāt, 1990.

Rabinowitz, Danni, 'Nostalgiya Mizraḥit: Eikh Hafkhu HaPalestinim Le'Arviyei Yisrael', *Te-oriya U-Vikoret*, 4 (fall 1993), pp. 141–51.

Rosen, Rolly and Ilana Hammerman, *Meshorerim Lo Yikhtevu Shirim*, Tel-Aviv, 'Am 'Oved, Proza Aḥeret, 1990.

al-Sakākīnī, Khalīl, *Kazeh Ani Rabotai! MeYomano Shel Khalīl al-Sakākīnī* (trans. Gideon Shilo), Jerusalem, Keter, Bidāyāt, 1990.

Schwartz, Michal, ''Al Ashmat Alef Bet Yehoshua VehaBabushka Shel Shammās', *Derekh HaNitzotz* (5 February 1986), pp. 6–7.

Shaked, Gershon, *HaSiporet Ha'Ivrit 1880–1980, BeḤevlei HaZeman*, vol. 4, Tel-Aviv and Jerusalem, HaKibbutz Ha-Artzi and Keter, 1993.

Shammās, Anton, *BeShnei Kolot*, Haifa, Beit Hagefen, 1974.

Shammās, Anton, *Krikha Kasha*, Tel-Aviv, Sifriyat HaPo'alim, 1974.

Shammās, Anton, 'HaSifrut Ha'Aravit BeYisrael Le-Aḥar 1976', *Skirot*, Tel-Aviv University, 2 (June 1976), pp. 2–8.

Shammās, Anton, *Shetaḥ Hefker, Shirim*, Tel-Aviv, HaKibbutz HaMeūḥad, 1979.

Shammās, Anton, *HaShakran Hakhī Gadol Ba'Olam*, Jerusalem, Keter, 1982.

Shammās, Anton, 'Rosh HaShana LaYehudim', *Ha'Ir* (13 September 1985), pp. 13–18.

Shammās, Anton, *'Arabeskot*, 2nd edn, Tel-Aviv, 'Am 'Oved, 1986.

Shammās, Anton, 'Avraham Ḥozer LaGola?' *'Iton 77*, 72–3 (6 February 1986), pp. 21–2.

Shammās, Anton, 'Ashmat HaBabushka', *Politika*, 5–6 (February–March 1986), pp. 44–5.

Shammās, Anton, 'Kitsh 22, O: Gevul HaTarbut', *'Iton 77*, 84–5 (January–February 1987), pp. 24–6.

Shammās, Anton, 'Yitzu Zemani Shel Ḥafatzim Nilvim', *Ha-aretz*, Sefarim (13 June 1989), p. 11.

Sharon, Moshe (ed.), *Sugiyot BeToldot Eretz Yisrael Taḥat Shilton Ha-Islam*, Jerusalem, Ben-Zvi Institute, 1976.

Shilo, Gideon, *'Arviyei Yisrael Be'Eynei Medinot 'Arav Ve-Ashaf*, Jerusalem, Magnes and the Truman Institute, 1982.

Sivan, Emmanuel, *Kana-ei Ha'Islam*, 2nd edn, Tel-Aviv, 'Am 'Oved, Ofakim, 1986.

Sivan, Emmanuel, *Mytosim Politiyim 'Arviyim*, Tel-Aviv, 'Am 'Oved, 1988.

Sivan, Emmanuel, 'Tarbut HaMuvla'at', *Alpaim*, 4 (1991), pp. 45–98.

Smooha, Sammy, 'Nikur Tarbuti BeYisrael', *Apiryon*, 2 (winter 1983/84), pp. 28–9.
Snir, Reuven, 'Petza' MePtza'av: HaSifrut Ha'Aravit HaPalastinit BeYisrael', *Alpaim*, 2 (1990), pp. 244–68.
Snir, Reuven, 'Banim Ḥorgim VeOhavim', *Moznayim*, 66:6 (May 1992), pp. 6–9.
Snir, Reuven, 'Reshito Shel HaTe-atron HaPoliti HaPalestini: Qaraqāsh Me-et Samīḥ al-Qāsim', *HaMizraḥ HeḤadash*, 35 (1993), pp. 129–47.
Somekh, Sasson, 'Sifrut 'Aravit BeTirgum 'Ivri' in *Meḥkarim Be'Aravit UveIslam* (ed. Jacob Mansour), vol. 1, Ramat-Gan, Bar-Ilan University, 1973, pp. 141–52.
Somekh, Sasson, 'Ma LeTargem Min HaShira Ha'Aravit', *Ma'ariv* (11 May 1979), p. 46.
Somekh, Sasson, 'Sifrut 'Aravit Be'Ivrit: Yesh LeHakhshir 'Atudat Metargemim', *Ma'ariv* (31 May 1979), p. 31.
Somekh, Sasson, 'Batim Gvohim, Karim: Dmut HaShakhen HaYehudi BeYetziratam Shel Sofrim 'Aravim MeḤaifa VehaGalil,' *Mifgash*, 4–5, 8–9 (winter 1986), pp. 21–5.
Somekh, Sasson, 'Ma LeTargem Min HaSifrut HaMitzrit', *Ma'ariv* (4 May 1989), p. 7.
Somekh, Sasson, *Tirgum BeTzidei HaDerekh*, Tel-Aviv and Giv'at Haviva, Tel-Aviv University and the Institute for Arab Studies, 1993.
Tawil, Raymonda, *Ma'atsar Bayit: Sipura Shel Isha Palestinit* (trans. Naomi Gal), Jerusalem, Adam, 1979.
Ṭūqān, Fadwā, *Derekh Hararit: Otobiografiya* (trans. Rahel Halabé), Tel-Aviv, Mifras, 1993.
Valentin, Avi, *Shahīd*, Tel-Aviv, Am Oved, 1989.
Yehoshua, Abraham B., 'Abraham B. Yehoshua: Teshuva Le-Anton', *Ha'Ir* (31 January 1986), pp. 22–3.
Yehoshua, Abraham B., 'Im Ata Nish'ar – Ata Mi'ut', *Kol Ha'Ir* (31 January 1986), pp. 42–3.
Yehoshua, Abraham B., *Mar Mani*, Tel-Aviv, HaKibbutz Hameuḥad, Hasifriya HaḤadasha, 1990.
Yinnon, Avraham, 'Kama Nos'ei Moked BaSifrut Shel 'Arviyei Yisrael', *HaMizraḥ HeḤadash*, 15 (1965), pp. 57–84.
Yinnon, Avraham, 'Nos'im Ḥevratyim BeSifrut 'Arviyei Yisrael', *HaMizraḥ HeḤadash*, 16 (1966), pp. 349–80.
Zaydān, Maḥmūd, *Ketovet BaḤalal*, Tel-Aviv, 'Eked, 1992.
Zilberman, Ifrah, *Mytos HaMotsa HaKena'ani Shel HaḤevra HaPalestinit*, Jerusalem, Jerusalem Institute for Israel Studies, 1993.

IN WESTERN LANGUAGES

Abu-Amr, Ziad, *Islamic Fundamentalism in the West Bank and Gaza, Muslim Brotherhood and Islamic Jihad*, Bloomington, Indiana University Press, 1994.

al-Ali, Nadje Sadig, *Gender Writing / Writing Gender: The Representation of Women in Selections of Modern Egyptian Literature*, Cairo, American University in Cairo Press, 1994.

Alcalay, Ammiel, *After Jews and Arabs, Remaking Levantine Culture*, Minneapolis, University of Minnesota Press, 1993.

Allen, Roger, *The Arabic Novel: An Historical and Critical Introduction*, Manchester, University of Manchester, 1982; 2nd edn, Syracuse, New York, Syracuse University Press, 1995.

Allen, Roger, Hilary Kilpatrick and Ed de Moor (eds), *Love and Sexuality in Modern Arabic Literature*, London, Saqi Books, 1995.

Allen, Roger (ed.), *Modern Arabic Literature*, New York, The Ungar Publishing Company, 1987.

Ashrawi, Hanan, *Contemporary Palestinian Literature Under Occupation*, Bir Zeit, Bir Zeit University, 1976.

al-Asmar, Fouzi, *Through the Hebrew Looking-Glass: Arab Stereotypes in Children's Literature*, London, Zed Books, 1986.

Badawi, Muhammad Mustafa, *A Short History of Modern Arabic Literature*, Oxford, Oxford University Press, 1993.

Badawi, Muhammad Mustafa (ed.), *Modern Arabic Literature: The Cambridge History of Arabic Literature*, Cambridge, Cambridge University Press, 1992.

Benvenisti, Meron, *Conflicts and Contradictions*, New York, Villard Books, 1986.

Berg, Nancy E., *Exile from Exile: Israeli Writers from Iraq*, New York, State University of New York Press, 1996.

Boullata, Issa J. (trans. and ed.), *Modern Arab Poets, 1950–1975*, Washington DC, Three Continents Press, 1976.

Boullata, Issa J. (ed.), *Critical Perspectives on Modern Arabic Literature*, Washington DC, Three Continents Press, 1980.

Boullata, Kamal (ed.), *Women of the Fertile Crescent: Modern Poetry by Arab Women*, Colorado, Three Continents Press, Colorado Spring, repr. 1994 (1st edn 1982).

Busse, Heribert, 'The Sanctity of Jerusalem in Islam', *Judaism*, XVII (1968), pp. 441–68.

Cachia, Pierre, *An Overview of Modern Arabic Literature*, Edinburgh, Edinburgh University Press, 1990.

Deleuze, G. and F. Guattari, *Kafka: Toward a Minor Literature*, Minneapolis, University of Minnesota Press, 1986.

Domb, Risa, *The Arab in Hebrew Prose, 1911–1948*, London, Vallentine Mitchell, 1982.

Elad [-Bouskila], Ami, 'Ideology and Structure in Fatḥī Ghānim's *al-Jabal*', *Journal of Arabic Literature*, Leiden, XX: 2 (1990), pp. 168–86.

Elad-Bouskila, Ami, 'En deux langues, la littérature moderne d'Afrique du Nord', in idem and Erez Biton (eds), *Le Maghreb, littérature et culture special issue*, *Apirion*, 28 (1993), pp. 86–7.

Elad [-Bouskila], Ami, *Writer, Culture, Text: Studies in Modern Arabic Literature*, Fredericton, York Press, 1993.

Elad [-Bouskila], Ami, *The Village Novel in Modern Egyptian Literature*, Berlin, Klaus Schwarzverlag, 1994.

Elad-Bouskila, Ami, 'La Littérature palestinienne d'Israël: Une littérature en quête de légitimation', *Levant*, 7 (1994–95), pp. 146–9.

Elad [-Bouskila], Ami, 'Al-Kâtib eine palästinensische Kulturzeitschrift als Forum der Intifāḍa-Literatur', *Orient*, 36 (1995), pp. 109–25.

Elad-Bouskila, Ami, 'Varieties of Language Usage in Dialogue in the Modern Egyptian Village Novel', in Ballas and Snir (eds), *Studies in Canonical and Popular Arabic Literature*, Toronto, York Press, 1998, pp. 77–86.

Elpeleg, Zvi, *The Grand Mufti, Haj Amin al-Hussaini, Founder of the Palestinian National Movement*, London, Frank Cass, 1993.

The Encyclopedia of Islam, 2nd edn, Leiden, E.J. Brill.

Gad, Ali, *Form and Technique in the Egyptian Novel, 1912–1971*, London Ithaca Press, 1983.

García Márquez, Gabriel, *One Hundred Years of Solitude* (trans. Gregory Rabassa), London, Penguin Books, 1970.

Goitein, Shlomo Dov, 'The Sanctity of Jerusalem and the Palestinians in Early Islam', in *Studies in Islamic History and Institutions*, Leiden, E.J. Brill, 1966, pp. 135–48.

Grunebaum, G. von, 'The Sacred Character of Islamic Cities' 'in Abd al-Rahman Badawi (ed.), *Mélanges Ṭāha Ḥusain*, Cairo: Dār al-Ma'arif, 1962, pp. 25–37.

Ḥabībī, Emile (= Habiby, Emile), *The Secret Life of Saeed, the Ill-Fated Pessoptimist: A Palestinian who became a Citizen of Israel* (trans. Salma Khadra al-Jayyusi and Trevor Le Gassick), New York, Vantage, 1982.

Hafez, Sabry, 'The Egyptian Novel in the Sixties', *Journal of Arabic Literature*, VII (1976), pp. 68–84.

Hafez, Sabry, *The Genesis of Arabic Narrative Discourse*, London, Saqi Books, 1993.

al-Ḥakīm, Tawfīq (= al-Hakim, Tewfik), *Maze of Justice* (trans. Abba Eban), London, Saqi Books, 1981 (1st edn 1947).

Hasson, Isaac, 'Muslim Literature in Praise of Jerusalem: *Faḍā'il al-Bayt al-Maqdis*', *The Jerusalem Cathedra*, I (1981), pp. 168–84.

Jabrā, Jabrā Ibrāhīm (= Jabra, Jabra Ibrahim), *The Ship* (trans. Adnan Haydar and Roger Allen), Washington DC, Three Continents Press, 1985.

Jayyusi, Salma Khadra (ed.), *Modern Arabic Poetry: An Anthology*, New York, Columbia University Press, 1987.

Jayyusi, Salma Khadra (ed.), *Anthology of Modern Palestinian Literature*, New York, Columbia University Press, 1992.

Kadi, Joanna (ed.), *Food for Our Grandmothers: Writings by Arab-American and Arab-Canadian Feminists*, Boston, South End Press, 1994.

Kanafānī, Ghassan (= Kanfani, Ghassan), *Men in the Sun and Other Palestinian Stories* (trans. Hilary Kilpatrick), Washington DC, Three Continents Press, 1978.

Kanafānī, Ghassān (= Kanafani, Ghasan), *Palestine's Children* (trans. Barbara Harlow), London, Heinemann, 1984.

Khalīfa, Saḥar (= Khalifeh, Sahar), *Wild Thorns* (trans. Trevor Le Gassick and Elizabeth Fernea), London, al-Saqi, 1985.

Khater, Akram F., 'Emile Habibi: The Mirror of Irony in Palestinian Literature', *Journal of Arabic Literature*, XXIV: 1 (March 1993), pp. 75–94.

Kilpatrick, Hilary, 'Tradition and Innovation in the Fiction of Ghassān Kanafānī', *Journal of Arabic Literature*, VII (1978), pp. 53–64.

Lloyd, David, *Nationalism and Minor Literature*, Berkeley, Los Angeles, University of California, 1987.

Maḥfūẓ, Najīb (= Mahfouz, Naguib), *The Thief and the Dogs* (trans. M.M. Badawi and Trevor Le Gassick), Cairo, American University in Cairo Press, 1984.

Malti-Douglas, Fedwa, *Woman's Body, Woman's World: Gender and Discourse in Arab-Islamic Writing*, Princeton, Princeton University Press, 1991.

Mansur, 'Atallah, *In a New Light*, London, Vallentine Mitchell, 1969.

Milson, Menachem, 'Najīb Maḥfūż and the Quest for Meaning', *Arabica*, 17 (1970), pp. 155–86.

Moreh, Shmuel, *Studies in Modern Arabic Prose and Poetry*, Leiden, E.J. Brill, 1988.

Nakhleh, Emile, 'Wells of Bitterness: A Survey of Israeli-Arab Political Poetry', in Boullata (ed.), *Critical Perspectives on Modern Arabic Literature*, pp. 244–62.

Neuwirth, Angelika, 'Kulturelle Sprachbarrienen Zwischen Nachbarm', *Orient*, 3 (1988), pp. 440–66.

Nicholson, Reynold A., *A Literary History of the Arabs*, Cambridge, Cambridge University Press, 1930.

Nijland, Cornelis, *Michail Nuaymah: Promotor of the Arabic Literary Revival*, Leiden, Brill, 1975.

Peled, Mattityahu, 'Annals of Doom: Palestinian Literature 1917–1948', *Arabica*, XXIX, 2 (1982), pp. 141–83.

Qleibo, Ali, *Before the Mountains Disappear: An Ethnographic Chronicle of the Modern Palestinians*, Cairo, Kloreus Book, 1992.

Ramras-Rauch, Gila, *The Arab in Israeli Literature*, Bloomington and Indianapolis, Indiana University Press, London, I.B. Tauris, 1989.

Rosenthal, Franz, *A History of Muslim Historiography*, 2nd edn, Leiden, E.J. Brill, 1968).

Ṣāliḥ, al-Ṭayyib [= Salih, Tayeb], *Season of Migration to the North* (trans. Denys Johnson-Davies), London, Heinemann, 1978 (1st edn 1969).

Schipper, Mineke (ed.), *Unheard Words: Women and Literature in Africa, the Arab World, Asia, the Caribbean and Latin America*, London, Allison Busby, 1985.

Schnell, Izhak, *Perceptions of Israeli Arabs: Territoriality and Identity*, Aldershot, Arebury, 1994.

Shammas, Anton, *Arabesques* (trans. Vivian Eden), New York, Harper & Row, 1988.

al-Sharqāwī, 'Abd al-Raḥmān (= Sharkawi, A.R.), *Egyptian Earth* (trans. Desmond Stewart), Delhi, Hind Pocket Books, 1972 (1st edn 1962).

Siddiq, Muhammad, *Man is a Cause: Political Consciousness and the Fiction of Ghassan Kanafani*, Seattle, 1984.

Siddiq, Muhammad, 'The Process of Individuation in al-Tayyib Salih's Novel *Season of Migration to the North*', *Journal of Arabic Literature*, XVII (1986), pp. 126–45.

Sivan, Emannuel, 'The Beginnings of the *Faḍā'il al-Quds* Literature', *Israel Oriental Studies*, I (1971), pp. 263–71.

Smooha, Sammy, *Arabs and Jews in Israel*, vol. 1, Boulder, Westview Press, 1989, vol. 2, 1992.

Snir, Reuven, 'We Were Like Those Who Dream: Iraqi-Jewish writers in Israel in the 1950s', *Prooftext* 11 (1991), pp. 153–73.

Somekh, Sasson, *Genre and Language in Modern Arabic Literature*, Wiesbaden, Otto Harrassowitz, 1991.

Sulaiman, Khalid, *Palestine and Modern Arab Poetry*, London, Zed Books, 1984.

Suleiman, Yasir, 'Palestine and Palestinians in the Short Stories of Samīra 'Azzām', *Journal of Arabic Literature*, XXII: 2 (September 1991), pp. 154–65.

Wild, Stefan, *Ghassan Kanafani: The Life of a Palestinian*, Wiesbaden, Otto Harrassowitz, 1975.

Young, Barbara, *This Man From Lebanon*, New York, Knopf, 1959.

Zeidan, Joseph, *Arab Women Novelists: The Formative Years and Beyond*, New York, State University of New York, 1995.

Index

www.ingramcontent.com/pod-product-compliance
Ingram Content Group UK Ltd.
Pitfield, Milton Keynes, MK11 3LW, UK
UKHW010019280225
455677UK00023B/684